HOW TO GROW A YOUNG READER
Books from Every Age for Readers of Every Age

Reading to the Children

Open books and open faces,
Loving times and loving places.

Loving words and loving looks,
Precious voices, precious books.

Open books for open eyes,
Snuggly stories, snug and wise.

Funny figures, funny rhymes,
Sunny pictures, sunny times.

Minds so drowsy, minds awake,
Hearts that give and hearts that take.

Questions new and questions old—
Answers silver, answers gold.

Pictures touched and pages turned,
Lessons offered, lessons learned.

Happy smiles and happy laughter,
Happy memories ever after.

Kathryn Lindskoog

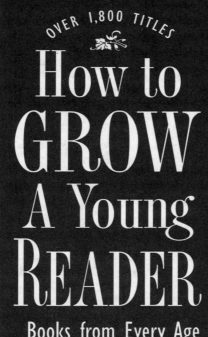

OVER 1,800 TITLES

How to GROW A Young READER

Books from Every Age
For Readers of Every Age

UPDATED & EXPANDED EDITION

Kathryn Lindskoog &
Ranelda Mack Hunsicker

HAROLD SHAW PUBLISHERS

WHEATON, ILLINOIS

Unless otherwise noted, Scripture quotations are taken from Today's English Version (The Good News Bible), © 1966, 1971, 1976, 1992 American Bible Society. Used by permission.

ISBN 0-87788-408-0

Edited by Miriam Mindeman and Elisa Fryling
Cover design by David LaPlaca

Library of Congress Cataloging-in-Publication Data

Lindskoog, Kathryn Ann.
    How to grow a young reader / by Kathryn Lindskoog and Ranelda Mack Hunsicker. — Rev. ed.
      p.   cm.
    Rev. ed. of: How to grow a young reader / John & Kathryn Lindskoog. ©1989.
      ISBN 0-87788-408-0 (pbk.)
      1. Children—English-speaking countries—Books and reading. 2. Children—United States—Books and reading. 3. Reading—Parent participation—English-speaking countries. 4. Reading—Parent participation—United States. 5. Children's literature, English—Bibliography. I. Hunsicker, Ranelda Mack, 1953- II. Lindskoog, John. How to grow a young reader. III. Title.
Z1037.A1L54 1999
011.62—dc21   98-51648
                                                  CIP

---

04   03   02   01   00   99

10 9 8 7 6 5 4 3 2 1

To our mothers,
Annie Inez Mack and Margarete Marie Stillwell.
They read to us.

Contents

Preface to the Revised Edition

My most delightful early childhood memories are of bedtime stories—especially fairy tales.

Then, when I was six years old, I made a most amazing discovery. One idle afternoon I suddenly realized that the mysterious rituals we had been practicing in first grade made it possible for me to read stories to myself. I didn't even have to say the words aloud; I could "hear" them more quickly through my eyes! I had a magic power of my own as wonderful as any in the fairy tales. I didn't have to wait for bedtime anymore.

Since then, good books have been both the bedtime and morning stories of my mental life–some giving me repose and others awakening me. Books bring me closer to people and to God. Books have informed me when I was ignorant and consoled me when I was suffering. They have guided me to joy and meaning and have actually healed me when I was sick. They have set off explosions of ideas in my mind. They keep me laughing and caring and growing.

Good books have made my life good. Through books I learn the wonder of the ordinary. And I walk next to all kinds of people, sharing their thoughts and experiences.

Cherished books have also brought me cherished friends. Twenty years ago a young teacher named Ranelda Hunsicker read and appreciated the first edition of my guide to children's books. Over ten years ago her love for the Narnian Chronicles attracted her to my graduate course on the writings of C. S. Lewis. A wonderful friendship developed with books at its heart. How pleased I am to have her as the coauthor of this revised and expanded edition of *How to Grow a Young Reader.*

Please take note of two practical items. First, our suggestions of age-appropriateness provide an approximate guide to when a child might best enjoy certain books. Most of the entries are left open-ended because a child too young for some books can never be too old for stories of excellence. Second, because books go in and out of print so rapidly, some of the titles mentioned may be unavailable in your bookstore. If so, they may be secured at a used bookstore or through your library.

Ranelda and I have both given the vast world of children's literature our best effort. But no book can be really complete in this life; it has to end where the authors' time and understanding end. There is always something left unsaid. I look forward to the life to come as the unending last chapter of all the good books I have ever read.

Kathryn Lindskoog

The Riches of
Children's
Literature Today

1 The Golden Age Is Now

It has always seemed clear to me that a good book for children must be a good book in its own right.

—John Rowe Townsend, *A Sense of Story*

Once upon a time the wisest man who ever lived warned grimly, "There is no end to the writing of books." (Ecclesiastes 12:12).

True, but little could King Solomon dream of the endless supply of books today. He lived about one thousand years before Christ, in what was the short golden age of the kingdom of Israel. With all his ambition, power, and intelligence—not to mention his one thousand wives and untold number of children—Solomon probably never imagined the possibility of even one book for children. And with all his silks and ivory and spices and gold— over twenty-five tons a year—he would surely have been amazed by the wealth of talent and beauty invested in children's books today. They are a new kind of treasure.

Solomon was rather a failure as a parent, according to the Old Testament. And, although he was the richest and wisest king, he was even somewhat a failure at that. But he was a great writer, judging from all the parts of the Bible attributed to him. One piece of advice he gave was, "Never ask, 'Oh, why were things so much better in the old days?' It's not an intelligent question" (Ecclesiastes 7:10). Solomon's implication is that things were not really better in the past, and the same is true in

11

children's literature. Today, not yesterday, is the prime time.

A modern-day author of children's books was browsing in a bookstore one day when a woman turned from the sale table in disgust and exclaimed, "It's not like the old days. They don't make good children's books anymore!" The secret author slyly suggested that there were some good ones on the shelf where his new book was sitting. "Oh no," the woman answered, "I don't even look at any books that aren't marked down to half price or less. Why waste money?" The author wondered how such people think authors of good books earn a living.

But this woman was not alone in her search for good books. Even parents who are willing to pay the price or who have a public library that pays the price for them might feel they need some of the wisdom of Solomon just to help their children find and read the right books today.

It is estimated that children between seven and fourteen will read no more than seventy books per year. That means a total of five hundred books read in their seven prime years of childhood reading. When we think of the inner growth that comes from rich childhood reading— the gains in security, insight, achievement, reverence, zest, delight, understanding, sympathy, affirmation, sensitivity, adventure, and moral courage—five hundred books does not seem like many.

In 1950 it seemed wonderful that fourteen hundred new children's books were being published in the United States yearly. This was twenty times as many as any child would read in a year, if one believes the supposition that children between seven and fourteen read no more than seventy books a year. In 1998, however, more than four thousand new children's books were published in the U.S., almost triple the number in 1950. Still more remarkable, because many books continue to be reprinted year after year—if not decade after decade—the number of children's books in print in the U.S. rose to 126,600 in 1998.

A Bird's Eye View of the U.S. Children's Book Industry

According to *Publisher's Weekly* (20 July 1998), sales of children's books in the U.S. rose steadily through the 1980s, took a dip in 1993, and peaked in 1996. That year almost 380 million were sold, amounting to almost one and a half billion dollars in receipts. Over half of these sales were rung up by mass merchandisers and book clubs. Fiction and picture books led in terms of kinds of books purchased (46 percent). Although the market has slowed since then, the children's book industry is definitely alive and well.

American children also benefit from books published in Great Britain, where thousands of new books for children are released yearly, and Canada, where approximately four hundred new children's and young adult books are published each year. Although some of these books are duplicates of new books in America, most are not. It is said that the twenty years between 1950 and 1970 gave British children the richest harvest of imaginative books any nation has ever produced. Today, an extraordinary revival of folktales, fairy stories, fantasies, and myths is occurring on both sides of the Atlantic.

Of course, only some of these thousands upon thousands of children's books are top quality. Children's books are profitable for hack writers and publishers who do not mind imitating others or reissuing books in inferior editions. After all, books are simply merchandise to many people in the publishing business. As the century turns, sales of hardcover and paperback children's books are predicted at yearly totals of well over a billion dollars (up from just 336 million dollars in 1985). In what has increasingly become a market-driven industry, many editors complain that sales concerns have eclipsed the art of fine book making. But if only a quarter of the children's books published today are really excellent, that still means 31,650 top-quality books are available in the United States alone—with more than one thousand added each year.

Some people may want to cry, "Stop the presses! Enough is enough!" If the gigantic children's publishing business should collapse, though, we would lose the new favorites that burst upon us every year. The real task of parents and teachers and lovers of children and books, then, is to find those books that are too good to miss. (This task may seem daunting, but this book gives tools to make it a dream-come-true adventure.)

Subscriptions soar to the few periodicals that describe new children's books to teachers and librarians, but these journals cannot begin to keep up with them all. Thousands of short reviews from various periodicals continue to be collected into reference volumes, and we now have not only lists of good books, we have lists of the lists of good books. The one list that gets the most publicity is probably that of Newbery and Caldecott award winners—American awards named, ironically, after two Englishmen.

John Newbery, who died more than two centuries ago, was the first major publisher of books for children. Every year since 1922, the American Library Association has chosen the most distinguished children's book by a U.S. author from the previous year to receive this award. There are usually several honor books named as well. The same committee of twenty-three librarians awards the Caldecott Medal for the best picture book by an American artist. This prize, which began in 1937, is named in honor of Randolph Caldecott, an English illustrator of a century ago whose pictures still delight children. Both the Newbery and Caldecott awards were originated by Frederic G. Melcher, who was editor of the influential American periodical *Publisher's Weekly*.

Curiously enough, the key award for good children's books in England is named after an American—Andrew Carnegie, the millionaire who contributed generously to libraries in both countries. Similar to the Newbery Medal, the Carnegie Medal is awarded to the author of a book published in the previous year. Since 1969 the winning author has not had to be a British subject, but the book must be in English and must have been printed first in the United Kingdom. England's counterpart to the American Caldecott Medal is the Kate Greenaway Medal, named in memory of one of England's favorite illustrators. As in the U.S., these English prizes are awarded by panels of librarians.

As Solomon said, "In this world fast runners do not always win the races, and the brave do not always win the battles" (Ecclesiastes 9:11). Likewise, the best books do not always win the prizes. *The Lion, the Witch and the Wardrobe* by C. S. Lewis won no award when it quietly entered the world in 1950. But for many people, it split the century in half.

"This is no thaw," a dwarf said to the winter witch in Lewis's story. "This is *spring*." And as we shall see, for children's books, 1950 really was.

The Enemies of Reading

2 But There Be Dragons

> Television captures the imagination but does not free it. A good book at once stimulates and frees the mind.
> —Bruno Bettelheim, "Parents vs. Television," *Redbook* (November 1963)

Ironically, 1950, the turning point for modern children's literature, was also the year that marked the takeover of family life by television. Between 1948 and 1952, television entered about fifteen million American homes. One cannot honestly think much about children's literature without considering television, which has not only usurped reading time but probably undermined reading ability. Today, along with TV, we have videos, electronic games, and the Internet affecting family life—over 80 percent of U.S. homes have a VCR, and over 20 percent are connected to the Internet.

These newer forms of entertainment are claiming ever larger chunks of our children's time, but television is still the front runner. Only one home in one hundred lacks television, and the other ninety-nine approach three sets per home. Preschool children spend more than a third of their waking hours watching TV—instead of talking and playing—and some researchers extend this total to over half their waking time. This means children spend more time watching TV before kindergarten than they will spend in four years of college classes.

In many American homes, TV viewing habits are

much more conservative, but reports consistently confirm that not nearly enough families are setting healthy limits. According to Albert Shanker, former president of the American Federation of Teachers, in 1990 one out of every four children nine years of age spent six or more hours a day watching TV. The National Assessment of Educational Progress reported that 71 percent of eighth-graders watch three or more hours of television a day, while only 27 percent read daily for pleasure.

Author and scientist Isaac Asimov brushed aside the menace of widespread TV addiction by claiming that, without television, people who watch a lot of it would be doing other things equally as empty—such as staring into space. He assumed that they would be passive even without their television sets, accomplishing nothing.

That is a radical assumption to make about the average adult who watches TV twenty-one to thirty-five hours a week. Thirty hours of nothing? Perhaps that is how average adults look to a phenomenal man like Asimov. But in fact, people who have to do without television for a time generally resort to reading, hobbies, games, studies, longer family dinners, earlier bedtimes, and even improved sex lives, according to some reports.

Asimov seems to be considering children as basically inactive because children watch television more than any other group. But when they are not watching television, children are about the busiest people in the world. They are constantly exploring themselves and their environment, chattering, reflecting, insisting, and probably keeping at least one adult very busy. Their brains, the most complicated things on earth, are developing daily. Most of their healthy growth activity falls into one category—play. Play is child's work.

And reading is child's work. When we read, our minds decode and manipulate the lines we see in a tremendously complex symbolic transformation. The cost to the reader is great concentration, and one of the benefits is enriched powers of imagination. The reading mind visualizes. The reading mind sets its own pace and even stops or goes back for better comprehension or deeper response. The reading mind is extremely active.

Needless to say, human beings are not apt to invest great concentration in this mental activity called reading if they have become dependent upon a fascinating machine which discourages analysis, imagination, and integration. Aside from floating in the womb, there are few states of mind more passive than TV watching.

As Marie Winn points out in her extraordinary book *The Plug-In Drug: Television, Children, and the Family,* the first television generation would have been about three years old in 1950 when television boomed. So we could expect to see the possible results in young people who approached college age in 1964 or 1965. Did that generation really show any new tendencies that could be a result of television?

It just happens that in 1964 the reading and writing ability of high school students who took college board exams suddenly dropped. And just as childhood television watching has steadily increased since 1950, so students' verbal abilities have steadily declined. This certainly does not prove that spending five to ten thousand hours watching TV before first grade interferes with the proper development of verbal ability, not to mention other abilities and attitudes and relationships. But the coincidence is suspicious.

Some people assume that hours of adult words and phrases pouring from a mechanical box should improve children's vocabulary and self-expression. But since this obviously has not happened, Marie Winn suggests that prolonged television viewing permanently retards the development of the brain's left side, where the center for logical speech is located. No matter what the program content, Winn maintains, looking at moving images produced on a screen by tiny dots is going to have some physiological effect upon the eyes and brain. She even suggests that video overstimulation of the brain's right half may cause the increased tendency toward drug abuse that became obvious in the 1960s. Such a theory may seem far-fetched, but so do many theories that prove true in the long run.

Reading specialist Dr. Jane M. Healy believes electronic media are responsible for more than children's reading problems. In her book titled *Endangered Minds: Why Our Children Don't Think*, she explains how the brain's left hemisphere controls auditory analysis and logical, sequential reasoning. When children watch TV or play electronic games, these parts of the brain get less practice than when they listen to a story or interact with a picture book. Sadly, television is robbing millions of preschool children of the most sensitive period for language development.

So far, the effect of six hours of flittering images a day on an immature, developing brain has never been scientifically studied. It would be too callous and cruel an experiment for scientists to inflict upon an innocent child, although kindly parents do it to their children all the time. So theories, statistics, and suspicions are almost all we have to go on. Of course, some people go on what they call common sense: E. B. White, author of one of this century's best books, *Charlotte's Web*, did not wait for any future analysis of children's brain development. He simply declared in *Newsweek*, "Short of throwing away all the television sets, I really don't know what we can do about writing." That was in 1975, in an article discussing "Why Johnny Can't Write."

No wonder Johnny can't write, since he has to be a good reader to be a good writer. And today we also have the problem of why Johnny's parents can't read—parents who grew up after the one-eyed dragon took the throne. Five adults out of a hundred in our country cannot read. And nearly three million adults can barely read. An estimated 70 percent of American families do not include reading among their regular pastimes.

In recent years, another one-eyed monster has reared its head. Over 40 percent of American homes now have a computer. Studies show that children play electronic games on computers or game systems an average of seven and a half hours a week. Add to this the hours spent surfing the Internet's World Wide Web. In this technology-filled environment, children in their formative years are being bombarded with enough information and sensory experience to keep them in constant overdrive. Meanwhile, educators and reading advocates are torn between viewing the computer as a learning tool and blaming it for children's lack of skill and interest in reading.

Some pediatricians and developmental psychologists are also concerned about the overstimulation modern technology is creating. Dr. Ronald Dahl, professor of psychiatry and pediatrics at University of Pittsburgh Medical Center, sees a steady increase of kids and teens who are hooked on thrills—the kind of intense, high-speed adventures they can experience on their computers. He observes, "As thrills displace needed rest, sleep-deprived kids have trouble with irritability, inattention, and moodiness. . . . Constant access to high stimulation may also create patterns of emotional imbalance." This concerned father of a four-year-old son and an eleven-year-old daughter is convinced families need to "rediscover slower, simpler pleasures before we all become burned out and bored to death" ("Burned Out and Bored," *Newsweek*, 15 December 1997).

Other researchers disagree. William D. Winn, director of the Learning Center at the University of Washington's

Human Interface Technology Laboratory points out that early exposure to game technology helps children develop "hypertext minds." He explains, "They leap around. It's as though their cognitive strategies were parallel, not sequential." Neil Gross, writing for *Business Week* ("Zap! Splat! Smash!" 23 December 1996), asks, "Does this mean games interfere with linear thinking or the ability to read a book? More research is needed. But some surveys show that games cut into TV time, not reading."

Proponents of a high-tech childhood argue that playing games on a computer causes kids to be more resourceful in seeking solutions to problems and enjoying hard challenges, skills that are essential to life-long learning. Since video games also produce intense concentration, they can help some distracted children learn to focus on specific goals and challenges. Frequent playing can actually remap the brain's neural network, a fact that encourages some observers and frightens others.

Concerned parents will be interested in the alliance between game companies and the U.S. Department of Defense. According to Gross, we have the military to thank for bankrolling most visualization technology used by game companies. And now the Armed Forces are benefiting from the game companies' development of video systems they can use in military training. This link may help to explain why electronic games are increasingly violent and realistic. Do we want our children's thinking shaped by the same exhilaration that prepares a soldier for battle? It's definitely a question worth pondering.

In a study at the University of Mississippi, researchers observed sixty seven- and eight-year-old boys. All sixty played video games, but some played games that were violent and others played games that were self-challenging. After twenty minutes, the boys were taken to a large toy-filled room. Those who had played the violent video games were much more physically and verbally aggressive with their playmates.

While politicians call for increased technology in our schools, children's advocate Fred Rogers, of "Mister Rogers' Neighborhood," is skeptical. He observes, "These days more and more children are exposed to fancier and fancier machinery. . . . But more often than not, computers are used as instruments for drill and practice. Right answer or wrong answer. . . . All too often the computer won't let me do what I want. It gets stuck and leaves me sitting there staring at a screen that won't listen to what I need. . . . I really do worry that the new technology adds frustration, a sense of being helpless, and powerless" ("Mister Rogers on Kids and Technology," *TECHNOS*, Winter 1996).

Caught in the web of images and sound bites, parents and children alike are suffering. In homes where audio and video reign, family reading is virtually extinct. And the problem transcends all socioeconomic categories. Children in affluent homes do not necessarily fare better in this regard than those who grow up in poverty. When ten kindergarten teachers in an affluent southern California community surveyed their students' families to see how many parents were reading aloud to their children, the responses were appalling. "In these $400,000 to $500,000 homes, they found only two parents who read aloud regularly—more than once a week—to their children," says Marilyn Carpenter, a former teacher and national reading consultant. These upscale parents were too busy or too tired to share books with their young children and opted for videos and television.

In fairy tale terms, children today seem to have inherited an incredible treasure of books but are held spellbound by a cold magic eye. Some children are born with reading disabilities. Others seem to derive disabilities of a sort from kindly electronic dragons with whom they keep close company at home. These electronic creatures were brought in as pets to pacify and entertain the children . . . but wise old stories warn us—dragons are definitely not to be trusted.

Family Reading
Possibilities

3 Battle Strategy

You may have tangible wealth untold:
Caskets of jewels and coffers of gold.
Richer than I you will never be—
I had a Mother who read to me.

—Stricklin Gillilan

No wise parent wants to pit books against TV and video games in a contest for a child's attention any more than one would pit vegetables and fresh fruit against dessert. In both cases parents who are concerned about a healthy diet have to use all their ingenuity and tact and forcefulness to keep arranging things for children so that dessert does not come first. It is a happy day when children actually come to prefer a fresh apple to a Snickers or when children forget about TV because they are absorbed in a wonderful book. No family can afford to wait for days like that, however. They must commit themselves to the battle for reading because they believe it is a good thing worth fighting for.

Obviously, the main enemies of reading are television and electronic games. Families who try to control over-indulgence in these addictive forms of entertainment have found a variety of strategies that help, as well as many that fail. It is wise to remember that different families need different solutions to such a problem.

The modest improvement that one family made was to cut the children's viewing down to three hours a day. For them, that was success. Many other families have tried—successfully or unsuccessfully—to set one hour a day as a maximum for TV, video, and computer game time. Needless to say, in some homes the one hour expands and expands because of wheedling, needling, whining, pleading, bargaining, and sneaking. Parents get worn down. Also, it is just about impossible for parents to limit television and Nintendo when they or their children are not home. Other families may have more permissive attitudes toward children's leisure time, and most baby sitters use TV to amuse themselves and the children. Many baby sitters simply are not used to TV rules and purposely ignore them. Television has become the baby sitter's baby sitter.

A few unusual families make television and video games a weekend indulgence only. And even then it may be limited to a few hours. This requires strong enforcement, as does the "rental" option, in which family members buy TV or electronic game time by doing chores or paying money into a book fund or reading books first.

In contrast to parents who allow TV sets in their children's bedrooms, some parents limit the family to one set and keep it in an inconvenient place, such as the basement or garage, where viewing is less comfortable. Others store a small TV in a closet and find that children are less apt to watch it if they have to get it out and then put it away afterward.

Another gambit that might work for a few parents is to watch television with the child, making value comments whenever needed. This sharing is good for the child and an eye opener for the parent. When the parent cannot or will not watch any longer, the set goes off. Michael K. Meyerhoff, Ed.D., head of a family advisory agency, believes most of the problems with TV stem from the failure to share the viewing experience. In the early days of television, families owned a single set and gathered around it to watch together. This provided common ground for discussions on a wide variety of topics. It also required family members to work out compromises about what they would watch. Today, Meyerhoff says, "too many kids are getting an overdose of the worst that television has to offer; and they are processing any and all messages sent via the airwaves good, bad, and neutral—without strong and persistent parental input to interpret, elaborate, buffer, or contradict what they see and hear" ("Television: Taming the Great Satan," *Pediatrics for Parents,* 1 January 1997). He tells parents to get rid of every TV set except the one in the family room.

Some parents have no intention of giving up their own favorite programs but want to greatly restrict their children's viewing. An honest thing to tell a child is this:

> I have probably watched 30,000 hours of television myself, but I want to keep you from investing a great deal of your life in it until you are old enough to be sure that is your real desire. I didn't read many good books or hear many good stories when I was a child, but I want you to do so. And I want to share them with you now to catch up on what I missed.

That makes sense and is reasonably fair to a child.

It is also sensible to create a weekly schedule for family activities, including electronic entertainment. As children mature, they can look through the television viewing guide with their parents and circle the programs they agree are worth watching. Then they must narrow their list to fit certain limited time slots in the family schedule. The lure of the screen can be reduced by the realization that it is robbing us of other enjoyable activities. This thoughtful approach encourages children and adults to become more discriminating viewers.

A natural method of limiting television use is to neglect to repair or replace an aging set. Poor reception discourages viewers who are not severely addicted. And the ultimate extension of that course of inaction is to neglect to replace a set when it expires. (There is a bleak passage in John Cheever's novel *Bullet Park* about an incompetent father who throws the family television set out into the rain and breaks it on the concrete because he does not know how to deal with his little boy's helpless dependence upon it.)

Turning off the television or a video game, however, does not automatically turn on books. The telephone, the doorbell, and all the clamor of demands and delights and discomforts are still there. Certain people will, it is said, keep reading even if the house is on fire. But in typical homes today the trick is to foster reading when the house is not on fire. In some homes that is a difficult trick that requires some planning.

TV Tales
Having difficulty getting your kids to turn off the tube? Then check out these books:

📖 *The Bionic Bunny Show* by Marc Brown and Laurene Krasny Brown. Wilbur Rabbit and his animal sidekicks create a TV show about a bunny who can make the impossible possible. This picture book can help young children understand how unreal things are made to look real.

📖 *The Problem with Pulcifer* by Florence Parry Heide. Pulcifer had a serious problem: he could not stop reading. His father was worried and disappointed that his son was not becoming a great TV watcher like dad.

📖 *Fix It* by David McPhail. Emma Bear's TV will not

work, and she is miserable . . . until she discovers reading.

📖 *Mouse TV* by Matt Novak. The mouse family argues about which TV programs to watch. Then the set goes on the blink, and they begin doing the things they once only watched.

📖 *The Wretched Stone* by Chris Van Allsburg. A captain and his crew discover a remarkable stone that captures their attention. They bring it on board their ship, where it gradually turns the crew into mesmerized monkeys. The captain must find a solution.

Out of the Womb and into Books

If you want your child to turn out to be a booklover, there are three secret steps that you need to take: first, be a very active booklover yourself; second, marry another booklover; third, make sure that you choose four grandparents for your child who are all booklovers. After you have taken these three basic steps, you are ready to have a child who loves books. Your chances will be above average.

One British expert claims slyly, "A reading child can be identified before conception." He means that reading children are usually born to reading parents. Reading, like a love of music and athletic skill, tends to run in families. There are exceptions, of course. Some people seem destined to love books just as surely as they were destined to have blue or brown eyes. They come to love books whether books are plentiful or scarce; they love books whether their parents love them or not. They love books no matter what happens.

But most of us and most of our children have to learn

this kind of love. Most booklovers are homemade. Parents who want to interest their children in reading and books can do all kinds of things easily and naturally to help their children become readers when they are ready.

The first way to prepare children for literature is to talk a lot to them and to take pleasure in human sounds with them from the beginning. Nancy Larrick, in *A Parent's Guide to Reading,* suggests four weeks as the right age to start preparing a child to become a reader. When words and love have always gone together in a child's life, he may grow up loving words themselves.

Mothers who talk to their babies all the time about everything are preparing them to be readers. Some parents supplement spoken words with big letters of the alphabet on the walls of the nursery so that their children grow up used to the shapes that they will later learn to read. Some people cut letters out of foam rubber for babies to touch. Many people provide sturdy books made out of cloth or heavy cardboard so that babies can learn to turn the pages as well as wave them, drop them, and chew on them.

But there is no question that for babies the only words that count are the words on the lips of people who love them, not the words in print. The reading that babies do is reading the faces of the people who care for them. If the people who care for them have fun with words, babies become more and more interested in words.

Toddlers and preschoolers are delightful and maddening to read to. There is a marvelous array of books for them in public libraries. At this age a child sometimes demands the same story so many times that the parent gets sick of it no matter how good it is. Also at this age, children sometimes enjoy it if readers pause fairly often in familiar stories and let them fill in key words that they know. (Some kids find it hilarious to fill in the wrong word intentionally.) They like to point to the pictures and turn the pages to get on to the next picture. When children this age imitate their parents and pretend they are really reading a book on their own, things are going well.

At Home with Reading

The basic way to interest children in good books is to have good books in the home. Ideally, children should see both parents reading and even hear their parents talk about books. Unless you have a good reason for not doing so, buy some good books. It has been said that the United States will not ever be a literate nation until we spend as much for books as we do for chewing gum. And chewing gum consumption has been increasing.

How many parents spend as much time reading as watching television? How many go to the library as often as the drugstore? Or to the bookstore as often as the shoe store? According to George Barna, about two-thirds of all adults (65 percent) say that they have purchased at least one book during the past twelve months. Of these purchases, about one-third were children's books. Other studies show that while older adults are buying more, younger adult book purchases are declining. Statistical analysis of national reading habits varies greatly from study to study, but it is fairly safe to say that less than a third of Americans read books.

Children notice where parents go and how they spend their money. Taking children along to libraries and kid-friendly bookstores can be fun for everyone. By the time children reach their teens, they should know the various bookstores and libraries in their vicinity. Family trips to the local children's library can give way to related family outings as the children grow older—trips to used book stores, to library book sales, to publishing companies, to book binderies, and to special libraries. Parents can pass along interesting book reviews to their adolescent children and let them know when interesting authors appear on television talk shows. Furthermore, some parents take their children to lectures by famous authors or plan their vacations around places that became important to them in books. But all of these activities are extras; the important activity is reading.

C. S. Lewis said his father bought all the books he read and never got rid of any of them. His description of their turn-of-the-century house in his autobiography, *Surprised by Joy*, is famous:

> There were books in the study, books in the drawing room, books in the cloakroom, books (two deep) in the great bookcase on the landing, books in a bedroom, books piled as high as my shoulder in the cistern attic, books of all kinds reflecting every transient stage of my parents' interest, books readable and unreadable, books suitable for a child and books most emphatically not. Nothing was forbidden. In the seemingly endless rainy afternoons I took volume after volume from the shelves. I had always the same certainty of finding a book that was new to me as a man who walks into a field has of finding a new blade of grass.

That must have been one of the most bookish homes a child ever grew up in. It is not surprising that C. S. Lewis and his brother kept reading books and talking about books together to the end of their lives. They both became Christians when they were adults, and C. S. Lewis became one of our century's best writers.

The Lewis home is one extreme. We see the other extreme all too often. Even if they own just a few books, many families keep them stashed away at the back of the closet. Bookworms seek them out anywhere, but for normal children books need to be visible in the home. Besides deserving a special shelf or bookcase, they can be purposely propped in public places to tempt people. Books should be seen and heard at home every day. That proves that they are necessary and wonderful.

One family built a book display rack for current interests beside their dining table. Another family has a full bookcase in their large bathroom. One bachelor interior decorator says that he leaves unusual books open in his glamorous New York apartment to make his rooms look "read in." Of course, his purpose is style rather than substance, but that proves that bookish houses need not be dowdy. A parent who cares can set out different books from week to week for variety, the way some people set out vases of flowers or dishes of candy.

The operative word in developing young readers is *pleasure*. If we want books to fall open and children to fall in, then we must present reading as a delight, not a drudgery. Some sincere but misguided parents and teachers attempt to force-feed certain books. For example, one well-meaning Christian school teacher told her seventh-grade class, "For your next book report you will read *In His Steps* by Charles Sheldon." A book that might have provided an enjoyable reading experience immediately went on these adolescents' blacklist. Compelling kids to read books that are "good for them" works about as well as spooning spinach into the mouth of a four-year-old who has decided not to swallow. A wide exposure to healthy books provides children with an opportunity to make choices and to discover their personal preferences. A boy who is fascinated by computer games may enjoy books about how they are created, and a girl who dreams of following in the footsteps of Sally Ride may appreciate stories about outer space. Millions of reluctant readers have been hooked on books because of the tempting bait strategically placed by wise adults.

Science writer Loren Eiseley told how much it meant to him to have his own book collection when he was a child. He knew that no one would throw away any of his worn-out or outgrown books. They were his private property as long as he wanted them, more like friends than like toys. They were few, but they were his own. Every child should have a personal library of books, no matter how small it is.

Once children start school, part of their response to books shifts into the hands of teachers. Fortunate are the children whose teachers read them stories in the classroom. At home, school children profit from a few standard reference books along with books for pleasure. Not every home has to have a set of encyclopedias or their CD-ROM multimedia siblings. But every home should have a good dictionary that gets used.

In very lively homes, avoid headaches and catastrophes around the bookshelves by simple planning. Expensive books and borrowed books should go on the top shelves where grubby little fingers will not pull them off onto the floor and smear them with peanut butter. Books meant for little children to use up and wear out should fill the bottom shelves where babies and puppies might reach them. The less scolding and spanking the better.

In many homes a space may have to be set aside so a child who does not read easily can have a quiet and well-lighted place. In a busy and crowded house where there is more than one child to a bedroom, a young reader could be given the privilege of reading alone in the parents' room. Some children like to read curled up in giant beanbags that plop on the floor anywhere. Daylight is the best kind of light for the eyes, when it is available. Many fluorescent light bulbs emit rays that are tiring and irritating to sensitive people and can cause hyperactivity or emotional strain. Parents should be cautious about using these lights where their children read. Simply watching for undue fatigue, restlessness, and crankiness will tell most parents if their children suffer from this common sensitivity, which could secretly spoil a reading area.

Recent scientific research on nutrition is serving up some surprises about what kinds of food make our brains work best. Researchers have found what some of us learned from personal experience: sugars and starches relax us and make us sleepy, while lean proteins energize us. The average child eats a breakfast and lunch so high in carbohydrates that reading during the day may be a chore rather than a delight. Instead of getting a boost from dopamine and norepinephrine, two of nature's best alertness chemicals available in lean proteins, young bodies are shifted into idleness by the soothing effects of the serotonin in carbohydrates. A high fat intake can create a problem because the blood that the brain needs for high efficiency is busy helping the body deal with these foods that do not digest easily. In addition, quite a few children become too restless to read well after eating sweets. The average American child eats an incredible thirty-two pounds of sugar a year. Perhaps that creates mental as well as dental cavities in some children. The ideal menu for alert readers features low-fat, high-protein foods.

Stories Here and Now

What is the single most important thing that parents can do to interest children of any age in reading? Journalist Jim Trelease has come up with a bestselling answer, and it is a very old-fashioned one: *Read aloud to children.*

In a helpful pamphlet about books and babies, Random House Children's Publishing notes,

At the President's Brain Summit in early 1997, researchers suggested that reading to children in their first few years, when the brain's circuitry is being formed, enhances the children's emotional and social development and lays the groundwork for vocabulary and later educational success.

Bedtime stories can become the highlight of the day. Parents can begin this ritual as soon as babies are ready to snuggle and listen to the sound of a loving voice. And they can continue throughout childhood. Bedtime stories, like clean sheets and fresh milk, are one of the best parts of childhood. But reading aloud to children can be difficult because restlessness interferes with listening. A relaxed pace and a pleasant—not preachy or sugary—tone of voice are always helpful. The better the oral reader, the better the attention.

Even calm young children like to participate when they are listening. A skillful reader can involve the child with short questions and answers and invitations to join in on refrains. It can also be fun to slip the listener's name in sometimes. Still, some children cannot ever listen until they are settled in bed for the night. And some hyperactive children listen best while they are soaking and swishing in the bathtub. Water is magically calming to them and enables them to enjoy a story better.

Countless story times have been destroyed by outside interruptions. At meals or at bedtime it is often worthwhile to let an answering machine take telephone calls and to hang a note by the doorbell in order to have privacy.

Reading aloud should be comfortable for parents if possible. Perching on the side of a bunk bed or a water bed is dreadful. On the other hand, lying down beside a child puts some tired parents to sleep. Some can keep on "reading" a few sentences of utter nonsense as they drift off—much to the listener's consternation. One father bought a sturdy old recliner chair for seven dollars at a garage sale for the sole purpose of reading to his son at bedtime. He realized that he had gradually given this up because they had physically outgrown their lap-sitting and bed-sharing days, and an upright chair or the floor was discouraging. The large comfortable chair helped.

In the home of writer Eve Lewis Perera, the time between dinner and the youngest child's bedtime is devoted to family sharing. Reading aloud fits naturally into this relaxed time of the day. Reading selections are suggested and informally decided upon. Each member of the family takes a turn reading—one paragraph for the youngest and several for older children and adults. Dinner guests are included in what has become an essential part of this family's routine.

Reading patterns should and do vary immensely from family to family. Some homes encourage reading at meals, and others consider it a vice. Some let babies tear up old magazines and let toddlers scribble in their picture books if they want to; others consider it a sacrilege. Some families can read in cars on trips, and others think it is bad for the eyes and/or nauseating. One book that would be fun to read aloud in the car is E. B. White's *Stuart Little*, a story about a mouse's auto journey.

For families who find story reading impossible in moving vehicles, audio-books provide a pleasant way to enjoy books on the road. Many audio-books available in bookstores are disappointing condensations of the original books, but most libraries offer unabridged children's books on tape, and some companies rent audio-books. (See chapter 13 for sources.) One mother who traveled thirty-six hundred miles in two weeks with her twelve-year-old son and nine-year-old daughter credited audio-books with providing an enjoyable journey. As they drove to visit relatives in four states, the family listened to *Watership Down, The Wind in the Willows,* and *The Prince and the Pauper.* There was not a single complaint on the entire trip. Another enriching diversion during travel time is group memorization of limericks and other favorite poems.

Books taken on vacations or visits can redeem spare moments. They give children pleasure in unfamiliar bedrooms and campsites. They can also enrich long waits on all kinds of ordinary errands. Books can make trips come alive as children discover the stories connected with the places they visit. A child who has read *Lily and Miss Liberty* by Carla Stevens or *An Ellis Island Christmas* by Maxine Rhea Leighton will see New York Harbor as more than just monuments and buildings. Books help children travel through time as well as space, appreciating the experiences and feelings of others.

Children's books can be especially valuable to children with disabilities who have limited activities and contacts. Little Cushla Yeoman was born with severe problems, and doctors said she was mentally retarded. As Dorothy Butler tells the story in *Cushla and Her Books,* Cushla's parents began reading to her when she was four months old, and when she was nine months old they could tell which books she liked best. They read her fourteen books a day. When she was three years old, she seemed to have normal intelligence. By the time she was five years old, she had taught herself to read and was clearly above average in intelligence. According to Dorothy Butler, books had been her therapy that worked wonders.

Every home is less than perfect, and even the most ideal families are sometimes handicapped by stress, disappointment, distractions, and pressures. Books not only offer escape and refreshment, but they often show us ways to cope with loneliness, fear, anger, and discouragement. They are therapy for all of us.

How long should parents continue to read aloud to their children? Long after the children can read well to themselves. Children enjoy hearing stories that are far beyond their reading level. They need that kind of stretching. The parent has the double pleasure of sharing old favorites and making new discoveries with a maturing child. For many children, there are few times more cozy and secure than when parents are reading to them. The physical closeness and the sound of that attentive voice continue to nurture the listeners, even in memories. And what parent does not cherish these special memories?

In today's hectic, high-pressure society—full of confused and neglected children and frustrated adults—the battle for family reading is one small part of the war that love is waging.

The Story of
Children's
Literature

4 Once Upon a Time

Dear, dear! How queer everything is today!
And yesterday things went on just as usual.
I wonder if I've been changed in the night?
—Lewis Carroll, *Alice's Adventures in Wonderland*

For fourteen centuries things went on as usual—there were no books for children. In fact, there were not many books for adults either. Then the printing press was invented in 1437, and a wonderful magic was unleashed. The first English printer, William Caxton, brought out a set of old animal stories called *Aesop's Fables* for adults. It became very popular with children and is still read today. He also gave families Thomas Malory's *Le Morte d'Arthur* and the fable *Reynard the Fox*. The idea that books could be good for children entered Caxton's mind, and in 1477 he published *The Book of Curtesye,* a collection of rhymes intended to teach youngsters manners.

The hornbook was invented about 1500 for children's education, but it was not really a book. It was a sort of wooden paddle on which school lessons were written— the alphabet, numerals, and the Lord's Prayer. Sometimes these paddles were also used on the playground for hitting balls, supposedly leading to the British game of cricket.

Chapbooks came into existence at about the same time. "Chapbook" was simply a way of saying "cheap book." These books were as flimsy as hornbooks were

39

sturdy, and they had nothing to do with education. They were little pamphlets usually sixteen pages long, illustrated with crude woodcuts and costing about one penny. Printed mainly for the poor—who made up 85 percent of the population—they consisted of condensed versions of well-known tales such as Robin Hood and King Arthur, legends, fairy tales, and nursery rhymes.

Much like primitive comic books, chapbooks were sold by peddlers or "chapmen," who carried them in bundles. Illiterate people were fascinated by the pictures and would gather to hear the stories read by someone who could read. Unfortunately, there was not much to read in these books. They remained popular with children and adults in England and America for two centuries.

Dreams for a Penny

In *Dream Peddler* (Dutton, 1993) Caldecott medalist Gail E. Haley has given children a captivating glimpse of eighteenth-century London and the world of the chapbook seller. By photocopying the endpapers of her book, readers can make their own chapbook.

The History of Making Books (Scholastic Voyages of Discovery, 1996) takes young readers from clay tablets and papyrus rolls to the printing press.

In the midst of this literary poverty, the first English translation of the Bible, by Miles Coverdale, was published in 1537. In 1611 the King James, or Authorized, version was published. Puritan children on both continents were limited to the Bible and a few acceptable books which they could only open with properly washed hands and a high regard for decorum. Books were brought out on Sundays and opened in silence, and reading was often followed by little oral examinations.

Boston minister John Cotton created a book especially for Puritan children. He titled it *Spiritual Milk for Babes* and filled it with catechism in a question-and-answer format. If fortunate, the children were allowed to read an adult favorite, *Foxe's Book of Martyrs,* which was popular in the 1600s, although it was a century old by then. This exciting book railed against the pope and was illustrated with copper engravings of dead and dying Protestants who gave their lives for God—highly entertaining violence with a Christian message.

The first real literature for children in England and America consisted of gloomy Puritan tales of sin, death, and hell, designed to steer children into eternal life. For example, in 1671 James Janeway wrote *A Token for Children: Being an Exact Account of the Conversion, Holy and Exemplary Lives, and Joyful Deaths of Several Young Children.* He urged children to live godly lives before dying joyfully with Christ's name on their lips. Godly living consisted of *not* doing a lot of things, such as playing with toys—especially Satan's favorite, the spinning top. Children who failed to live right would go to hell. But those who succeeded would be rewarded by an early and joyful death and everlasting bliss. Janeway himself died at 38—how joyfully is not recorded.

In the same year a typical "courtesy book" for teenagers of the day was written by Caleb Trenchfield, Gent., and titled *A Cap of Gray Hair for a Green Head: or, The Father's Counsel to His Son, an Apprentice in London.* Like Charles Shedd's *Letters to Philip,* this book gave advice to a young man concerning proper behavior after marriage. Trenchfield cautioned, "Women can with no patience endure to be mew'd up till Mid-night while you are clubbing it at a Tavern; and you cannot think it a wonder, if at such times they sport with your Servants at home. . . . How long is Love to last, where the blundering Husband comes home like a sous'd Hogshead."

The greatest Puritan book besides Milton's master-piece, *Paradise Lost,* was John Bunyan's *Pilgrim's Progress,* written for adults but relished by children. Published in 1678, it sold at least a hundred thousand copies in Bunyan's lifetime. It will be discussed more fully in chapters 5 and 14.

Shortly after *Pilgrim's Progress,* American Puritans produced the *New England Primer* to teach children to read. Its rhyming alphabet begins:

> *A* . . . In Adam's fall
> We sinned all.
>
> *B* . . . This life to mend
> God's book attend.

The primer, subtitled *An Easy and Pleasant Guide to the Art of Reading,* appeared in varied editions. About seven million copies were sold, and it was used for over a century. Besides the rhyming alphabet it included other sections, such as a long message from a Christian martyr, John Rogers, accompanied by a picture of him burning up while his wife and ten children watched, held back by a guard.

In contrast, across the Atlantic in 1715 Isaac Watts published *Divine Songs* for children. Watts was a Puritan clergyman and hymn writer whose lyrics contained an unusual softness and beauty. His many songs included the well-known "Cradle Hymn" ("Hush! my dear, lie still and slumber"), "When I Survey the Wondrous Cross," "Joy to the World," and "O God, Our Help in Ages Past."

Soon after the lovely Watts hymns, two adult books were published that quickly became children's favorites because children still had no stories of their own. These were Daniel Defoe's *Robinson Crusoe* (1719), which is strongly Christian in its full-length version, and Jonathan Swift's *Gulliver's Travels* (1726).

Then a certain trickle entered England that would later become a flood. In 1729 a popular French book was translated into English, Charles Perrault's collection of eight fairy tales entitled *Tales of Mother Goose*. Children loved it. It was a far cry from their old Puritan books—although morals were tacked onto the tales, such as this one at the end of "Little Red Riding Hood":

Little girls, this seems to say,
Never stop upon your way.
Never trust a stranger-friend;
No one knows how it will end.
As you're pretty, so be wise;
Wolves may lurk in every guise.
Handsome they may be, and kind,
Gay, or charming—never mind!
Now, as then, 'tis simple truth—
Sweetest tongue has sharpest tooth!

After thousands of years of reading and writing, this was the earliest piece of literature for children that intended to entertain more than instruct. It came only 250 years ago.

Next came the first man to successfully produce books for children: John Newbery. His motto was "Trade and Plumb-cake for ever. Huzza!" That meant "Business and entertainment—hurrah!" A farmer's son who married a printer's widow in Reading, England, Newbery took over his wife's first husband's business and moved to London. Soon he became a publisher, a bookstore owner, and an author. It is now known that he hired two great London authors as ghost writers to help him turn out the books he printed: Oliver Goldsmith and Dr. Samuel Johnson.

A growing number of people had the time, money, and education to buy books and read. Middle-class farmers were becoming more home and family centered. And children were being recognized as special human beings. Newbery was the first to realize what a market there was for books produced especially for children. Starting in 1744, he published over thirty children's books.

A shrewd businessman, Newbery died rich, but most of his wealth was gained from the sale of patent medicines rather than books. His best-known remedy, Dr. James's Fever Power, is mentioned often in his children's books. In fact, a tragic death occurred in one story because the sick person was unable to obtain this marvelous medicine.

The first Newbery book announced on its title page:

> *A Little Pretty Pocket Book,* Intended for the Instruction and Amusement of Little Master Tommy and Pretty Miss Polly with Two Letters from Jack the Giant Killer, As Also A Ball and a Pincushion, the use of which will infallibly make Tommy a good Boy and Polly a good Girl.

Amusement is the key word. Newbery wanted to amuse while teaching. The book cost sixpence, and the ball or pincushion two pence extra. Pins were to be stuck into the ball's one side or other to record the child's good and bad deeds. The book contained a series of games with rhymed directions, such as pitch and hussel, cricket, and leap frog. It also included proverbs, rules of behavior, a rhyming alphabet, and a few poems.

Newbery invented characters and imaginary authors including Woglog the Giant, Giles Gingerbread (a boy who lived on learning), Nurse Truelove, Peregrine Puzzlebrains, and Primrose Prettyface. His best publication was *Goody Two-Shoes,* described on the title page as "The History of Little Goody Two-Shoes, otherwise called Mrs. Margery Two-Shoes, with the means by which she acquired her Learning and Wisdom. . . . See the original Manuscript in the Vatican at Rome, and the Cuts by

Michael Angelo." Of course, the original manuscript of this story was not at the Vatican. But Newbery enjoyed little jokes, such as his pretense about Michelangelo.

In 1751 Newbery brought out the first children's periodical of all time, *The Lilliputian Magazine,* which pretended to be produced by the Lilliputian Society and its secretary R. Goodwill. Four years later Newbery published the first children's Bible, *The New Testament Adapted to the Capacities of Children.* The Puritans had not done that!

At about the time of the American Revolution, Isaiah Thomas of Massachusetts pirated Newbery's books and made them available to American children, apparently without paying Newbery a penny. But books from another British source had more widespread appeal and influence over the development of children's literature in America. Their author was Maria Edgeworth, a firm believer that young minds are best influenced by stories that convey "the history of realities written in an entertaining manner." Once again, moralizing won out over imagination and entertainment. But to Maria's credit, her instructive tales had real plots with suspense and surprise endings.

At the turn of the century, Christian tract societies were established in England and North America to minister to adults and children. Sunday School Unions were being formed then also. In 1820, the Tract Society of New York (later the American Tract Society) warned that books of fiction and fancy were a bad influence and that books of war, piracy, and murder led children into crime.

In 1825, the Philadelphia Sunday School Union published *The Glass of Whiskey* for children. It said,

> There is a bottle. It has something in it which is called whiskey. Little reader, I hope you will never take any as long as you live. It is poison. So is brandy, so is rum, so is gin, and many other drinks.

> They are called strong drink. They are so strong
> that they knock people down and kill them.

It is not surprising that most American children preferred to read Washington Irving's Knickerbocker Tales.
The stories of "Rip Van Winkle" and "The Headless
Horseman" offered a different but equally intoxicating
kind of strong drink.

In the early 1800s most educated people disapproved
of imaginative literature for children. They preferred
factual information about science, history, geography, or
travel to fairy tales or other "absurd" books. Samuel
Griswold Goodrich agreed with them, and in 1827 he
published *Tales of Peter Parley About America*. It was so
popular that he wrote 120 other information books under the pen name of Peter Parley. Sales reached seven
million, and there were numerous imitations in both
America and England.

Not everyone agreed with this trend. British author
Charles Lamb complained to his friend Samuel Taylor
Coleridge about the shortage of books like *Goody Two-
Shoes.* He wanted young readers to experience the romance of language and ideas, to laugh and cry over
human experience, to be inspired to virtue rather than
coerced into it. In this spirit, Lamb and his sister Mary
Ann gave children's literature one of its enduring classics, *Tales from Shakespeare* (1807).

At about the same time, the Grimm brothers' collection of German folk tales was translated into English for
readers of all ages. The Grimms were German language
scholars who claimed they discovered traditional fairy
tales among the humble peasants. (Over a century later,
researchers discovered that the Grimms had fooled everyone about where the stories came from. In 1985 John
Ellis explained the hoax in his book *One Fairy Story Too
Many.* See chapter 5 for more information.)

In 1837, Victoria took the throne of England, and before her reign was over the tide had turned—children's literature had exploded with creative fiction and fantasy. Two years after Victoria was crowned, the earliest modern fairy story was written by Mary Sinclair in her book *Holiday House*. Called "The Wonderful Story," it tells about a lazy, greedy boy named Master No-book, and it begins, "In the days of yore, children were not all such clever, good, sensible people as they are now." As you can tell, the story is cheerful satire.

Two years later a twelve-year-old girl named Euphemia Gray challenged the young adult John Ruskin to write a fairy story for her. She thought it would be impossible, but Ruskin promptly wrote *The King of the Golden River*. When it was published ten years later, he and Euphemia were already married. Unfortunately, the marriage did not end as happily as the fairy story. ("The Wonderful Story," "The King of the Golden River," and several other fine stories from the 1800s are now in the collection *Modern Fairy Stories*, edited by Roger Lancelyn Green.)

In 1844, Francis Paget published *The Hope of the Datzekopfs: or, The Sorrows of Selfishness*, thinking that a tale of enchantment might teach wisdom to young people. Paget was rebelling against "the unbelief of this dull, plodding, unimaginative, money-getting, money-loving nineteenth century." Two years later, Hans Christian Andersen's *Fairy Tales* was translated into English. The incomparable Andersen had collected and retold folk tales from various lands and added fairy stories of his own.

Four years after Andersen's stories came to England, the public library movement began there in 1850. That may seem like a dull fact, but this movement would eventually make good books available to vastly more children and would be a great support to children's book publishers. In 1851, Ruskin's *The King of the Golden River* was published, and for fifty years after that children's literature continued to flourish.

During Queen Victoria's reign, children also read the highly popular adult novels of Walter Scott and the Leatherstocking Tales of James Fenimore Cooper. Then there were the great books by Mark Twain, *The Adventures of Tom Sawyer* (1876), *Life on the Mississippi* (1883), and *Huckleberry Finn* (1884).

Series books also became extremely popular at this time. Children enjoyed adventure series, mystery series, biography series, and series on sports, science, and occupations. In the books of the American Horatio Alger, a poor boy always makes good through hard work: the epitome of the American ideal. Beginning with *Ragged Dick* in 1868, Alger wrote over a hundred books, mostly in series of six. Unlike his heroes, Horatio Alger did not get rich. He did, however, become famous; for generations his name was a household word.

Another category of literature that came into its own in the Victorian age was the domestic drama. One quiet spinster who created these family stories was Charlotte Mary Yonge. C. S. Lewis said of her, "[She] makes it abundantly clear that domesticity is no passport to heaven on earth but an arduous vocation—a sea full of hidden rocks and perilous ice shores only to be navigated by one who uses a celestial chart." Yonge was an ardent Christian and a gifted storyteller who won the hearts of readers with *The Heir of Redcliffe* (1853) and *The Daisy Chain* (1856). A prolific writer, she gave the world over two hundred books and edited a magazine called the *Monthly Packet*.

On the other side of the Atlantic Ocean, Susan Warner's domestic novels were a similar sensation. Writing under the pseudonym of Elizabeth Wethrell, Warner wrote *The Wide, Wide World* in 1850. Another devout Christian, Warner made her home with her sister Anna in a cottage on Constitution Island (which they owned), directly across from West Point. The sisters devoted much of their time to teaching Sunday school and ministering to cadets. The rest was spent in literary pursuits. Anna is best remembered for giving children the favorite hymn, "Jesus Loves Me, This I Know." Susan's bestseller, *The Wide, Wide World,* was second in sales only to *Uncle Tom's Cabin.* While one was an impassioned tract against slavery, the other was an equally fervent tract for Christianity.

When Louisa May Alcott wrote *Little Women* (1868), she was following in the footsteps of Yonge and Warner. In the British edition of *Little Women,* Jo March cried over Yonge's *The Heir of Redcliffe.* In the American edition, she cried over Warner's *The Wide, Wide World.* Some critics note a strong similarity between Jo and Yonge's character Ethel May.

Martha Finlay came next with her series Elsie Dinsmore (1867), books about the most goody-goody heroine in all fiction. In addition to being very rich and beautiful, this little girl is extremely tearful. She cries sixty-three times in the first book alone. In his book *Written for Children,* author John Rowe Townsend says,

> The most fascinating thing about Elsie is that although she is so pure, and the tone of her books is religious and uplifting, the reader nevertheless can wallow in emotion and sensuality while contemplating those beautiful large soft eyes, forever filling with tears; that slender frame forever being clasped to Father's breast for kisses and fondlings. This perhaps is the literary equivalent of "tonic wine," which you can drink without guilt but which is quite highly alcoholic.

In 1881 *The Five Little Peppers and How They Grew* by

Margaret Sidney appeared, telling about a resourceful family and the mother who works hard tailoring and mending to pay their rent. The first book led to a series of six and sold over a million copies.

Frances Hodgson Burnett's *Little Lord Fauntleroy* (1886) went through nine editions in nine months and is said to have swept England like a sickly fever. It is the story of a wonderful little boy, but people who have not read it have the mistaken impression that it is about an obnoxious prig. Burnett's *A Little Princess,* also known as *Sara Crewe* (1888), and *The Secret Garden* (1909) are still favorites with readers young and old.

One of the most powerful and imaginative Victorian fantasy writers was George MacDonald, a Congregationalist minister turned author, who had an enormous influence on C. S. Lewis years later. His works for children include *The Golden Key* (1867), *At the Back of the North Wind* (1871), *The Princess and the Goblin* (1872), *The Princess and Curdie* (1883), *The Light Princess* (1893), and several short stories. Here is a Christian author who wrote serious yet exciting fairy stories.

Some other highlights in the floodtide of children's literature between 1850 and the very early 1900s are Charles Kingsley's *Water-Babies* (1863), Lewis Carroll's *Alice's Adventures in Wonderland* (1865), Kate Greenaway's *Under the Window* (1879), Robert Louis Stevenson's *Treasure Island* (1880) and *A Child's Garden of Verses* (1885), Rudyard Kipling's *Jungle Books* (1894, 1895) and *Just So Stories* (1902), E. Nesbit's *The Story of the Treasure Seekers* (1899), and Beatrix Potter's *Peter Rabbit* (1901). Queen Victoria died in 1901.

With a few notable exceptions, children's literature became far less exciting in the first half of the twentieth century. Then around 1950, another flood of outstanding books appeared. The children's wealth of the atomic age rivals that of the Victorian age or exceeds it. The books of the twentieth century will be discussed in later chapters. Aside from quality, their numbers alone are staggering.

Juvenile literature has become big business. In 1940 Random House, one of the largest publishers in the United States, had no separate juvenile department. But by 1973 its juvenile budget alone was thirteen million dollars, and that department was its most profitable. For many years it has had entire warehouses covering several acres to store the books of just one of its most popular authors—Dr. Seuss.

Dr. Seuss began as the mere Theodor Geisel, a Hollywood screen artist and successful advertising cartoonist. He wrote his first book by accident, setting words to the rhythm of the ship's engines on a long crossing of the Atlantic. Twenty-nine publishers rejected that book—*And to Think That I Saw It on Mulberry Street* (1937)—but the thirtieth publisher accepted it. Children loved it. His first two books under the pen name *Dr. Seuss* were so popular that he became a full-time children's author.

Geisel wrote a total of forty-eight books, translated into twenty languages, and he received a Pulitzer Prize citation for his contribution to American family life. It is said that during his lifetime he sold more books than any other living author and was probably the richest writer alive. That makes him one of the richest authors in the history of the world. According to biographers, by 1984 his yearly royalties averaged one and a half million dollars or more. Since his death in 1991, sales have remained as strong as ever. Geisel attributed his success to three qualities his books shared—verse, absurdity, and fun.

Three hundred years ago little American children were reading in their New England Primers:

Xerxes must die
And so must I.

Today they are reading:

> We looked!
> Then we saw him step in on the mat!
> We looked!
> And we saw him!
> The Cat in the Hat!

Twenty years after *And to Think That I Saw It on Mulberry Street*, Dr. Seuss wrote *The Cat in the Hat* with only 223 carefully chosen words, a "controlled vocabulary" for beginners which Random House supplied. "I read the list three times and I almost went out of my head," Seuss told *Arizona Magazine*. "I said, 'I'll read it once more, and if I can find two words that rhyme, that'll be the title of my book.'" He decided later that controlled vocabulary was a poor idea. But he continued to believe that we would not have so many illiterates today if they had been given interesting reading materials as children.

An incredible literary heritage bridges Perrault's *Mother Goose* and Dr. Seuss. Our children who sample the literature in between are richer for it.

Children's Literature Timeline

1450: Printing press was working, but not for children
1550: Still nothing for children
1650: Puritans began printing instruction books for children
1750: Newbery began the fun-filled children's book business
1850: Rich period of fantasy books for children began in England
1950: Second very rich period of books for children began in England and the U.S.

Old Books for Young People

5 Tried and True

If one man's meat is another man's poison, certainly one man's book may be another man's boredom.

—May Hill Arbuthnot, *Children's Books Too Good to Miss*

Here is a browser's guide to over forty of the best books from the past for children today. They are not better than today's books just because they are older. But they are part of our heritage and too good to forget. Some young readers will enjoy exploring these classics on their own, but more enjoy them as family reading experiences. By sharing these books with your children, you will form important links between the past and the present, lay the foundation of a rich cultural heritage, and create a treasure trove of happy memories.

Early copies of these beloved books are extremely valuable, but current editions of the books are affordable, plentiful, and sometimes more attractive than older editions. Dover Publications sells facsimiles of children's classics from eighteenth-century chapbooks on. All are high quality at low prices. (For publisher addresses, see appendix 4.)

More recently the Antique Collectors' Club has launched a line of children's classics with "new contemporary illustrations, fine printing, good paper, and traditional binding in cloth with dust jackets."

The writers of this literature of the past were not all innocent, domesticated, pious, and happy, although one was Queen Victoria's chaplain. One was a political spy, one took his pen name from his job as a rowdy riverboat pilot, and one was the successful but sad secretary of the Bank of England. One wrote in prison, and one died in prison. Those who wrote some of the greatest children's books of all time were as varied as the books they produced. The same is true of those who write great books for children today.

In addition to glimpses at the authors and what they wrote about, we have included references to some recent editions of these classics that you and your family may enjoy.

Aesop's Fables (translated into English in 1484)
In folklore, animals and humans often speak a common language and learn from one another. A folktale becomes a fable when it has an obvious moral purpose. Most of our familiar fables come from Greece and are attributed to Aesop. According to one legend, Aesop, whose name means black, was a slave at Samos in the sixth century B.C. However, most scholars think that Aesop's fables originated with Demetrius Phalerus, founder of the Alexandrian Library (300 B.C.). G. K. Chesterton compared Aesop to the fictional Uncle Remus. While we cannot unpuzzle his life history, we know that Aesop's fables were translated into Latin, then French, followed by an English translation published in 1484 by William Caxton, England's first printer.

Fables have fallen into disfavor with those who think their moralizing detracts from their effectiveness as stories. It is important to remember, as Jean de la Fontaine the famous French fable-teller observed, "We yawn at sermons, but we gladly turn / To moral tales, and so amused, we learn."

Young readers can enjoy *Aesop's Fables* beautifully illustrated by Heidi Holder (Viking, 1981). For a more complete selection, try V. S. Vernon Jones's translation with classic illustrations by Arthur Rackham (Franklin Watts, 1968).

Pilgrim's Progress by John Bunyan (1678)
Just seventeen years after the King James Bible broke upon the world, a baby boy was born into a very poor family in an obscure English village. They gave him England's most common name—John—and sent him to the free school in the village long enough for him to learn to read and write. Then he became a tinker (a traveling mender of metal household utensils). John was drafted into the army as a teenager, escaped death by a hair, returned to be one of the village rowdies, and then married a poverty-stricken but virtuous girl when he was about twenty-one.

Bunyan's young bride had nothing but a couple of religious books that she had inherited from her father, and the two read them. Soon John was studying the King James Bible, was converted, and at twenty-five became a lay preacher. When he was thirty-two, Bunyan was caught preaching—a violation of England's Restoration Law. He was thrown into the county jail for twelve years. There he wrote several great books and preached to his visitors. When he was forty-four, the law changed, allowing laymen to preach, and Bunyan returned to his wife and children. But the law was soon reversed, and he was locked up in the town jail for six months. It was during this second time in prison that he wrote his immortal classic, *Pilgrim's Progress*. In the first sentence he said he entered a den and dreamed a dream. The den was really his prison cell; the dream, the allegorical story he was inspired to write.

Bunyan waited until 1678 to publish the book because some friends had advised against it. Beloved by both children and adults, it sold 100,000 copies in ten years while Bunyan was a busy Baptist pastor. It is said that for over two centuries most homes in England had two books if no others—the King James Bible and *Pilgrim's Progress*, two of the finest works of English literature. Since Bunyan's flowing prose is utterly superb—except when he stops to preach a bit—families who can do so without undue frustration would do well to read *Pilgrim's Progress* as Bunyan wrote it, not in Mary Godolphin's quaint version that uses only words of one syllable. As C. S. Lewis said, "We must attribute Bunyan's style to a perfect natural ear, a great sensibility for the idiom and cadence of popular speech, a long experience in addressing unlettered audiences, and a freedom from bad models." It is nice to keep in touch with roots like that. (For more about *Pilgrim's Progress*, see chapter 14.)

Arabian Nights (translated into English in 1706)
The stories of Ali Baba, Aladdin, and Sindbad the Sailor originated in Persia, Arabia, India, and Egypt. They were collected and set down in Arabic in the late 1400s, and they serve as an excellent reminder that imaginative storytelling was going on for centuries all around the world. Many of these folktales are not appropriate for children, but every child should know a few of them.

The first English translation of *Arabian Nights* was derived from a contemporary French translation. One of the earliest children's editions was edited by Andrew Lang in 1898. Children loved the magic password, "Open sesame," the genie in an oil lamp, and the wonderful flying carpets. Since that time, countless editions of Queen Scheherazade's fabulous stories have appeared. The influence of *Arabian Nights* on Western imaginative literature is considerable.

Children today can enjoy these ancient stories as retold by Amabel Williams-Ellis and illustrated by Pauline Baynes in 1957. Many of the tales also appear individually as picture books. One of the best is *Aladdin and the Enchanted Lamp* (1985) by Marianna Mayer, illustrated by Caldecott medalist Gerald McDermott.

Tales of Mother Goose or *Stories from Olden Times* by Charles Perrault (translated into English in 1729)
After a brief career as a lawyer, Charles Perrault devoted himself to the world of literature. He believed that the arts and sciences were at their peak in his time and place, seventeenth-century France under the reign of Louis XIV. This was an unusual idea because most educated people in Europe and America believed that ancient Greek and Roman culture had been the highest summit of all.

Perrault created his collection of fairy tales for Elizabeth Charlotte d'Orleans, niece of Louis XIV. It contained eight folktales, including "Little Red Riding Hood," "Blue Beard," "Puss in Boots," "Cinderella," and "Hop o' My Thumb." Although Perrault invented the term *Mother Goose,* she is now associated almost exclusively with nursery rhymes rather than Perrault's courtly fairy tales.

Since this book was first translated into English in 1729, its beloved stories have been retold by many outstanding writers and illustrated by some of the world's most talented artists. Two of the best are Trina Schart Hyman's interpretation of *Red Riding Hood* (a Caldecott Honor Book) and Marcia Brown's *Cinderella* (Caldecott Winner). You and your child will find it interesting to compare the many different ways people present the same stories.

Robinson Crusoe by Daniel Defoe (1719)
A major character in a great detective novel says,

> When my spirits are bad—Robinson Crusoe. When I want advice—Robinson Crusoe. In past times,

when my wife plagued me: in present times, when I have had a drop too much—Robinson Crusoe. I have worn out six stout Robinson Crusoe's with hard work in my service.

When this adult Christian novel burst into a bleak book world, it became the favorite adventure story for readers of all ages. It is the story of a young fool who ran away from wealth, security, and family love for a rough life at sea—and came to his senses too late, stranded alone on a tropical island.

Defoe's story is loosely based on the real adventures of Alexander Selkirk. It begins when Robinson Crusoe is shipwrecked on an island near the Orinoco River of Venezuela. Adjusting to the primitive conditions by practicing self-reliance and ingenuity, he builds a shelter, raises corn, makes a raft, and finds great comfort reading the Bible. He becomes a strong Christian. After twenty-four years of solitude, one Friday he saves a black man from cannibals and thus acquires an excellent companion, whom he names Friday. Later on, other shipwreck survivors join him, he eventually returns to England, and he has more adventures.

Defoe recorded thirty-five years of suspense, surprises, and setbacks, from the day Crusoe ran away to sea until the day that he was rescued from his island. As a result, the book is so long—475 pages of fine print in the 1885 edition—that few people are aware of the second half, in which Crusoe returns to his island, travels clear around the world, and returns to England in old age to peacefully await "a longer journey than all these." Abridged editions of the first half tend to leave out Crusoe's long struggle with God and his slow transformation into a faith-filled Christian. Kathryn Lindskoog's Young Reader's Library edition of this classic (Multnomah, 1991, now available through the on-line bookstore, Amazon.com) retains the complete story and its Christian message.

Defoe was the son of a London butcher and was raised a Presbyterian. His education was intended to prepare him for the ministry, but he became a hosiery merchant instead. That was another false start because he was a talented journalist, not a talented businessman. He wrote countless political pamphlets and single-handedly produced a journal called *The Review* three times a week for ten years. At times he also moonlighted as a political spy. One of his political pamphlets was a satire urging high-church Anglicans to be more severe in their persecution of Non-conformists. When the Anglicans realized that he was really attacking them for their intolerance, Queen Anne had him severely fined, pilloried, and cast into Newgate Prison.

Defoe was almost sixty when he wrote this first novel and discovered his gift for vivid fiction. After his success with *Robinson Crusoe,* he wrote seven more novels in his last ten years, obviously turning them out as fast as possible for fun and profit. *Robinson Crusoe* is one of the most popular adventure stories ever told.

Gulliver's Travels by Jonathan Swift (1726)

This books appeals to adults because of its satire and to children because of its fantasy. In its first three weeks it sold ten thousand copies.

Jonathan Swift was dean of St. Patrick's Cathedral in Dublin, Ireland, but spent a great deal of time in London and was active in political life. He was passionately devoted to the welfare of the oppressed and wrote this book to attack all manner of evils, lampooning the English in particular. Because it is a masterpiece, they loved it anyway, and it made Swift a hero in his native Ireland.

The book has four parts:

1. Lemuel Gulliver, a ship's surgeon, sails from Bristol, is shipwrecked, and swims ashore to find himself on the island of Lilliput, whose inhabitants are foolish and petty and only six inches tall.

2. Gulliver next finds himself in Brobdingnag where he treats those citizens as the Lilliputians treated him. This portion is a satire on politics.

3. The islands of Laputa and Lagado are the scene for less memorable adventures that satirize the endeavors of philosophers and scientists.

4. Finally Gulliver visits the land of the Houyhnhnms, where a race of intelligent and kind horses rules over a race of stupid and filthy humans known as Yahoos. After trying to describe our civilization to the Houyhnhnms, Gulliver realizes that all humans are Yahoos! But he remains curious, hopeful, and ready for new adventures—an outlook we wish for our children in an often disappointing world.

In its entirety, *Gulliver's Travels* is too negative for many adults and certainly too harsh for children. But there are good expurgated versions that both children and adults can enjoy. Swift's masterpiece is imaginative and witty, simply written, and dear to the hearts of those who hate pretension. Introduce children to Swift's fantastic story as retold by Ann Keay Beneduce and illustrated by Gennady Spirin (Philomel Books, 1993).

Tales from Shakespeare by Mary and Charles Lamb (1807)
Here twenty plays by Shakespeare are turned into stories for young readers. They are retold simply and with faithfulness to the originals, emphasizing the moral of the

central situation in each play. Shakespeare's own language has been woven into the text wherever possible. Mary wrote the fourteen comedies; Charles the six tragedies.

Charles and Mary were a devoted brother and sister who inherited brilliance and the family tendency toward insanity. Charles lost his mind and was committed to an institution once, and he never knew if the illness would recur.

Once, after his recovery, he returned home and found Mary holding a bloody knife: she had just injured their father and killed their mother. Charles became Mary's legal guardian and cared for her from then on, thus sparing her life in an asylum but forfeiting marriage for himself. When she was not suffering occasional relapses, Mary was a loving and delightful companion. Charles supported them both by working as a clerk in the accounting department of London's East India House. In his spare time, he wrote his popular essays, his part of *Tales from Shakespeare,* and wonderful letters to his friends.

Swiss Family Robinson by J. D. Wyss (1814)
Of the many imitations of Defoe's *Robinson Crusoe,* this is the favorite. Wyss was pastor of the Protestant Reformed Cathedral in Berne, Switzerland, and wrote this story to read aloud to his four sons. One of those boys grew up to be a noted professor of philosophy at the University of Berne and adapted his father's story for publication.

Fairy Tales by Jacob and Wilhelm Grimm (translated into English in 1823)
Because of their political views, these noted German linguists became interested in editing German folktales. They pretended they had gone from village to village and house to house collecting the spoken tales. In fact, however, their major sources were educated, middle-

class, and French. The brothers gathered tales from well-to-do friends and relatives, radically rewrote them, and passed them off as genuine German folktales. (For the full account of their deception, read *One Fairy Story Too Many* by John M. Ellis, professor of German literature at the University of California, Santa Cruz.) With this publication, folktales supposedly told by poor people suddenly became fashionable among rich people. In spite of the hoax that was being perpetrated, the stories had a spellbinding quality that made them extremely popular.

The first English edition of their work, called *German Popular Stories*, contained fifty-five tales in two volumes. It was illustrated by George Cruikshank, whose vigorous but eerie etchings enhanced the stories. (Years later Cruikshank became a crusader against alcohol and rewrote some of the stories as propaganda for abstinence.)

The Grimms's stories are not full of fairies. They include tales of kings and princes, ordinary folk such as tailors and soldiers, and apprentices in search of their fortune. Magic abounds; goblins weave spells; and birds, beasts, and people avenge bad deeds or aid the good-natured. Some stories are pure beast fables. Others are familiar stories in a new guise, such as "The Sleeping Beauty," and "Cinderella."

One less familiar tale well worth reading is *The Water of Life* retold by Barbara Rogasky and illustrated by Trina Schart Hyman (Holiday House, 1986). Do not miss the marvelous picture book *Rapunzel*, retold and illustrated by Paul O. Zelinsky (Dutton, 1997; Caldecott Winner for 1998).

"The Pied Piper of Hamelin" by Robert Browning (1842)
Browning is considered one of the major poets of the Victorian era, and his story-poem about a clever piper

is one of his best-known works. The poem is derived from a thirteenth-century German folktale. Browning wrote "The Pied Piper of Hamelin" for a friend's little boy who was ill, and he made the language very colorful and the descriptions vivid so that the boy could have fun illustrating it. Children are charmed by the rhythm and rhyme and delighted when the mistreated piper outwits the stingy town.

A Christmas Carol by Charles Dickens (1843)
This story of nineteenth-century England has delighted young and old for over a century. Novelist Dickens wrote his Christmas Books series for family reading in five years, and *A Christmas Carol* became the most popular. His little *Life of Our Lord,* which he wrote for his own children in 1849 and not for publication, was finally printed in 1934 but is not widely known.

A Christmas Carol tells about miser Ebenezer Scrooge, who dreams he is visited on Christmas Eve by spirits that enable him to see his past life, his miserliness, and his danger of eternal hell. On Christmas Day, he awakens a changed man. The carol ends with the joyful cry of Tiny Tim, the crippled son of Scrooge's needy clerk, Bob Cratchet, "God bless us, every one!" Award-winning illustrator Roberto Innocenti has given young readers a magnificent visual experience to go with Dickens's original text for *A Christmas Carol* (Stewart, Tabori & Chang, 1990).

Dickens is best known for such novels as *Oliver Twist* (1838), *David Copperfield* (1850), *A Tale of Two Cities* (1859), and *Great Expectations* (1861). Some older children enjoy these books as well, but others find them too complex and depressing. Dickens wrote four stories for children that were published as *A Holiday Romance* (1874). Two of them—"Captain Boldheart" and "The Magic Fishbone"—are presented in one volume with illustrations by Hilary Knight (Macmillan, 1964). Both stories are melodramatic spoofs filled with outrageous events meant to bring boos, hisses, hurrahs, and laughter from the entire family.

Fairy Tales by Hans Christian Andersen (translated into English in 1846)

Hans Andersen, the gangling and awkward son of a poor Danish washerwoman and a shoemaker, was often ridiculed and mistreated by his peers. His profound love of children and compassion for their suffering is evident in his *Fairy Tales*. Although he loved books and the theater from childhood and dreamed of becoming famous, he was "the Ugly Duckling"—a failure in the trades his mother chose for him, and as an actor, singer, and dancer. His determination won him a sponsor and an education. He made a modestly successful beginning as a poet and novelist. Then in 1835 he wrote four short stories for the daughter of the secretary of the Academy of Art. The Ugly Duckling at last had become a Beautiful Swan.

In the next forty years, Andersen wrote more than 150 stories for children, and they have been translated into more than eighty languages. His early stories were based on old folktales, but around 1843 he began to create his own stories. His frequent travels, love of nature, memories of childhood, and everyday events became the "seeds" for his fairy tales. "They lay in my thoughts as a seed-corn," he said, "requiring only a flowing stream, a ray of sunshine, a drop from the cup of bitterness, for them to spring forth and burst into bloom."

Andersen's *Fairy Tales* are considered to be among the most beautiful, sensitive, and powerful tales ever told. Fancy and reality blend in these stories, which include "The Little Match Girl," "The Ugly Duckling," "The Little Mermaid," "The Emperor's New Clothes," and his masterpiece, "The Snow Queen." His tales contain sweetness and sadness, gravity and sunshine. One especially beautiful edition of *The Snow Queen* is a retelling by Amy Erlich with pictures by Susan Jeffers (1982).

The Water Babies by Charles Kingsley (1863)
Charles Kingsley was a scholar in mathematics and classics at Cambridge University and after ordination became the parish priest at Eversley. He immediately set out to reform the parish. He was a co-founder of the Christian Socialist movement in Britain and a professor at Cambridge. In 1859 he became chaplain to Queen Victoria.

He wrote *Water Babies* for his youngest child, Grenville. The hero is a neglected little chimney sweep named Tom who drowns in a river and becomes a water baby, to be helped by good fairies. Tom swims to the home of other water babies, where he meets the two fairies Bedonebyasyoudid and Doasyouwouldbedoneby, who slowly teach him to be good. The theme of this strange moral fantasy is redemption: Tom's sin is washed away. A new edition of *The Water Babies*, retold by Josephine Poole and illustrated by Jan Ormerod (Millbrook, 1998), may once again draw children into the magical waters that have grown murky with time.

Alice's Adventures in Wonderland by Lewis Carroll (1865)
The Rev. C. L. Dodgson (Lewis Carroll) taught mathematics at Oxford University. He was a bachelor who was interested in logic, photography, and playful nonsense. He was also an ordained minister, but preaching was difficult for him because he had a stammer. On 4 July 1862, Dodgson took three little girls rowing on the river. They were daughters of Henry George Liddel, dean of Christ Church College where Dodgson taught. During

the boat ride he began telling the girls a story. Later he wrote it down at the request of his favorite, Alice, calling it *Alice's Adventures Underground*. This handwritten, illustrated manuscript is in the British Museum.

Once Dodgson decided to publish the book, he chose the famous *Punch* magazine cartoonist Sir John Tenniel to do the pictures. By then the real Alice was becoming a teenager and had changed a good deal; thus the original elfin, brunette Alice was replaced by the young, blond girl we know so well. But Dodgson had one special copy of the new book bound in white vellum as a gift for Alice.

In spite of the fact that Dodgson had to pay a publisher to issue the book, and the fact that some reviewers disliked it, the story was immediately successful among children. By the 1880s it had been introduced in most European countries, including Russia where the title became *Sonya in the Kingdom of Wonder.*

Out of demand for an Alice that very young children could enjoy, Dodgson wrote *The Nursery Alice*, also illustrated by John Tenniel. In 1966, McGraw-Hill released a new edition of this work. In saluting its reappearance, Roger Lancelyn Green said, "It is one of the mysteries of publishing that this charming book . . . has been out of print for so many years. As a book for children under five, it is only surpassed by the best of Beatrix Potter."

Alice has been of immense interest to adults, but many children today are bored or disturbed by it. Most of the wit is lost to modern children and much of it to adults, unless they read an annotated version that explains the jokes and puns. This book and its 1872 companion, *Through the Looking Glass,* are the sources of numerous familiar quotations.

In 1876, Dodgson wrote an Easter message to every child who loves Alice. Here is an excerpt from his letter:

Dear Child:

Please fancy, if you can, that you are reading a real letter from a real friend whom you have seen, and whose voice you can seem to yourself hear, wishing you, as I do now with all my heart, a happy Easter.

. . . I do not believe God means us . . . to divide life into two halves—to wear a grave face on Sunday and to think it out of place to even so much as mention Him on a weekday. Do you think He cares to see only kneeling figures, and to hear only tones of prayer; and that He does not also love to see the lambs leaping in the sunlight, and to hear the merry voices of the children as they roll among the hay? Surely their innocent laughter is as sweet in His ears as the grandest anthem that ever rolled up from the "dim, religious" light of some solemn cathedral.

And if I have written anything to add to those stories of innocent and healthy amusement that are laid up in books for the children I love so well, it is surely something I may hope to look back upon without shame and sorrow (as how much of life must then be recalled!) when my turn comes to walk through the valley of shadows.

This Easter sun will rise on you, dear children, feeling your "life in every limb," and eager to rush out into the fresh morning air—and many an Easter Day will come and go before it finds you feeble and gray headed, creeping wearily out to bask once more in the sunlight. But it is good, even now, to think sometimes of that great morning when the "Sun of righteousness shall arise with healing in his wings."

Surely your gladness need not be less for the thought that you will one day see a brighter dawn than this—when lovelier sights will meet your eyes than any waving trees or rippling waters—when angel hands shall undraw your curtains, and sweeter tones than ever loving Mother breathed shall wake you to a new and glorious day—and when all the sadness and the sin that darkened this life on this little earth shall be forgotten like the dreams of a night that is past!

Your affectionate friend,
Lewis Carroll

You may want to introduce your family to Carroll's classics by reading *The Other Alice: The Story of Alice Liddell and Alice in Wonderland* by Christina Bjork (author of the bestselling *Linnea in Monet's Garden*) and Inga-Karin Eriksson (R & S Books, 1993). It helps children understand what it was like to be a child in Victorian England and to have a friend like Mr. Dodgson. Alice Liddell (the real Alice) died in 1934, but lived long enough to celebrate the Lewis Carroll centenary in 1933 and to autograph a copy of the book for the present Queen Elizabeth. The story of her adventures in Wonderland has been translated into 120 languages, second only to the Bible.

Hans Brinker, or The Silver Skates by Mary Mapes Dodge (1865)
In her twenties, Mary "Lizzie" Mapes married a lawyer named William Dodge and had two boys. When her husband died, she moved back in with her parents and decided to become a writer. She brought out a book of children's stories, and then a publisher friend of her father asked her to write a book about an American boy in the Civil War.

At first she agreed, but she had heard a lot about Holland from some Dutch neighbors, and she wanted to write about a Dutch boy instead of an American boy.

Editors warned her that young Americans would not want to read about Holland, but she proved them wrong. *Hans Brinker* came out when she was thirty-one and made her famous. She moved into an apartment that looked out on New York's Central Park and kept on writing.

At age thirty-nine, Mrs. Dodge became the first editor of a new children's magazine called *St. Nicholas*. Children loved it. Contributors included Louisa May Alcott, Henry Wadsworth Longfellow, Rudyard Kipling, Emily Dickinson, and John Greenleaf Whittier. Under Dodge's thirty-two-year editorship, *St. Nicholas* was the best children's magazine in the world.

Hans Brinker is the story of a poverty-stricken brother and sister who long to restore their disabled father to his right mind. Secrets get sprung, risks get taken, a great ice-skating race is won, a treasure is found, and mysteries get solved before the splendidly happy ending. It is a tale of courage, faithfulness, aspiration, and generosity.

For an introduction to Dodge's masterpiece, *Hans Brinker*, read *The Hole in the Dike* retold by Norma Green and illustrated by Eric Carle (Crowell, 1974). This story from *Hans Brinker* led the Dutch to erect a statue in Spaardam "dedicated to our youth to honor the boy who symbolizes the perpetual struggle of Holland against the water."

Little Women by Louisa May Alcott (1868–1869)
Louisa May Alcott was born into an unusual family and grew up in Boston. She was surrounded by stimulating people, conversations, ideas, and books—and also by impracticality. Her philosopher father was a dreamer who started a utopian communal farm called Fruitlands. The farm soon fell apart because its transcendental residents liked talking better than farm labor.

Louisa was practical. She served as a nurse during the Civil War and then settled down to make a living for her family with her pen. Her first attempts, fantasies, were failures; then her editor talked her into writing a girl's story instead. Alcott thought the book might be too dull, but it was an immediate bestseller. She followed it with *Little Women, Part II, Little Men* (1871), and *Jo's Boys* (1886). Royalties from her books made it possible for Alcott to support her parents until their deaths.

The little women are the four very human daughters of the memorable March family in New England: Jo, Beth, Meg, and Amy. This nineteenth-century family struggles with various problems, including the prolonged absence of the father and the death of loved ones. The four fun-loving sisters use *Pilgrim's Progress* and the Bible as their guides to life. Jo, the strong young heroine, becomes a writer like Alcott and goes on to lead a full and active life. The chapters are full of laughter and tears and surprises, and they make us cherish the idea of home. This is the first great family story.

In the Young Reader's Library edition (a two-volume set, beginning with *Four Funny Sisters* and followed by *The Sisters Grow Up*), Kathryn Lindskoog has retained the original plot and author's style, while making the story easier for today's readers to enjoy. She also clarifies the importance of *Pilgrim's Progress* in the story, a theme that is often left out or misunderstood. (This edition is now available from *www.amazon.com*)

Sir Gibbie by George MacDonald (1879)

In the world of children's literature, George MacDonald's contributions are often overlooked or underrated. When he is mentioned, it is primarily for his works of fantasy. But MacDonald was also a master of realistic storytelling, as evidenced by *Sir Gibbie*. In *George MacDonald and His Wife*, MacDonald's son and biographer,

Greville MacDonald, writes, "*Sir Gibbie* is, I think, at once the most direct and most beautiful of all George Mac-Donald's novels. . . . Children as much delight in its magic as they cherish the enchantment of his fairy tales."

Sir Gibbie is a heart-gripping adventure story set in Scotland over a century ago. It is the tale of a ragged orphan who triumphs over hunger and homelessness, murder and misery, with a valiant spirit and a heart full of love.

One hundred years after MacDonald wrote the book, Lindskoog met *Sir Gibbie* through an abridged edition by Elisabeth Yates. At the time Yates edited the book, it had been out of print for about thirty years. She short-ened it almost by half. Since Lindskoog knew that the complete *Sir Gibbie* was a favorite of her favorite author, C. S. Lewis, she searched out a copy of the full 1914 Everyman edition, which is probably the one Lewis read. To her dismay, she discovered that along with the old Northern Scots dialect and a key part of the plot, Yates had cut out much of MacDonald's Christian teaching (treating it as a digression from the story).

So Lindskoog immersed herself in the book and adapted it from scratch, faithfully condensing each of the sixty-two chapters to make it as readable for today's American children and adults as it was for British chil-dren and adults a century ago. The resulting edition of *Sir Gibbie* was published as part of Multnomah's Young Reader's Library in 1992 and won a Gold Medallion Award from the Evangelical Christian Publishers Asso-ciation.

Although MacDonald was a minister plagued with poverty, illness, and bereavements, he was also a cele-brated literary figure and public speaker. He was so spec-tacular on an 1872 lecture tour in the United States that he was offered the pastorate of a church on New York's Fifth Avenue with a salary of twenty thousand dollars a year. Leading American authors eagerly befriended him.

MacDonald's literary talent can't compare with that of his friend Mark Twain, but his power of imagination makes him at least Twain's equal. Mark Twain intentionally copied things from George MacDonald's Christian *Sir Gibbie* (1879) when he wrote his non-Christian *Adventures of Huckleberry Finn* (1885). Lindskoog made this discovery when she was studying *Huckleberry Finn* for its centennial. Specific details in *Sir Gibbie* repeatedly appear in *Huckleberry Finn*.

Extensive literary detective work by Lindskoog revealed that when MacDonald and his wife visited the United States in 1872, they became friends of Mark Twain and his wife. The two authors discussed the idea of literary collaboration as a way to protect copyrights and combat transatlantic piracy.

In 1873, Twain and his wife visited the MacDonalds in England. From 1876 to 1883 the two authors sometimes exchanged their works. In 1880 Twain bought MacDonald's new novel *Sir Gibbie*. In 1883 MacDonald invited Twain to co-author the sequel to *Sir Gibbie* but Twain declined. Then in 1885 Twain published *Huckleberry Finn*.

Evidently, *Huckleberry Finn* was Twain's tart answer to *Sir Gibbie*. Both *Huckleberry Finn* and *Sir Gibbie* include humor, horror, irony, and sorrow; but *Sir Gibbie* is permeated by the sweetness of MacDonald's profound trust in God. In contrast, Twain's view of God varied from skeptical to bitter. Gibbie is a moral prodigy and a Mozart of Christian sensibility; in contrast, Huck Finn has keen moral intuition but no sense of God's goodness.

Twain liked George MacDonald and he and his daughter Susie loved MacDonald's fantasy *At the Back of the North Wind* (1871). In this extremely powerful story reminiscent of Andersen's Snow Queen, Little Diamond, a coachman's son, has two parallel lives—one in the harsh world of working-class London and the other in a dream world where he travels with the North Wind, who is a beautiful woman. He is carried through thirty-eight adventures, some with the North Wind and some with earthly friends or enemies—a continual change back and forth between the fantastic and the realistic. Little Diamond reforms, rescues, and guides several people. Then he gets sick and passes through the North Wind to the country lying at her back. Because of its sad beauty, this book is probably for very few children; but it is superb for adults.

One of MacDonald's greatest gifts was his ability to gently draw his readers' hearts toward God. He depicts God as a loving father and mother whose power is mingled with tenderness, and he often portrays wise women as agents of God's grace and discipline. In his poem "Mother's Hymn" he wrote:

> My child is lying on my knees;
> The signs of Heaven she reads:
> My face is all the Heaven she sees,
> Is all the Heaven she needs.
>
> I also am a child, and I
> Am ignorant and weak;
> I gaze upon the starry sky,
> And then I must not speak.
>
> And so I sit in thy wide space
> My child upon my knee:
> She looketh up into my face,
> As I look up to thee.

MacDonald's *The Princess and the Goblin* (1872) and *The Princess and Curdie* (1883) are a wonderful pair of stories for readers of any age. They are easy and exciting enough for children and wise enough for elderly professors. Twenty of MacDonald's other stories are available in a two-volume set called *The Gifts of the Child Christ: Fairy Tales and Stories for the Childlike* (Eerdmans, 1973). The favorites in that set are "The Golden Key" and "The Light Princess." MacDonald said, "For my part I do not write for children, but for the childlike, whether five or fifty or seventy-five."

MacDonald was good friends with Lewis Carroll and Carroll sent his *Alice in Wonderland* manuscript to MacDonald to see how his family would like it. So MacDonald was the first parent in the world to read *Alice* to his children. (He had eleven children of his own and had adopted two more who needed a home.)

C. S. Lewis was strongly influenced by MacDonald's writing. As a Christian he said that he owed more to MacDonald than any other single writer. In *The Great Divorce,* a short fantasy for adults, Lewis pictured himself meeting George MacDonald on the outskirts of heaven and telling the wise old man how his writing led Lewis to Christianity.

20,000 Leagues Under the Sea by Jules Verne (1873)
Jules Verne is considered the father of science fiction. Although his novels were not written for children, many young readers find them fascinating. As a young man, Verne studied law in Paris and then spent fifteen years writing opera lyrics and plays. It was not until he began to write science fiction that his work became popular. His most popular books in the order of their publication in French are *Journey to the Center of the Earth* (1864), *From the Earth to the Moon* (1865), *20,000 Leagues Under the Sea* (1870), *Mysterious Island* (1870), and *Around the World in 80 Days* (1872). In 1995 Grammercy made all five novels available in a one-volume edition. Even more enjoyable for children is Viking's The Whole Story edi-

tion of *Around the World in 80 Days* with its helpful annotations on history and science and colored illustrations.

Families can have fun reading these stories and talking about Verne's hits and misses in predicting the future. Submarines, helicopters, guided missiles, space flight, and air conditioning were among his educated guesses.

The Adventures of Tom Sawyer by Mark Twain (1876)
Samuel Clemens worked as a young riverboat pilot on the Mississippi and derived his pen name, Mark Twain, from a call that reported the depth of the water. The symbolism of the Mississippi River in Twain's writing has been overworked by some critics, and his attack upon racism has been illogically mistaken for racism by some readers. Twain would no doubt make fun of both groups. He was one of the great humorists of all time, but under the humor one finds an increasingly sad, serious, and even bitter man.

The Adventures of Huckleberry Finn (1884) is one of America's greatest works of fiction, but most children enjoy the story of Tom Sawyer far more. It is full of pranks, escapades, hilarious happenings, and spine-tingling adventures. Twain makes a habit of portraying churchgoers as hypocrites; therefore, Tom Sawyer provides an excellent springboard for parents and teachers to talk with children about the need for authentic Christian living. There is much that children can learn from Tom about resourcefulness, loyalty, and perseverance.

Black Beauty by Anna Sewell (1877)
Anna Sewell did not consider herself an author; she was a spunky Quaker, a great animal lover, an artist with unusual talent in science, and a practical helper of people in need. Unfortunately, she was gradually crippled by symptoms that match those of multiple sclerosis.

When she was fifty and totally bedridden, she decided to write a story that would "induce kindness, sympathy, and an understanding treatment of horses." In the months when she could not hold a pencil, she dictated to her mother.

In seven years the story was finished, a lucky publisher bought it for only thirty pounds sterling, and it was published. Anna Sewell died three months later. *Black Beauty* was the first animal story of major importance. It has been translated into over a dozen languages and has sold more than forty million copies.

The horse, Black Beauty, tells this story full of accounts of cruelty to animals—certainly not exaggerated. Some adults chuckle because the horse-narrator all too often expresses the tastes and opinions of a refined lady of the 1800s. Nevertheless, Sewell wrote with compassion and courage, condemning war, fox hunting, greed, and alcohol abuse. Her story fosters kindness to human beings as well as animals, and encourages clean living and regular church attendance.

Most readers today assume they are reading *Black Beauty* as it was originally written. That is usually not the case. As enduring as it and other children's classics are, their Victorian language and verbosity are difficult to comprehend or enjoy. Unfortunately, some modern editions have removed uplifting moral and spiritual content. A more satisfying alternative is the Young Reader's Library edition (now available through *www.amazon.com*).

The Peterkin Papers by Lucretia Hale (1880)
One day Lucretia Hale and some friends were about to go for a drive, but their horse refused to budge. After trying every method possible to get the horse to move, they discovered they had forgotten to untie it from the hitching post. This event is supposed to have provided the idea for Hale's Peterkin stories. The Peterkin family

manages to complicate all sorts of simple situations. These problems are always solved by a certain practical lady from Philadelphia. Obviously, the humor is robust and simple.

For an introduction to these witty stories, check out *The Lady Who Put Salt in Her Coffee,* adapted and illustrated by Amy Schwartz (Harcourt Brace Jovanovich, 1989).

Uncle Remus: His Songs and His Sayings by Joel Chandler Harris (1880)

For almost twenty-five years, Joel Chandler Harris was a newspaperman for the *Atlanta Constitution.* During this time he collected about seven hundred African-American folktales from former slaves in his native state of Georgia. He attributed them all to the excellent memory of his fictitious storyteller Uncle Remus, a plantation slave. The tales center around Brer (Brother) Rabbit, who repeatedly triumphs over other animals. Harris was careful to present the stories in the Gullah dialect of the black storytellers.

The most familiar version of the Uncle Remus stories was adapted by Margaret Wise Brown and called *Brer Rabbit* (Harper, 1941). But today's children have several fine new retellings from which to choose. Award-winners Julius Lester and illustrator Jerry Pinkney have teamed up to create four wonderful volumes of Uncle Remus stories. Van Dyke Parks, a Mississippi composer, put the stories to music in an album called *Jump!* Then he and illustrator Barry Moser chose some of the most enjoyable Brer Rabbit stories for a picture book titled *Jump! The Adventures of Brer Rabbit* (Harcourt Brace Jovanovich, 1986) and its sequel, *Jump Again!* As Parks comments,

No where will you find a better example of pluck and cleverness triumphing over brute strength. . . .

Harris has been both applauded and deeply criticized for his portrayal of life in the Old South. But the lessons in these stories are universal, and there are few corners in life they do not illuminate. Tempered by hardship and nourished by hope, these tales are a testament to the belief that no one can be wholly owned who does not wish it.

The Boys' King Arthur by Sidney Lanier (1880)
Around 1470 Sir Thomas Malory is thought to have written *Le Morte d'Arthur* while imprisoned for political crimes. It is derived from French and English legends, and Malory's compilation filled twenty-one volumes. William Caxton published the tale in 1485. Not everyone thinks that the King Arthur stories are appropriate for children, but the romance and chivalry of these tales have made them enduring favorites with many young readers. Poet Sidney Lanier, who had grown up with the aristocratic Old South's traditions of chivalry, retold the Arthur legends for his sons and to make some quick money. Filled with beauty, imagery, and the burning idealism of knights and fair maidens, Lanier's version is still one of the most enjoyable versions available. Illustrations by N. C. Wyeth make it a true classic.

The Merry Adventures of Robin Hood by Howard Pyle (1883)
Howard Pyle became well known for his illustrations in *Harper's Weekly* and other magazines. In addition to his artistic skills, he was also a gifted storyteller. Fascinated with medieval folklore, Pyle carefully researched the clothing, weapons, and buildings of the Middle Ages. His black-and-white illustrations are realistic, and his characters are portrayed with rich emotion.

Following his success with *The Merry Adventures of Robin Hood,* Pyle wrote a gruesome story about the robber barons of Germany called *Otto of the Silver Hand* (1888); *Men of Iron* (1891), an enduring story of a boy's training for knighthood; and *The Story of King Arthur and His Knights*.

In a fairy tale vein, Pyle wrote and illustrated *Pepper and Salt* (1885) and *The Wonder Clock: Or Four and Twenty Marvelous Tales* (1887), a favorite for reading aloud. The clock is a magical device that carries the storyteller to the next tale and binds the twenty-four stories together. Each story is short and filled with adventure. For generations of young readers, Pyle's stories and illustrations are inseparable. But a new generation of readers can compare the effectiveness of his artwork with that of more contemporary illustrators. Trina Schart Hyman has brought new magic to *Bearskin* (1997), the first story in *The Wonder Clock*. Another of Pyle's wondrous tales, *The Swan Maiden*, appears in a 1994 retelling by Ellin Greene with illustrations by Robert Sauber.

Treasure Island by Robert Louis Stevenson (1883)
This Scottish novelist, essayist, and poet gave the world of children's literature several classics. As a young man Stevenson contracted tuberculosis, and he spent much of his forty-four years traveling in hopes of relieving the condition. He took a canoe trip through Belgium and France, traveled by donkey through the French mountains, sailed to California (where he married), took a cruise to the South Pacific, and finally settled in Samoa.

On a cold, windy, and wet Scottish vacation with his parents and his stepson Lloyd, Stevenson drew a map of an imaginary island and began writing a story about it to entertain his stepson. Stevenson's *Treasure Island* is a tale filled with mystery, mutiny, and hard-core adventure. All the rules for writing children's stories are broken. Blood flows, morality sometimes disappears, and the rum flows freely. But this captivating pirate story offers young readers in today's violent world some reassurance that goodness eventually will triumph over treachery. Its vivid, well-developed characters also provide an opportunity for parents to talk with children about the mixture of strength and weakness, virtue and vice, that is so much a part of the human condition. In the captain's handling of his crew and his counsel to young Jim, there is a powerful illustration of the importance of discipline and responsible behavior.

Heidi by Johanna Spyri (English translation, 1884)
This story, set in Switzerland, is about a happy girl who loves life in all its fullness and overcomes misfortune. Following the wholesome tradition of *Hans Brinker, or The Silver Skates,* it portrays the land and people well. Spyri (pronounced Spee-ree) began writing at the age of forty-three because she wanted to help victims of the Franco-Prussian War. Her success caused her to make writing a lifelong career. Heidi is her best work and the product of several years of labor. It was inspired by Spyri's own childhood experience; because of her poor health, her parents decided she should leave her home near Zurich for a summer in the mountains.

The Happy Prince and Other Fairy Tales by Oscar Wilde (1888)
The tales told by Oscar Wilde are highly polished and full of imagery. The most famous is "The Selfish Giant," which audaciously brings Jesus into a fairy tale that combines gentle humor with overwhelming sweetness. The stories in *The Happy Prince* and *A House of Pomegranates* (1892) were written for Wilde's two sons.

The Dubliner Oscar Finall O'Flahertie Wills Wilde led a life as flamboyant as his name. He claimed that he poured his genius into his eccentric lifestyle and only put his talent into his writing. Although he was hailed as a master of adult wit and drama, he died a broken man only twelve years after he published his fairy tales. While serving a prison sentence, Wilde wrote *De Profundis (From the Depths,* 1905), an apology for his life. Before his death he became a Roman Catholic. The fruit of his life was bitter, but Wilde's beautiful fairy tales should not be missed. Readers will find them surprisingly rich in the finest of human values.

Ed Young, one of today's most distinguished children's illustrators, has interpreted *The Happy Prince* (Simon & Schuster, 1989) for today's young readers.

The Blue Fairy Book by Andrew Lang (1889)
Andrew Lang was a brilliant classical scholar, historian, and expert in folklore. He believed that universal human emotions accounted for the development of similar stories in widely varying cultures. To support his theory, he collected fairy tales from many lands and ethnic groups. Then he turned to Mrs. Lang and others who retold the stories for children. Thus, Lang actually served as editor for the series known as the Colour Fairy Books that bears his name. The first one was *The Blue Fairy Book,* featuring tales from Grimm and Perrault, old chapbook stories, some selections from *The Arabian Nights,* some Scottish tales, and an abridged version of *Gulliver's Travels.*

Lang wrote in the introduction to *The Pink Fairy Book:*

> We see that black, white, and yellow people are fond of the same kind of adventures. Courage, youth, beauty, kindness, have many trials, but they always win the battle; while witches, giants, unfriendly cruel people, are on the losing side. So it ought to be, and so on the whole it is and will be; and that is the moral of all fairy tales.

His subsequent yearly color books, which ended in 1910

with *The Lilac Fairy Book,* branched out and included traditional folklore from all over the world. In addition to collecting fairy tales, Lang wrote several of his own. The best of them is *The Gold of Fairnilee,* based on the Scottish legends and ballads of his childhood.

Pinocchio by Carlo Lorenzini (translated into English in 1891)
Carlo Lorenzini lived in Florence, Italy, and worked as a government official. After his retirement, he began to write stories for children under the pen name Carlo Collodi. Because puppet shows began in Italy, it is appropriate that Lorenzini's best-loved story brings a puppet to life. *Pinocchio,* written in 1883, has been popular in the United States ever since it was first translated into English.

Children enjoy the wickedness of Pinocchio and his eventual transformation from a bad puppet into a good boy. It is a playful story full of humor and the kind of unconscious misdeeds most children readily identify with. Christian readers also will see, quite possibly, a parallel between the grief Pinocchio causes his creator, Gepetto, and the sorrow of God over His misbehaving children. The Blue Fairy, a mother and guide to the prodigal puppet, may also be interpreted as a symbol of the Holy Spirit, who creates in us a desire for godliness. Pinocchio at last becomes human through the power of love.

Two Italian illustrators have given children wonderful new editions of this beloved book—Sergio Rizzato (Golden Press, 1963) and Roberto Innocenti (Knopf, 1988).

The Jungle Books by Rudyard Kipling (1894–1895)
These two volumes are much more interesting than most animal stories because Kipling's writing is unusually inventive and colorful. He was the first English author

honored with a Nobel Prize (1907). His writing owes much to his deep understanding of and identification with India, the land of his birth. It also reflects his strong belief in a life of vigorous activity.

The story of the boy Mowgli, raised by wolves and destined to become leader of the jungle, is well-known. Although these stories are said to teach children about nature—highlighting the similarities and differences between human beings and animals—they certainly do not give the most accurate portrayal of animal life. Instead, they express Kipling's own code of masculine behavior.

The first story in *The Jungle Book* is pictured in *Mowgli's Brothers,* illustrated by Christopher Wormell, one of Britain's finest wood engravers (Creative Editions, 1993). Caldecott Honor artist Jerry Pinkney has adapted and illustrated another *Jungle Book* story in his *Rikki-Tikki-Tavi.* If the young readers at your house enjoy these two books, then be sure to treat them to Viking's The Whole Story edition of *The Jungle Book* (1996). Its illustrations and annotations greatly enrich the reading experience.

Kipling wrote a series of fanciful animal tales for younger children, the *Just So Stories* (1902), which are good to read aloud. There is, however, keen objection to the self-concept of the black boy in "How the Leopard Got His Spots."

The Story of the Treasure Seekers by Edith Nesbit (1899)
Edith Nesbit knew both wealth and poverty. When she was young her widowed mother lost all her money, and later her husband lost his business capital because of a dishonest partner. She had to support the family herself, which she did in a variety of ways, including hand coloring Christmas cards and, eventually, writing books for children.

The Treasure Seekers was her first book and the beginning of a series about the Bastable children. They dig for treasure, sell poems, serve as detectives, rescue a princess, and borrow money. The principal character is Oswald Bastable, the oldest boy and also the narrator. Although he does not say that he is the narrator, it is obvious because he refers to Oswald as "a boy of firm and unswerving character" and makes other self-congratulatory remarks.

The other two Bastable stories are *The Wouldbegoods* and *New Treasure Seekers*. Nesbit wrote a second set of three books about a family of children who fall into fantastic adventures: *Five Children and It* (1902), *The Phoenix and the Carpet* (1904), and *The Story of the Amulet* (1906). C. S. Lewis mentioned the Bastables at the beginning of his own children's book, *The Magician's Nephew*. He was particularly fond of *The Story of the Amulet*.

In 1998 Britain's Royal Mail paid tribute to fantasy literature with a series of stamps entitled "Magical Worlds." The stamps illustrate scenes from *The Hobbit*, *Through the Looking Glass*, *The Lion, the Witch and the Wardrobe*, and *The Borrowers*. In the brochure which accompanied the stamps, Nesbit is credited with opening up the way for real children to step effortlessly between their world and the world of fantasy.

The Wizard of Oz by L. Frank Baum (1900)
Here is a highly moral fantasy of Midwestern America that is often underrated. Ironically, many U.S. libraries have refused to carry it, thinking it junk literature, but the English saw its value.

L. Frank Baum was a kind of rollicking wizard himself. While he was still in his teens, he became a journalist and established his own weekly newspaper, at the same time selling fiction and humorous verse to magazines. He wandered the Middle West as a traveling salesman, became a successful producer of several dramas, wrote for various large newspapers, and founded the National

Association of Window Trimmers. With a wife and four sons to support, he also worked as a hack writer for a fiction factory, turning out twenty-four girls' books as Edyth Van Dyne and more books as Susanne Metcalf, Laura Bancroft, Floyd Akers, Capt. Hugh Fitzgerald, and other unlikely people.

In 1889 Baum's own book, *Father Goose, His Book,* which told stories about nursery rhyme characters, sold 90,000 copies in ninety days. With the profits Baum built a summer home on Lake Michigan called "The Sign of the Goose," made his own furniture, decorated the house with goose trim, and crowned the project with an immense stained-glass window featuring a goose. (Then he wrote a book about decorating.)

The next year, *The Wizard of Oz* came out and was quickly made into a New York musical. Baum got the name Oz from the O–Z drawer on a filing cabinet. The story of Dorothy's adventures with the Scarecrow, the Tinman, and the Cowardly Lion has always been popular with children and has even spawned a fanatic Oz following among adults.

In 1905 Baum moved to Southern California, eventually settled in Hollywood in a home called Ozcot, and became the dahlia-growing king of California. After several successive Oz books such as *The Land of Oz* and *Ozma of Oz,* he tried to end the series with *The Emerald City of Oz,* but pressure from children kept the series going until there were fourteen. After Baum's death, even more were produced by inferior writers.

The Tale of Peter Rabbit by Beatrix Potter (1901)
Beatrix Potter (1866–1943) was the best writer and artist of picture-story books at the turn of the century. She grew up a lonely, shy child of very wealthy and neglectful parents in London. They took little or no interest in her love of nature, her art, and her small books for children.

Her dear editor/fiancé died shortly before their wedding. Finally in middle age she married an English farmer and developed into quite a crusty and unsentimental major landowner in the Lake District. She never had any children.

Her classic *Tale of Peter Rabbit* and other stories created a little world of amusement and delight. Young children fall in love with Hunca Munca, Squirrel Nutkin, Mrs. Tiggy-Winkle, Jemima Puddle-Duck, and the others. Potter's watercolor illustrations show cozy little animals dressed up like humans, pursuing their busy lives in meadows and lanes and doll houses. The clear, precise art of the text makes her work a milestone in children's literature. It is claimed that *Peter Rabbit* is the beginning of the modern picture-story: a total blend of picture and text.

In a satirical essay, the contemporary author Rumer Godden creates an imaginary correspondence between a tasteless modern editor and the ghost of Beatrix Potter. She is urged to simplify her vocabulary and change the story for modern children. She replies, "I have too much common sense to think that Peter Rabbit could ever be magnificent; he is an ordinary small brown rabbit."

In a letter to *The Horn Book* in May 1929, the real Beatrix Potter wrote, "My usual way of writing is to scribble, and cut out, and write again and again. The shorter and plainer the better. And read the Bible (unrevised version and Old Testament) if I feel my style wants chastening."

Johnny Crow's Garden by L. Leslie Brooke (1903)
Leslie Brooke gave young children three entertaining picture books about a decidedly English crow who loves to have parties in his garden. All of Johnny's guests are animals, and Brooke's humorous, detailed drawings present each feathered and furry creature in an engaging

and believable way. He remembered his father reciting a rhyme about Johnny Crow to him in childhood. As a father himself, Brooke expanded on Johnny Crow's adventures, and the third volume in this series was written for his grandson. Few parents or children today know about these little treasures, but they should. Look for *Johnny Crow's Garden* (1903), *Johnny Crow's Party* (1907), and *Johnny Crow's New Garden* (1935). Brooke also illustrated a collection of Mother Goose rhymes titled *The Golden Goose Book* (1905).

Rebecca of Sunnybrook Farm by Kate Douglas Wiggin (1903)

A twelve-year-old New Englander named Kate Smith had the pleasure of meeting Charles Dickens on a train traveling to Portland, Maine. She and her family were making the journey to hear Dickens read his work. At twenty-one, she published her first story in *St. Nicholas Magazine*. As a young woman she studied children's education in Los Angeles and started a kindergarten in San Francisco—the first one west of the Rockies.

In 1886, Wiggin's first book, *The Birds' Christmas Carol*, was published to raise money for her kindergarten. Today she is best remembered for giving us *Rebecca of Sunnybrook Farm*, a book she wrote after she returned to her childhood home, "Quillcote," in Hollis, Maine. At the nearby Tory Hill Meeting House a Celtic cross honors Wiggin, who wrote this colonial church into one of her stories. The cross is inscribed with the title of the last chapter of her autobiography, "The Song Is Never Ended."

In an era when both American nostalgia and concern for female self-esteem are flourishing, this sweet, light-hearted, and witty novel deserves a reading. It is the story of an exuberant young girl who has to be brought up in a small town by her two rigid, gloomy, and suspicious aunts. Guess who brings up whom!

Peter Pan by James M. Barrie (1904, 1911)

Sir James Matthew Barrie, a Scottish playwright and novelist who became chancellor of the University of Edinburgh, thought of life as a romantic adventure. Two of his favorite themes were the importance of holding on to the innocence of childhood and what he saw as the natural feminine instinct for motherhood. These themes come together in his classic *Peter Pan*.

Barrie later made the play into a book, *Peter and Wendy* (1904). The book has never been as popular as the play because its language is a bit subtle for children. A musical version of the play starring Mary Martin was produced when the play was about fifty years old.

The story features Peter Pan, the boy who will not grow up; Captain Hook; the fairy Tinker Bell; and three Darling children who go off to Never Never Land with Peter. *Darling* really is a family name, but *Wendy* was never heard of until Barrie invented it for his young heroine. Few, if any, other writers have invented a new name that has been bestowed upon so many children.

Artist Scott Gustafson spent four years creating fifty oil paintings to illustrate *Peter Pan* (Viking, 1991). It is a visual treat the whole family will enjoy.

Freckles by Gene Stratton Porter (1904)

Gene Stratton Porter named her Indiana home "Limberlost" after the swampy woods nearby. On its wide porch she wrote about the wonders of nature, and she often trekked into the wilds with her forty-pound camera and tripod to capture the flora and fauna that fill her books. When the Limberlost swamp was drained, this world-renowned author and photographer built a large two-story log cabin in Wildflower Woods bordering the Limberlost. Her writings include twelve adult novels, one book for children (*Morning Face*, written in 1916), ten nature studies, and three volumes of poetry and essays.

Her two best novels are *Freckles* and *A Girl of the Limberlost* (1909), and they make enjoyable family reading experiences.

It is estimated that fifty million readers have read Porter's books, and eight of her novels have been made into movies. While her fiction seems sentimental and melodramatic today, it still has the power to captivate nature lovers. It is rich in inspiration, with frequent references to faith, prayer, and characters who triumph over adversity by making moral choices.

White Fang by Jack London (1906)

This is a story of fierce animal heroism. White Fang is a crossbreed dog who is cruelly trained to be a ferocious fighter. Later a kind owner domesticates him, and he eventually gives his life to save this man.

Author Jack London lived a short, rough, and extremely adventurous life that began in poverty and ended tragically, due to his struggle with alcoholism. He left his home state of California to take part in the Alaskan gold rush. When he returned to San Francisco, he became a newspaperman and began to write about his experiences. In the course of his life, London wrote more than fifty books. His writing enjoyed great popularity in his day. He combined vivid, exciting, and sometimes brutal realism with feelings of kindness and compassion.

Another dog story of his, *The Call of the Wild* (1903), is probably his greatest single work; it, too, is enjoyed by many children. Viking's The Whole Story series enriches *The Call of the Wild* with excellent illustrations and annotations on history, geography, social customs, and the animal world.

The Wonderful Adventures of Nils by Selma Lagerlöf (translated into English 1907)

For ten years, Selma Lagerlöf taught school in

Landskrona, Sweden. In 1891 she published a collection of folktales, and by 1895 she had left teaching for a career as a writer. The National Teachers' Associate of Sweden asked her to write a geographical reader about Sweden, and she spent three years studying the folklore and natural history of the provinces. Then, *The Wonderful Adventures of Nils* came out in 1906, and *The Further Adventures of Nils* in 1907. Now they are combined in one volume.

Lagerlöf presents Sweden's climate, landscape, wild creatures, people, and traditions through the experiences of young Nils, a farmer's son. Nils is bad-tempered and unkind to animals. He becomes an elf who rides on the back of a wild goose and is soon enlightened. One favorite episode is the great crane dance on a mountain near the sea. In Lagerlöf's fantasy stories, good is seen triumphing over evil. One of her tenderest fantasies is "Robin Redbreast," an unforgettable little story about Christ's crucifixion.

In 1909 Lagerlöf received the Nobel Prize in Literature; she was the first woman to receive that honor.

The Wind in the Willows by Kenneth Grahame (1908)
Here is a book that evokes nostalgia, one that can be read to young children or savored by older readers. The author was a country gentleman who loved the outdoors. His father abandoned him and three other children to their grandmother after their mother died. Instead of getting the education he was suited for, Grahame grew up and went into banking, becoming wealthy before he retired to the country.

Grahame enjoyed telling long tales to his son "Mouse" at bedtime. Once when Mouse was to go to the seaside with his nurse, he put up a terrible fuss because he would miss the story's continuation. His father persuaded him with the promise that he would mail him a chapter a day. The nurse wisely saved these chapters for the Grahames. They became *The Wind in the Willows,* still named as the most cherished book of British readers.

Each chapter contains an adventure of four animal friends—Mole, Water Rat, Badger, and Toad. Morality, though never mentioned, permeates all the action and conversation of the animals—really "people in fur" representing human types.

The animals live a lovely pastoral life along the river. But not far from there is the Wild Wood and beyond that the Wide World, where river animals would never go if they had any sense. Toad does not have any sense and gets himself into all kinds of trouble. He is rescued in the end by his friends, and the idyllic life is once again resumed.

The first chapter of *The Wind in the Willows* is available as a picture book titled *The River Bank* (Scribner's, 1977). It is illustrated by Adrienne Adams, recipient of the Rutgers Award for Distinguished Contribution to Children's Literature. An especially fine edition of the entire story is the Golden Anniversary Edition (Scribner's, 1959), with eight new color pictures by the original illustrator, Ernest H. Shepard, who got pointers from Kenneth Grahame. Equally delightful is the outstanding edition illustrated by Michael Hague (Henry Holt, 1980).

Anne of Green Gables by Lucy Maud Montgomery (1908)
Lucy Maud Montgomery was raised by her grandparents on Prince Edward Island. Her girlhood experiences inspired a series of bestsellers about an orphan named Anne who adopts the aging owners of Green Gables.

Montgomery began writing as a child, and, in addition to a brief career as a teacher, she worked for a year as a reporter on the *Halifax Daily Echo.* She published numerous stories and poems in newspapers and children's magazines, and her first novel, *Anne of Green Ga-*

bles, immediately won the hearts of Canadian and American readers. Its sequels are *Anne of Avonlea* (1909), *Anne of the Island* (1915), *Anne of Windy Poplars* (1936), *Anne's House of Dreams* (1917), *Rainbow Valley* (1919), and *Rilla of Ingleside* (1921). Less well-known but equally satisfying are *Emily of New Moon* (1923) and its sequels, *Emily Climbs* (1925), and *Emily's Quest* (1927) about another young orphan. Emily, an aspiring writer, is a favorite of Madeleine L'Engle, who found in her "a hero who allowed me to be different." All of Montgomery's heroines are feisty, independent, and imaginative. For a picture book introduction to this author, see *Lucy Maud and the Cavendish Cat* by Lynn Manuel (1997).

Old Mother West Wind by Thornton W. Burgess (1910)
Thornton Burgess was a syndicated storytelling columnist for forty-four years, and he is credited with writing ten thousand animal stories for children. In homes all over America, children gathered round for mothers and fathers to read about Jimmy Skunk, Bowser the Hound, Reddy Fox, and Danny the Meadow Mouse. Each story had a clear moral, but the animals' antics captivated youngsters. They are still enjoyable for some children today, especially when presented with Michael Hague's illustrations (Henry Holt, 1990).

The Secret Garden by Frances Hodgson Burnett (1909)
This is the wonderful story of a miserable, isolated boy named Colin and the two children who work a change in him. Colin, his rich father, and his new friend Mary—the heroine of the book—all burst through from darkness and grief to light and joy, with the help of the secret garden and a special family on the moors. The story has delicious mystery and enchants its readers. Tasha Tudor's illustrations (Lippincott, 1962) are the most familiar, but when the story's copyright expired in 1985

several new editions appeared at once from different publishers, with a variety of illustrations and a wide range of prices.

The story of Frances Hodgson Burnett is almost as much "a dream come true" as the ones she wrote. Her fatherless family moved from England to Tennessee when she was sixteen. She started to write stories in a cold little attic room there, and they eventually made her rich and famous. She published over fifty books, but the most beloved are *Little Lord Fauntleroy* (1886); *A Little Princess*, also known as *Sara Crewe* (1888); and *The Secret Garden*. She said of herself, "With the best that was in me, I have tried to write more happiness into the world."

In the Conservatory Garden of New York City's Central Park, there is a fountain honoring Burnett for her children's classics—a particularly fitting tribute to the woman who gave us an enchanted story garden.

Children's literature is like a secret garden to many adults. They do not know how welcome they are to enter and how pleasant it is to linger there with or without a child.

The classics described in this chapter are all from before World War I. Most of the first children who enjoyed even the latest of them are probably great-grandparents now or have passed away. But these books and dozens of other good ones from long ago are still ours to enjoy. If you choose to dive down the rabbit hole into this part of our past, you will, like Alice, find quite a wonderland.

6 Flights of Fancy

A fairytale, dear sir, in relating miraculous happenings as though they were the normal events of everyday is a humble acknowledgment of the fact that this universe is a box packed full of mysteries. . . . Heaven alone knows what will pop out of it next.

—Elizabeth Goudge, *The Blue Hills*

Fantasy hints of the greater reality that lies behind the scientific fact and ordinary practicality of our day-to-day lives. Such literature often thrusts the reader into new dimensions of space and time, worlds of wonder, and strange powers. Books of fantasy are sometimes gentle, sometimes wild, sometimes humorous, and sometimes deadly serious.

Kenneth Grahame, author of *The Wind in the Willows*, cheerfully contrasted dragons with dinosaurs once by claiming that a dragon is "a more enduring animal than a pterodactyl. I have never yet met anyone who really believed in a pterodactyl."

Fantasy writer Lloyd Alexander pointed out that just as the great humorists tend to be melancholy people, so fantasy writers tend to be hard-headed realists.

Many authors have praised fantasy, including those whose Christian faith is central to their work. J. R. R. Tolkien called fantasy the most perfect art form and described Christ's birth, life, death, and resurrection as the greatest fairy tale of all. And, wonder of wonders, it is true.

G. K. Chesterton said that fantasy reminds us that "the universe is wild and full of marvels. . . . In the fairy tales the cosmos goes mad, but the hero does not go mad. In the modern novels the hero is mad before the book begins, and suffers from the harsh steadiness . . . of the cosmos."

C. S. Lewis said, "It would be nice if no little boy . . . were ever at all frightened. But if he is going to be frightened, I think it better that he should think of giants and dragons than merely of burglars."

Albert Einstein once said that the best reading for children is fairy tales, more fairy tales, and more fairy tales. And William Kilpatrick, Boston University professor and author of *Why Johnny Can't Tell Right from Wrong*, commends fantasy literature for providing children with adventure, appealing pictures of home life, and assurance of the world's underlying moral order.

But fantasy literature also has its detractors, many of whom are extremely passionate and outspoken in their opposition. Some people characterize all fantasy as illogical and escapist, and others believe it is demonic. Stories that mention magic, dragons, witches, wizards, ghosts, or other supernatural elements are labeled New Age, pagan, and occult. Parents are told to forbid such books in their homes and to do whatever they can to have them removed from libraries and classrooms. These accusations are supported by reports of how young people's lives have been ruined by fantasy books and games.

Responding to such fears of fantastic tales, Focus on the Family editor Ray Seldomridge points out the parallels between some works of fantasy and the Scriptures: "Such stories help young readers grasp at a deeply emotional level the fact that evil cannot ultimately win." And to the well-meaning Christian parents who avoid anything to do with fire-breathing dragons, he offers a reminder that "this symbol for evil is used in the Bible itself—in Revelation 12:7. What matters is that the dragon is defeated!" (*Focus on the Family,* July 1988).

Marian Bray, who writes stories for young adults, says, "For many people who are antagonistic toward God and the church, science fiction and fantasy can be a marvelous light. In my own conversion, I can see how Madeleine L'Engle's stories helped me begin to sort out various issues concerning my relationship to God."

Teacher Eve Lewis Perera tells an amusing story about a student who set out to write a paper on why reading fantasies is a waste of time for someone preparing to be a pastor. "He ended up writing his paper on the opposite side after he read C. S. Lewis's *Great Divorce.*"

"I find myself literally driven to tears by a good fairy-story," writes Lutheran pastor Rod Rosenblatt. "And not simply because I am a romantic, quite the contrary! [He was an undergraduate science major.] It is because I now see how a good fairy-story points back two thousand years to the time when God really delivered me from the power of [evil] through the death and resurrection of Jesus Christ, the deliverer."

George MacDonald, who is for many readers the patron saint of children's fantasy literature, would be delighted with these tributes. He once said,

> If I can wake in any human heart just a little fluttering of life, if I can help any human soul to feel . . . that there is an eternal world, a world of life, of truth; a world of duty, of hope, of infinite joy. . . . If I can make the clouds just part the least bit, and give a glimpse of the blue sky, of the infinite realities of things, then I hold that it is worth doing.

Here are some basic guidelines for selecting positive fantasy and science fiction:

◆ It focuses on the heroic thoughts and deeds of seemingly ordinary characters. For example, in *The Lord of the Rings,* a comfort-loving creature named Frodo is given an overwhelming task. When he protests that he is not equal to it, the wizard Gandalf tells him, "This quest may be attempted by the weak with as much hope as the strong. Yet such is oft the course of deeds that move the wheels of the world: small hands do them because they must while the eyes of the great are elsewhere." Encouraging words for hobbits and small humans!

◆ It emphasizes the importance of personal choice. In *The Lion, the Witch, and the Wardrobe,* Edmund's decision to conspire with the White Witch has far-reaching consequences that are not easily or painlessly reversed. It is a principle that can help readers of all ages resist temptation. Edmund complained, when he was still secretly siding with the Witch for his own gain, "Which is the right side?" But deep down he really knew. And eventually he was named "the Just" for his ability to know and do what was right.

◆ It alerts the reader to the presence of evil in the world and the need for vigilance on the part of those who love truth. Sometimes, as in the case of George MacDonald's Curdie, those called to heroic acts are given special gifts that enable them to detect the presence of evil. In *The Princess and Curdie,* after Curdie thrust his hands into the rosefire, the Princess told him that his real hands [spiritual perception] were now so near the outside of his "flesh gloves," he would be able to feel and identify the beasts into which evil men and women were growing. Better yet, he could perceive hidden goodness in others. With these gifts, he and today's children can fulfill their purpose in life.

◆ It contributes to a clearer understanding of oneself and society without resorting to preaching or moralizing. For instance, in "The Emperor's New Clothes," by Hans Christian Andersen, readers can laugh at the folly and pride of the Emperor, who believes he is resplendently dressed when he is actually naked, and at the people who refuse to admit his error. It is the kind of story that subtly pricks our conscience and brings life into sharper focus.

◆ It leaves the reader with hope. In the words of Hans Christian Andersen,

> the Ugly Duckling felt quite glad of all the misery and tribulation he had gone through; he was the better able to appreciate his good fortune now, and all the beauty which greeted him. . . . He rustled his feathers and raised his slender neck aloft, saying with exultation in his heart: "I never dreamt of so much happiness when I was the Ugly Duckling!"

A fantasy that keeps faith with the reader leaves the promise of growing up to be a beautiful swan, of having cinders and shame replaced by royal splendor, and even of having beastliness tamed and transformed by love.

Top Ten Contemporary Fantasies

Fantasy for children has blossomed in the decades since World War I, particularly after World War II. Unfortunately, there has been a trend toward negativity and despair in some contemporary fantasy and science fiction (as well as other genres). Here are ten especially good contemporary fantasies that meet our five criteria for excellence.

1. Doctor Dolittle Stories by Hugh Lofting (1920, Grade 3 and up)*

Lofting, who served in the front lines in World War I, hated to tell his family what he was really experiencing. Being disturbed by what happened to animals that were used in the war, he made up happy animal stories and sent them to his children in the United States.

After the war, he put the letters together and hesitantly submitted them to a publisher. They were accepted and became *The Story of Doctor Dolittle*. Two years later, the second book, *The Voyage of Doctor Dolittle,* won the Newbery Award. At one point after that Lofting tired of the continuing series and quit, leaving Doctor Dolittle on the moon. But pressure forced him to write more—twelve books in all.

In the first book, Doctor Dolittle is offending his human patients because he has too many pets. His one last human patient suggests that he should become an animal doctor. His pet parrot convinces him to do just that and teaches him animal language. This new profession is challenging: it takes a much brighter person to treat animals than to treat humans.

Hugh Lofting has been criticized in recent years for a kind of benign racism and national chauvinism. Africa's Prince Bumbo begs to be turned white, and King Koko is often pictured sucking a lollipop. Most readers remember that Lofting wrote eighty years ago and overlook these lapses. He was, like most of us, a product of his own culture and did not see beyond it at all points. Those who prefer to have the racially offensive material

---

*Authors' Note: Children's reading abilities and interests defy all attempts to relegate books to certain grade levels. We offer suggestions of age appropriateness only as an approximate guide to when a child might best enjoy certain books. Most of the entires are left open-ended because a child too young for some books can never be too old for stories of excellence.

removed can choose Delacorte's 1988 editions of *Story* and *Voyage*.

2. *Winnie-the-Pooh* by A. A. Milne (1926, all ages)
One of the pleasures of parenthood is reading Pooh books to children. Their lyrical quality and colorful descriptions are as fascinating as the adventures of one "silly old bear," Winnie-the-Pooh, who is especially fond of eating honey.

Winnie-the-Pooh was written for A. A. Milne's small son Christopher Robin—fondly called Billie Moon—who wished to hear stories about his toy animals. A child's natural love of cuddly stuffed animals and his desire to make them live pervade Milne's narrative. He describes Pooh's friends—Piglet, the melancholy donkey Eeyore, Rabbit, Kanga, and Baby Roo. Pooh attempts to catch a Heffalump and track a woozle, and he discovers the North Pole. A sequel, *The House at Pooh Corner* (1928), contains further adventures and introduces a new friend, Tigger.

Alan Alexander Milne was educated at Cambridge University and served as assistant editor of *Punch* magazine before World War I. His children's stories are sunny and simple, full of good-natured affection and light humor.

Pooh has universal appeal. When Lindskoog and her husband were on an educational tour behind the Iron Curtain in 1960, they spotted a metal street sign near the University of Warsaw with Winnie-the-Pooh on it. Pooh has been greatly loved in Poland for generations, even through the dark Nazi and Communist years. (There he is called "Kubus Puchatek.")

3. *The Hobbit* by J. R. R. Tolkien (1937, Grade 4 and up)
John Ronald Reuel Tolkien was born to English parents

in South Africa, was bitten by a tarantula when he was a toddler, and learned to read when he was three. His father died the next year when young Tolkien, his mother, and his baby brother were visiting relatives in England.

Mrs. Tolkien taught her son Latin and French, and he came to love the stories of George MacDonald and Andrew Lang. When he was seven, he started to write a story about a green great dragon, and his mother told him it had to be a great green dragon instead. He wondered why the rest of his life. When Tolkien was twelve, his mother also died. He later won various scholarships and became a philologist—always learning, studying, and even inventing languages.

In the early 1930s this scholar of language, literature, and mythology wrote *The Hobbit* to read to his sons after supper. Eventually, one of his ex-students told an editor about it. It was published in September 1937, was reviewed enthusiastically in *The Times* by C. S. Lewis, and sold out before Christmas. *The Hobbit* tells of the harrowing but humorous adventure of Bilbo Baggins, a homey creature who is tricked into embarking on a dangerous quest to rescue stolen treasure from Smaug the Dragon and becomes a hero because of his simple virtues.

The publisher wanted Tolkien to write another hobbit book right away. He had a huge book, *The Silmarillion,* which he had been working on all his adult life; but that had no hobbits, and the publisher did not want it. So Tolkien began another hobbit story, which soon became related to *The Silmarillion* (which was not published until 1977). Instead of being ready in one year, as planned, this hobbit story grew to a half-million words in thirteen years of writing and was finally published in 1954–55 in three volumes as *The Lord of the Rings*. It would never have been finished without Lewis's encouragement and prodding.

The Lord of the Rings, which brought to our world new realms of myth, is largely about Bilbo's heir, Frodo Baggins, and his quest. It was not, in Tolkien's opinion, cheerful enough to be suitable for children. The publisher brought it out half-reluctantly, expecting it to sell only a few thousand copies. As publication day neared, Tolkien said, "I have exposed my heart to be shot at." Nevertheless, the favorable responses outweighed the attacks. Sales and interest rose steadily until 1965, when popularity exploded in the United States. By the end of 1968 about three million copies had been sold. During the next thirty years, total sales rose to over seven million copies.

The Hobbit can be read to children as young as five, and *The Lord of the Rings* can be enjoyed by children as young as twelve. In 1976 a new book for children came out: *The Father Christmas Letters,* a selection of illustrated story-letters that Tolkien wrote to his children for more than twenty years. They tell of Father Christmas's annual adventures with his helper the North Polar Bear. Two other delightful stories by Tolkien are *Smith of Wooton Major* (1967) and *Farmer Giles of Ham* (1949).

4. The Narnian Chronicles by C. S. Lewis (1950, Grade 3 and up)
Like J. R. R. Tolkien, Clive Staples Lewis was first a brilliant child whose boyhood was shattered by bereavement, was then a student at Oxford University, later a professor of literature there, and, eventually, a great writer for children as well as adults. Unlike Tolkien, Lewis was an atheist and an agnostic until his conversion to Christianity—with some help from Tolkien—when he was thirty-two.

The Christianity in Tolkien's books is inherent but never obvious. In contrast, the Christianity in Lewis's books often shines through very clearly. Ironically, Lewis was an enthusiastic reader and reviewer of Tolkien's fantasies, but Tolkien did not like Lewis's books for children at all.

A scene that gave rise to *The Lion, the Witch and the Wardrobe* first popped into Lewis's head when he was seventeen. (All his fiction sprang from pictures in his mind.) Then in 1949 he suddenly wrote the whole story with Aslan the golden Lion at its center. Lewis thought that was all. But he soon wrote *Prince Caspian, The Voyage of* The Dawn Treader, *The Horse and His Boy, The Silver Chair,* and *The Magician's Nephew.* The final book in the series, *The Last Battle,* won the Carnegie Award for 1956. Lewis received many letters begging for more tales of Narnia, but he said that there were only seven. He died seven years after *The Last Battle* was published, on the day President Kennedy was assassinated.

The Lion, the Witch and the Wardrobe tells how four English children stumble into the marvelously beautiful world of Narnia, where talking animals are wrongly ruled by a white witch until Aslan overthrows her. *Prince Caspian,* the least popular of the series, tells how the children return a year later to find that many centuries have passed and that the rightful prince needs their help. *The Voyage of* The Dawn Treader tells of a dangerous trip to the end of that world. *The Horse and His Boy* flashes back to the time of the first book and tells of a great adventure that happened during the children's first visit. In *The Silver Chair* two children seek a captive prince and find much more. *The Magician's Nephew* carries two children back to the creation of Narnia. *The Last Battle* brings the children and all of Narnia to and beyond death.

Critic Roger Lancelyn Green said of the chronicles,

> They have a fourth dimension, that of the spirit. More than almost any other children's books, they

have at their best this kind of reality, and this it is which gives them their quality of vividness, and makes them leave behind an echo and a taste that do not fade.

The Chronicles of Narnia are enjoyed by children as young as six and are good for reading aloud. Some bookstores have kept them in their adult fantasy and science fiction section because of their overwhelming popularity with young adults. A 1998 survey of favorite children's books conducted by the BBC and Waterstone's bookshops found that adults (those over age sixteen) ranked Lewis's *The Lion, the Witch and the Wardrobe* as second only to *The Wind in the Willows.*

Young people who are mature readers will also enjoy *Out of the Silent Planet* and *Perelandra,* two of Lewis's three science fiction novels for adults.

5. *Charlotte's Web* by E. B. White (1952, Grade 3 and up) Elwyn Brooks White was born in 1899 in Mount Vernon, New York. After serving in World War I, he joined the staff of the *New Yorker* and met and married a former editor. In 1929 White co-authored a book with fellow humorist James Thurber called *Is Sex Necessary?*, a satire on popular psychoanalysis. In 1938 his family moved to a farm in Brookline, Massachusetts, where he lived out his life.

When *Charlotte's Web* was published in 1952, it received unusual acclaim from reviewers and critics in both adult and children's sections of important literary magazines. Since then it has sold millions of hardback copies and was reprinted by Britain's prestigious Puffin Books six times in one six-year period. All this public affection is for the humorous but heart-gripping story of a spider named Charlotte who saves the life of a fat little pig named Wilbur by spinning words of praise about him into her web. It is a barnyard fantasy about good country people and the loyalty of animal friends—a story, in one sense, of human strengths and weaknesses and mortality.

White's other books for children are *Stuart Little* (1945), about a mouse who is not just a mouse but the child of human parents, and *Trumpet of the Swan* (1970). Both books are funny but serious.

6. *The Borrowers* by Mary Norton (1952, Grade 3 and up)

Mary Norton was born in London in 1903 and grew up in a Georgian house in Bedfordshire much like the one that appears in *The Borrowers*. She had a career as a Shakespearean actress long before becoming a popular writer. Her flair for the dramatic and her appreciation for the effective use of setting and props are apparent in her stories. *The Borrowers*, her original contribution to English folklore, was the product of her childhood fantasies. As a nearsighted child, she focused on the lavish details of the microcosm around her—house, hedgerow, field, and stream.

The Borrowers are tiny people who live in hidden places in quiet old country houses. They take their names from the large objects near their homes—such as a clock, a chest, or a harpsichord—and they "borrow" little things permanently from the house's large occupants. Evidence of their presence is abundant in the number of items humans can never find after carelessly laying them aside.

In *The Borrowers*, a boy who visits the country actually meets one of the brave and resourceful borrowing families and does some borrowing on their behalf—until the exterminator arrives. Norton tells more about the doughty borrowers in other books including *The Borrowers Afield*, *The Borrowers Afloat*, and *The Borrowers Aloft*.

In 1998, the British paid tribute to *The Borrowers* with

a postage stamp, recognizing it as one of the four favorite classic fantasy books for children. In the brochure introducing the "Magical Worlds" stamp collection, the British Philatelic Bureau wrote,

> The fantasy author's concern with the small often involves the exploration of the strangest and most dangerous universe of all: our own world seen from a different perspective which is, usually, much lower down. . . . In Mary Norton's Borrowers books, the classic "little folk" are now thoroughly and literally at home, inside the walls. In a big world with many dangers, the small can band together and succeed.

7. The Green Knowe Books by Lucy Boston (1954, Grade 4 and up)

Lucy Boston first became a writer in 1954 when she was over sixty years old. She was born to wealthy but strict English parents who discouraged her love of pleasure and beauty. When she was twenty-three, she saw an old farmhouse called the Manor at Hemingford Grey in the English countryside and was impressed by it. Boston moved to continental Europe to paint. Twenty-four years later, she returned to England and bought that manor house.

Boston was fascinated with the house and spent years removing various remodeling jobs that had been added through the centuries. The original walls she uncovered were made of mortarless blocks of stone three feet thick, dating back about eight hundred years. After twelve years of living in this historic house and loving it, Boston began to write about it to express that life and love. In her fiction she calls the house Green Knowe. Her son Peter illustrated her books.

Critic and author J. R. Townsend claims that Boston is unsurpassed by any English children's writer and rivaled only by one, Philippa Pearce. Boston herself said that she would like to remind adults of the obsolete concept of joy and to encourage children to use and trust their senses.

In her first two books, *The Children of Green Knowe* (1954) and *The Treasure of Green Knowe* (1958), a small boy named Tolly stays with his great-grandmother, Mrs. Oldknow. There he finds the children who lived in her house three centuries ago. Sometimes he only sees them in a mirror, but other times he talks to them, moving back and forth in time. In *The Treasure of Green Knowe,* blind Susan and her servant friend Jacob appear to Tolly from the eighteenth century.

A young refugee from Burma—Ping—appears in three of the later books, *The River at Green Knowe* (1959), *Stranger at Green Knowe* (1961), and *An Enemy at Green Knowe* (1964). It was *Stranger at Green Knowe* that won the Carnegie Award. Who would have dreamed that a story about a gorilla who escaped from a zoo could be so tender, so evocative, and so exciting?

Lucy Boston also wrote *The Castle of Yew* (1965), *The Sea Egg* (1967), *Nothing Said* (1971), *Memory in a House* (1973, a memoir for adults of her restoration of the Norman Manor immortalized as Green Knowe), *The Fossil Snake* (1976), and *The Stones of Green Knowe* (1976).

8. *Tom's Midnight Garden* by Philippa Pearce (1959, Grade 4 and up)
In contrast to Lucy Boston, Philippa Pearce intended to be a writer from childhood on. She was the youngest of four children of a very successful flour miller and corn merchant. She grew up in a large seven-bedroom home called Mill House, in Great Shelford near Cambridge.

After college, Pearce spent thirteen years as a scriptwriter and producer in the School Broadcasting Department of BBC. In 1951 she contracted tuberculosis and spent a summer in a Cambridge hospital, longing for her parents' home five miles away on the river. After her recovery, she decided to try her hand at setting children's stories in that old home that was so vivid in her mind. The river is the setting for her first book, *Minnow on the Say* (1955), and the old house and its garden appear in *Tom's Midnight Garden,* with an extra upstairs added for the character Mrs. Bartholomew.

Critic John Rowe Townsend says that *Tom's Midnight Garden* is as close to being a perfectly constructed book as any he knows. Tom has to stay with his Uncle Alan and Aunt Gwen in their apartment in an old converted house while his brother is quarantined with measles. The landlady, Mrs. Bartholomew, lives at the top of the building. Unhappy Tom sets out to check the old grandfather clock on the ground floor one night when it strikes thirteen. He finds his way into a garden at the back of the house, a garden which is certainly not there when he checks the next day.

This garden belongs to the house and its past, and Tom enters the past through it each night. He is invisible to all the people who inhabit the garden except for a little girl named Hatty. Time passes more quickly in the past, and as Tom visits Hatty each night, she grows up. On the last night of Tom's visit, he learns that old Mrs. Bartholomew is his friend Hatty and that she has been dreaming him into her own past life.

This masterpiece gives children a concept of the continuity of generations as well as a sense of wonder.

9. *A Wrinkle in Time* by Madeleine L'Engle (1962, Grade 5 and up)

L'Engle grew up as the only child of a well-to-do writer. She was educated mainly in Europe, went into drama, married an actor, raised a family, and is now the writer in residence at the Cathedral of St. John the Divine in

New York City. She has written nineteen children's books and twenty adult books and is a great favorite of many readers. When asked recently to compare her writing with that of C. S. Lewis, L'Engle said, "[He] has more answers than I do. And I have more questions."

A Wrinkle in Time is a spiritual science fiction story about the young heroine Meg Murry, her precocious little brother Charles, and their friend Calvin. They rescue Meg's father, a scientist, from the great brain that controls the zombie population of Comazotz. Three good witches—actually angels—named Mrs. Who, Mrs. Which, and Mrs. Whatsit assist the children in their triumph over evil. *A Wrinkle in Time* won the Newbery Award in 1963, and L'Engle has published three sequels, *The Wind in the Door* (1973), *A Swiftly Tilting Planet* (1978), and *Many Waters* (1986). In 1998, thirty years after winning the Newbery Medal for *A Wrinkle in Time*, L'Engle received the Margaret A. Edwards Award for her lifetime contribution to teen literature. In celebration of this milestone, a new edition of the Time quartet has been released with beautiful covers by Caldecott-winning illustrator Peter Sis.

10. *Earthfasts* by William Mayne (1967, Grade 7 and up)

As a boy, Mayne attended Canterbury Cathedral Choir School, the setting for four of his more than forty books.

Earthfasts was his first book to include the supernatural. Two scientifically minded schoolboys see strange movements and hear drumming one evening on a Yorkshire hillside. Then a drummer-boy marches out of the hillside—from 1742 into now—carrying a candle that burns with a cold flame. He has been looking for King Arthur's burial place. After talking with the two schoolboys and seeing his old house, which is still standing, he marches back. Soon there are strange happenings in the area, and one of the two boys disappears.

In *Hill Road* (1968) Mayne has present-day characters visiting the distant past, the opposite of *Earthfasts*. Both books deal with how human beings relate to time, but their greater theme is how human beings relate to one another. Through his characters, Mayne stresses the importance of treating one another with dignity and compassion rather than with the cold curiosity of a scientist experimenting with a rat.

Mayne says that most people who read his books are adults—"whatever their age."

Twenty More Contemporary Fantasy Writers

The previous ten authors and books rank near the top of twentieth-century fantasy for children by almost anyone's standards. The following twenty authors are also superb in a variety of ways.

📖 Richard Adams, *Watership Down* (1972), *Tales from Watership Down* (1997); Grade 6 and up

This is a detailed story about rabbits who leave their endangered warren, make their way across enemy territory under the leadership of Hazel, and are drawn into war with a dictatorial warren ruled by General Woundwort. Although the rabbits are much like people, Adams based his story on the behavior of real rabbits as recorded in *The Private Life of the Rabbit* by R. M. Lockley.

Adams began telling this story aloud to entertain his two young daughters when he drove them back and forth to Shakespeare plays at Stratford. It is a wonderful selection for family reading times, especially for children ten and older. Adams says, "Right and wrong have been revealed to us for all time by our Lord Jesus Christ," and he believes that much evil is being published today that is very bad for its readers. He aims for his writing to benefit his readers.

📖 Joan Aiken, *The Wolves of Willoughby Chase* (1962, Grade 5 and up)
Daughter of a famous poet, Joan Aiken is called a first-class lightweight writer. Her books are full of drama, humor, and outrageous imagination. They are set in a past that never existed because she rewrites history. For instance, *The Cuckoo Tree* (1971) tells of a plan to roll St. Paul's Cathedral of London down into the Thames River on rollers.

In *The Wolves of Willoughby Chase*, Aiken skillfully mixes Victorian melodrama, suspense, and whimsical exaggeration. The result is a captivating story about how two young girls survive wolf attacks and the plottings of a wicked governess. The whole family can enjoy rooting for the brave and resourceful children and, of course, hissing and booing at the villains.

Aiken's other books include *The Whispering Mountain* (1968), which won the Guardian Award in Britain, *Black Hearts in Battersea*, *Night Birds on Nantucket*, *All But a Few*, *A Happy of Fishiness*, *The Kingdom Under the Sea*, *Winterthing*, *A Small Pinch of Weather*, *A Necklace of Raindrops*, and *Midnight Is a Place*.

📖 Lloyd Alexander, The Prydain Novels (1964–68, Grade 5 and up)
Alexander's books tell Welsh legends in a modern folktale style. They have strong characterization and humorous dialogue. This series is excellent for reading aloud to children ages ten and up.

The five books in his series are *The Book of Three*, *The Black Cauldron*, *The Castle of Llyr*, *Taran Wanderer*, and *The High King*. The latter won the Newbery

Medal in 1969. These books tell of Arawn, Lord of Annuvin, and the forces of evil, which are defeated by Taran and the Sons of Don. In the end Taran marries the princess and becomes the High King.

Alexander has also written a picture book, *The King's Fountain*, illustrated by the Caldecott-winning artist Ezra Jack Keats, and *The Cat Who Wished to Be a Man*.

📖 Natalie Babbit, *Tuck Everlasting* (1975, Grade 4 and up)
During her childhood Natalie Babbit spent much of her time reading fairy tales, drawing, and painting. Her amateur artist mother gave her art lessons, and Natalie grew up thinking of herself as an artist rather than a writer. She entered the world of children's literature in 1966, illustrating her husband's book, *The Forty-Ninth Magician*. Then Samuel Babbit became a college administrator and didn't have time to write any more stories. Natalie decided to try writing her own books and, consequently, readers are much the richer.

In *Tuck Everlasting* ten-year-old Winnie Foster longs for adventure. What she gets is a chance to drink from the Fountain of Youth. She meets a fascinating family named Tuck and discovers their secret—a spring hidden in the woods that has keeps them from ever growing old or dying. Unfortunately, she is followed by a sinister man in a yellow suit who wants to use the spring to get rich. Before the story ends, Winnie must decide whether to join the Tucks' world or remain in her own, growing up and growing old. Family members can enjoy this book together and then explore their own thoughts and feelings about immortality, aging, and death.

Other worthwhile books by Babbit are *The Search*

for Delicious (1969), a celebration of her love for word-play, and *Kneeknock Rise* (1970), the story of a village that is terrorized by a non-existent ogre.

📖 John Christopher, The White Mountains Trilogy (1967–1968, Grade 4 and up)
Christopher wrote science and adult fiction before turning to children's literature. He is an excellent storyteller whose books deal with human problems. This trilogy has been highly popular with both children and critics.

The trilogy is made up of *The White Mountains, The City of Gold and Lead,* and *The Pool of Fire.* In these stories the world is ruled by masters from another planet. These rulers enforce their rule by "capping" the inhabitants, a kind of mental castration. A few uncapped men struggle to overthrow the rulers, who think of them as lower creatures, before the rulers can succeed in changing the earth's atmosphere to benefit only themselves.

Christopher has followed these books with a second trilogy made up of *The Prince in Waiting, Beyond the Burning Lands,* and *The Sword of the Spirits.* Other books of his include *The Guardians* and *The Lotus Caves.*

📖 Susan Cooper, *The Grey King* (1975, Grade 5 and up)
Cooper, an English writer who now lives in the United States, has written a series of five fantasies set in Cornwall and Wales. In this series, supernatural evil is rising, and ordinary mortals along with those who are immortal join the battle between dark and light. The secret son of King Arthur, a boy who lives in our day instead of the past, plays a part in the mysterious and powerful struggle. The

titles are *Over Sea, Under Stone; The Dark Is Rising; Greenwitch; The Grey King,* which won the Newbery Award in 1976; and *Silver on the Tree.* Cooper uses some biblical allusions in her stories, but she presents a dualistic world where good and evil are eternally coexistent. Some children will be troubled by the mingling of darkness and light portrayed in some of the characters.

Helen Cresswell, *The Piemakers* (1967, Grade 5 and up)
This English author has taught children and worked for the BBC. *The Piemakers,* her first memorable book, is a mock-heroic account about how the Roller family of Danby Dale fulfilled the challenge of the king by creating the largest pie in the history of the world—a pie of epic grandeur. Both *The Piemakers* and *The Signposters* are set in a jolly and charming England of the indefinite past.

In the Bagthorpe Saga series, Cresswell introduces an eccentric clan of outrageous characters involved in hilarious stories and wild plots. The series begins with *Ordinary Jack* (1977), and continues in *Absolute Zero* (1978), and *Bagthorpes Unlimited.* Cresswell's other books include *The Night Watchmen* (1969), *Up a Pier* (1971), *The Bongleweed* (1973), *A Game of Catch* (1977), and *The Secret World of Polly Flint* (1984).

Cresswell's writing has been compared to James Thurber's because of her "ability to harness words and syntax for a fully satisfying comic effect."

Ronald Dahl, *Charlie and the Chocolate Factory* (1964, Grade 4 and up)
Dahl was born to Norwegian parents in Wales. He was a World War II hero in East Africa; after the war he became a successful writer of adult short

stories, publishing often in the *New Yorker* maga-zine. In 1961 Dahl published *James and The Giant Peach,* about a magic peach that carries a good boy across the ocean and is finally eaten up by ten thou-sand children in New York City.

Dahl happened to love chocolate, and his sweet tooth paid off—*Charlie and the Chocolate Factory* has sold millions of copies. This is the story of a poor but virtuous boy who finds the fifth and final golden ticket in a candy bar wrapper and gets to tour Willy Wonka's Chocolate Factory. The other four winners are spoiled and selfish children who disappear one by one, leaving Willy to win the final prize.

Not all critics think this is a good book. One calls it a "thick rich glutinous candy-bar of a book . . . nauseating." Some readers charge that the happy black Oompa-Loompas who work in the factory are a belittling caricature of the African pygmies. Oth-ers charge that Dahl's stories are misogynist, fre-quently portraying women as evil.

Dahl began receiving about five hundred letters a week from children all over the world asking for another Charlie book, so he wrote *Charlie and the Great Glass Elevator,* which included a ridiculous American president and therefore is not allowed in some libraries. Dahl had in mind all American presi-dents except his two favorites and says that he dis-approves of the super-patriotic respect children are taught to give the president and the government.

Dahl is perhaps the children's author most widely read around the world. In 1986 *Charlie and the Chocolate Factory* debuted in China with an initial printing of two million copies.

📖 Peter Dickinson, *Heartsease* (1969, Grade 5 and up) Dickinson, an editor of *Punch* magazine in England

and an author of adult mysteries, turned to children's fiction in the late 1960s.

His three books *The Weathermonger, Heartsease,* and *The Devil's Children* all take place in an England of the near future—an England in which all machines have been outlawed, the weather is controlled by magic, and ignorance and intolerance are on the increase. In *Heartsease,* a couple of English children who have not been caught in the strange national enchantment find a victim of the local hysteria, a young American who was taken for a witch and left for dead by violent villagers. They save his life and help him escape on the tugboat called *Heartsease.* Brotherhood and love are strong values in these books.

📖 William Pène Du Bois, *The Twenty One Balloons* (1947, Grade 3 and up)
This is the story of the last days of Krakatoa Island. Professor Sherman sets off in a balloon to see the world and lands on a volcanic island inhabited by skillful inventors of amazing gadgets, including a machine for escape should the volcano erupt. It does, and they escape by balloon.

📖 John Gardner, *Gudgekin the Thistle Girl and Other Tales* (1976, Grade 3 and up)
Literary historian, novelist, and short-story author John Gardner wrote three farfetched, not-quite-slapstick fairy tale books for children, somewhat in the James Thurber tradition. They have plenty of magic, a very light touch, and a hint of good-natured satire. Gudgekin, the heroine of one of the stories, seems to be a parody of Cinderella. In the end she gets what she deserves, which is a handsome prince and a dose of healthy respect for her-

self and others. Gardner's other books for children are *Dragon, Dragon* and *The King of the Hummingbirds and Other Tales.* Unfortunately, Gardner died young in a motorcycle accident, so readers cannot look forward to more books from him.

📖 Roger Lancelyn Green, *Old Greek Fairy Tales* (1958, Grade 5 and up)

R. L. Green devoted most of his life to children's literature. He read voraciously as a child, often home from school because of illnesses. At Oxford University he wrote his thesis about Andrew Lang, the great fairy tale collector. Green served as a schoolmaster, dealer in rare books, actor, and college librarian.

In addition to his books for adults, some of which are about children's authors, he wrote or edited about thirty books for children. Two of them, *The Luck of the Lynns* (1952) and *The Theft of the Cat* (1954), take place in his own home, Poulton-Lancelyn, the manor where his ancestors lived for nine hundred years.

Besides creating his five children's novels, editing *The Complete Fairy Tales of Mary De Morgan* and *The Diaries of Lewis Carroll,* and writing *The Story of Lewis Carroll* and *Kipling and the Children,* Green published *The Adventures of Robin Hood, King Arthur and His Knights of the Round Table, Myths of the Norsemen* (recommended by Harold Bloom as essential reading), *The Tale of Troy, Tales of Ancient Egypt, Tales of the Greek Heroes,* and other collections of legends, myths, and folktales that are part of our heritage. Reading authoritative and detailed renderings of these old fantasies enables children to understand many contemporary fantasies that refer to the older stories that readers are expected to know.

Old Greek Fairy Tales is unusual because Green re-told sixteen Greek myths without the difficult names and pseudo-historical relationships that usu-ally encumber them. Thus children can learn the basic stories much as they were first enjoyed in an-cient Greece.

📖 Robert Heinlein, *Podkayne of Mars* (1963, Grade 6 and up)

Heinlein wrote many extremely popular books on interspace travel. They are good for beginning readers of science fiction as well as more seasoned ones because he was technically accurate but not difficult. Heinlein was well-versed in mathematics, astronomy, and space technology.

He used both boys and girls as heroes. In *Pod-kayne of Mars,* a sixteen-year-old girl is kidnapped on a stopover at Venus during her first trip to Earth. Some of his other juvenile science fiction books are *Rocket Ship Galileo, Have Space Suit—Will Travel, Space Cadet, Starman Jones,* and *Citizen of the Galaxy.* His adult novels are not appropriate for children.

📖 Norton Juster, *The Phantom Tollbooth* (1961, Grade 6 and up)

Juster is a practicing architect by profession. In his major book, a bored boy named Milo finds himself traveling through Dictionopolis and other strange lands to save the lost princesses Rhyme and Reason. With his newfound friends, a watchdog named Tock and a genuine Humbug, he braves many obsta-cles—the Doldrums, a Point of View, the Valley of Sound, the Isle of Conclusions, Digitopolis, and the Mountains of Ignorance. In the process he becomes a better boy. The book is an outrageous *tour de force* full of wordplay and idea-play, a kind of rollicking cautionary tale.

📖 Robert Lawson, *Rabbit Hill* (1944, Grade 3 and up)
Lawson won both the Caldecott and the Newbery Awards within five years. As a boy he never tried his hand at art until he decided to enter a poster contest in high school and won first prize. After serving in France in World War I, he became an advertising artist until the Depression temporarily ruined the advertising business.

Fortunately, Lawson was hired to illustrate a book at that time and so discovered his true calling. He published his own first book in 1939, *Ben and Me*, the story of Ben Franklin told by his pet mouse Amos. *Mr. Revere and I* (1953) is the story of Paul Revere told by his horse. *Rabbit Hill* and its sequel *The Tough Winter* (1954) foster a tender interest in small wild animals such as those that surrounded Lawson's own country home, Rabbit Hill. Lawson's fictitious animals are all individual personalities who think and talk a great deal but do not, of course, wear clothes.

📖 Ursula LeGuin, *A Wizard of Earthsea* (1968, Grade 7 and up)
LeGuin is an American who has been compared to Tolkien and Lewis because she too is a great writer who has created another world. Earthsea is like Earth in some ways, although it is made up of archipelagos. It lacks machines but has magic. Every village has its local second-rate sorcerer, and high magic is taught at the central university of wizardry. A magician named Ged increases in power and lets loose a nameless evil that he himself cannot control. It roams, and Ged eventually has to meet it head

on in an unforgettable confrontation. *A Wizard of Earthsea* is the first in a trilogy. The other two books are *The Tombs of Atuan* (1971) and *The Farthest Shore* (1972).

📖 Andre Norton, *Dark Piper* (1968, Grade 7 and up)
This is a rather grim science fiction story in which pirate bands roam the skies after intergalactic civilization crumbles. The last human beings on a certain planet—a group of children and young people—are rescued by taking refuge underground with their leader Griss Lugard, who is a latter-day Pied Piper. Lugard and one of the children die, and the rest are left to face life on the abandoned planet. It is strong stuff but well written and full of invention.

Andre Norton used to be a children's librarian in Cleveland, Ohio. She studies folklore, history, anthropology, religion, and archaeology for background information for her books, hoping to entice young people into learning more about subjects she introduces.

📖 James Thurber, *The Wonderful O* (1957, Grade 3 and up)
This famous American humorist from Columbus, Ohio, was a staff member of the *New Yorker* most of his career. His wistfully inept cartoons, droll anecdotes, and satire made him extremely popular with adult readers. Thurber gradually lost a long battle against blindness and reportedly spent his last years in some emotional as well as physical darkness. His first book for children was *Many Moons* (1943), the story of a king who tried to get his daughter the moon. Only the jester knew how to succeed.

The Wonderful O is made up of humor and word play. When pirates totally eliminate the letter *O* from the island of Ooroo, all sorts of amazing consequences follow. Finally goodness returns, full of Os, and the moral is clearly spelled out at the end of the book.

Thurber's other books include *The White Deer,* a spoof about enchantment, and *The Thirteen Clocks,* a traditional fairy tale in extravagantly playful English.

P. L. Travers, *Mary Poppins* (1934, Grade 4 and up)
Pamela Travers spent her childhood in rural Australia buying one-penny books of fairy tales and soaking up her parents' love for Ireland and mythology. Her love for fairy tales increased with age, and she believes that collectors, anthropologists, and (worse yet) psychoanalysts try to dissect and drain them, but that their meanings cannot be exhausted.

Mary Poppins herself slides up banisters and sails through the air with an umbrella. She is a nursemaid who is brought to the Banks family by an east wind and leaves by a west wind. However, she returns in several sequels, including *Mary Poppins Comes Back, Mary Poppins in the Park,* and *Mary Poppins Opens the Door.* The only objection to these books is that when Mary Poppins visits the United States, she meets some Southern blacks portrayed as inappropriate stereotypes. In the 1964 version and subsequent editions this objectionable material has been removed.

Walter Wangerin, Jr., *The Book of the Dun Cow* (1978, Grade 7 and up)
Walter Wangerin, Jr., is a Lutheran minister whose first novel, *The Book of the Dun Cow,* won the American Book Award and was called the best children's book of the year in the *New York Times.* It is a wrenching fable about Chaunticleer the Rooster

and his barnyard friends. They live above the monster Wyrm, who is breaking free with his army from his prison below. This monster is Evil itself, and the proud, foolish, lovable barnyard animals have to fight the best they can. One reviewer wrote, "As adeptly as he breaks the reader's heart, he warms it over adeptly still, evoking the most tender emotions as vividly as one is likely to find them evoked in American fiction." The sequel, *The Book of Sorrows*, appeared seven years later. It received the *Campus Life* magazine Editor's Choice Award. These two books are for older children and adults.

Wangerin's *Potter* is a picture book (illustrated by Daniel San Souci) that aims to expand the horizons of children, but it is probably a book for the most mature children and adults. *Potter* gets to joy by the only true route, right through sorrow.

Other children's books by Wangerin are *Thistle* (1983, chosen as Best Book of the Year by *School Library Journal*), *In the Beginning There Was No Sky* (1986, re-release 1997), *Elisabeth and the Water-Troll* (1991), *Branta and the Golden Stone* (1993), and *Probity Jones and the Fear-Not Angel* (1996).

Wangerin pastored an inner city church in Evansville, Indiana, for eleven years and has taught theology and literature at Christ Seminary in Chicago. He and his wife Thanne (a nickname for Ruthanne) have four children. In 1985 he left his pastorate to devote more energy to writing and childrearing. In 1991 he became a professor of English and theology at Valparaiso University.

More Than Sixty Other Recommended Fantasy Writers

Atwater, Richard and Florence, *Mr. Popper's Penguins* (1938, Newbery Honor)—An entertaining read-aloud book to delight listeners of all ages. Mr. Popper, a kindhearted house painter, loves penguins. One day his friend Admiral Drake sends him a penguin named Captain Cook. What happens next is a barrel of laughs and goodwill. Grade 4 and up.

Bailey, Carolyn Sherwin, *Miss Hickory* (1946, Newbery Winner)—Miss Hickory is a little doll whose head is a hickory nut and whose body is a tree twig. Her owner moves to Boston and leaves Miss Hickory behind in New Hampshire. The brave little doll makes it through winter with the help of Crow. A lesson in facing adversity. Grade 4 and up.

Banks, Lynne Reid, *The Indian in the Cupboard* (1981)— Omri, the youngest of three brothers, receives three birthday gifts: a used plastic Native American figure, a discarded tin medicine chest, and an old-fashioned key. When Omri locks the Native American figure inside the cupboard, the figure comes to life. The magic cupboard brings Omri some difficult moral choices and provides readers with a look at decision-making and values. Grade 3 and up.

Bianco, Margery Williams, *The Velveteen Rabbit* (1926)— This sentimental story is one of many fantasies about toys that come to life. In this case, a little boy's beloved rabbit suffers with the child through a dangerous illness and is made real by love. Bianco's enchanting definition of what is "real" has become a favorite among teens and adults as well. When the copyright expired on this popular work, many new editions began to appear. Look for a facsimile of the original version illustrated by William Nicholson. All ages.

Bibee, John, *The Magic Bicycle* (1983)—In his Spirit Flyer series John Bibee weaves a magical and mysterious story about ordinary American boys and girls in the ordinary town of Centerville. When these children discover the amazing powers of their Spirit Flyer bicycles (a vehicle for some great Christian truths), they face a struggle against the Kingdom of Darkness and Goliath Industries. Grade 4 and up.

Bond, Michael, *A Bear Called Paddington* (1960)—A bear from "Darkest Peru" comes to live with the Brown family in London. His chief talent is getting into trouble, and his adventures are filled with preposterous humor and gentle satire. The first ten books in this series are good choices for beginning readers. Bond has also given children *Olga De Polga*, a fantastic and funny guinea pig. Grade 1–4.

Bond, Nancy, *A String in the Harp* (1976, Newbery Honor)—A widowed father and his three children move from North America to a remote area of Wales following the death of the children's mother. They become fascinated with the Welsh legends of Taliesen, a sixth century bard, and a magic harp key allows one of them to travel back in time. A good selection for reading aloud with upper elementary and middle school children.

Cameron, Eleanor, *The Wonderful Flight to the Mushroom Planet* (1954)—The story of two boys who stow away in a small space ship. Although it cannot be read as science fiction, it is an enjoyable book for some children who go on to read the other three books in the series. Also by Cameron is *Court of the Stone Children* (1973), in which a girl solves a mystery from the time of Napoleon through time-travel. Grade 4 and up.

Catling, Patrick Skene, *The Chocolate Touch* (1952)—John Midas finds an old coin and trades it for a box of his favorite thing—chocolate! After eating this enchanted candy, however, he finds that everything he touches turns into chocolate. He discovers that one *can* have too much of a good thing. Grade 3 and up.

Coatsworth, Elizabeth, *The Cat Who Went to Heaven*

(1958)—This book may be helpful in introducing children to Japanese culture, including Buddhism. Less well known but more satisfying for Christian families is Coatsworth's *The Wanderers* (1972), a story about a wandering monk and his traveling companions. Grade 4 and up.

Colum, Padraic, *The Golden Fleece: And the Heroes Who Lived Before Achilles* (1962), *Children of Odin* (1920), *The Arabian Nights, Tales of Wonder and Magnificence* (1953), *The Children's Homer: The Adventures of Odysseus and the Tale of Troy* (1918)—Wonderful prose retellings of Greek myths by an outstanding Irish poet, these books were made available in paperback during the 1960s. Grade 4 and up.

de la Mare, Walter, *Collected Stories* (1945), *The Three Mullah Mulgars* or *The Three Royal Monkeys* (1910)—Classic fantasies that reflect De la Mare's belief in the beauty and goodness of life. Grade 4 and up.

Druon, Maurice, *Tistou of the Green Thumbs* (1958)—The son of wealthy, beautiful parents, Tistou is born with the proverbial silver spoon in his mouth. His problems begin when he is sent to school. Although he is bright, he falls asleep in class and is expelled because "he is not like other people." Grade 4 and up.

Eager, Edward, *Half Magic* (1954)—Four children find a magic coin that grants half-wishes. Also in the series are *The Time Garden* (1958) and *Magic or Not?* (1959). Try reading these aloud during a "boring" summer vacation. Grade 4 and up.

Enright, Elizabeth, *Tatsinda*, illustrated by Katie Thamer Treherne (1963)—A charmingly illustrated fairy tale about a mountain kingdom and a lovely weaver who is stolen by an evil giant. This story is full of love and courage. Grade 3 and up.

Erickson, Russell E., *A Toad for Tuesday* (1974)—A daring toad leaves his cautious brother behind and goes in search of adventure. This easy-to-read animal fantasy is followed by *Warton and Morton* (1976), in which the two brothers go adventuring together, and *Warton King of the Skies* (1978). Grade 2 and up.

Field, Rachel, *Hitty, Her First Hundred Years* (1929, Newbery Winner)—An old-fashioned story about an old-fashioned doll, but one that is still loved by many young girls, mothers, and grandmothers. Grade 3 and up.

Fleming, Ian, *Chitty Chitty Bang Bang, the Magical Car* (1964)—An old racing car gets another life and takes to the air with an adventurous family. Grade 3 and up.

Gallico, Paul, *Snowflake* (1953)—An allegory on the meaning of life, this story follows a little snowflake from its birth to its final destination. Charming and poetic, it is ideal for reading aloud. Gallico portrays change, loss, and death as a natural part of fulfilling our God-given purpose. Out of print, but worth searching for. Gallico also wrote *The Snow Goose* and *Thomasina* and several other books that make good read-aloud selections. Grade 5 and up.

Gannett, Ruth S., *My Father's Dragon,* illustrated by Ruth Chrisman Gannett (1948, Newbery Honor)—Good for reading aloud to young children, or for beginning readers to enjoy alone. A dad uses his wits to rescue a baby dragon from Wild Island. Grade 1 and up.

Garner, Alan, The Stone Quartet (1967)—Garner is recognized as one of the most outstanding writers of juvenile fantasy, but his work is extremely dark and could prove distressing to many children and teens.

Godden, Rumer, *Four Dolls* (1983)—A collection of four treasured stories by a great writer: *Impunity Jane* (1954), *The Fairy Doll* (1959), *The Story of Holly and Ivy* (1959), and *Candy Floss* (1960). Young girls who like dolls will be charmed by these stories lovingly illustrated by Pauline Baynes. Godden also wrote *The Doll's House*

(1948), a story about a great-grandmother's dollhouse and the dolls inside who believe they are the Plantagenet family. Grade 2 and up.

Goudge, Elizabeth, *The Little White Horse* (1946, re-release 1992)—Goudge was a master at fusing fantasy, realism, and spirituality. (She was a devout Anglican.) Her stories are a bit slow-moving by today's standards, but they are worth the effort. *A Pedlar's Pack*, a collection of excerpts from her novels, offers a sampling. Then try reading aloud *The Little White Horse, Smoky House, A City of Bells,* and *The Blue Hills.* Grade 4 and up.

Grahame, Kenneth, *The Reluctant Dragon* (1938)—Not all dragons enjoy breathing fire and hoarding stolen treasure. One dragon longs for a peaceful life and makes friends with a little boy. Look for a facsimile of the original edition with illustrations by Ernest H. Shepard or the edition illustrated by Michael Hague. Like Grahame's *The Wind in the Willows*, this story is rich in moral value. Grade 2 and up.

Graves, Robert, *Greek Gods and Heroes* (1960), *The Siege and Fall of Troy* (1963), *Two Wise Children* (1966)—Best known for *I, Claudius,* Graves does a marvelous job of acquainting children and adults with Greek mythology. His prose is captivating as well as informative. Grade 6 and up.

Griffin, Penni R., *Switching Well* (1993)—In San Antonio, Texas, a girl of 1891 trades places with a girl of 1991. The girl of long ago wants to vote and fly, while the girl of today wants a world without air pollution, drugs, and divorce. Both learn there is no perfect time to be alive. Grade 5 and up.

Heide, Florence Parry, *The Shrinking of Treehorn* (1988)—Acclaimed for its outstanding illustrations by Edward Gorey and for its funny and wistful story about a boy whose problems and needs are overlooked by adults. Grade 2 and up.

Hoban, Russell, *The Mouse and His Child* (1967)—The adventures of a mechanical mouse and his father. Its layers of meaning make it popular with all ages.

Hodges, Elizabeth Jamison, *The Three Princes of Serendip* (1966)—The princes are sent by their father to find a secret formula called "Death to Dragons." In the process of searching, the princes discover many treasures they were not expecting. During their travels they grow in wisdom, kindness, and courage. In *Serendipity Tales* (1966), Hodges shares seven mysterious stories heard by the three princes of Serendip (Ceylon) in a Persian palace. Each tale is complete in itself, and they all come from the fifth century A.D. Grade 5 and up.

Hughes, Ted, *The Iron Giant: A Story in Five Nights* (1968)—This spellbinding book by one of America's best known poets was made to be read aloud. When a mechanical monster terrorizes the neighborhood, a young boy named Hogarth takes on the job of solving the problem. The story has a happy ending for the people and the Iron Man. Grade 4 and up.

Jacques, Brian, the Redwall series—An epic fantasy about the adventures of Martin, a monk mouse who becomes a warrior. These well-plotted stories are popular with children and teens because they combine swashbuckling adventure, comedy, and a strong sense of belonging. "No one has to be a latchkey kid at Redwall [Abbey]," says Jacques. "There's plenty of friends and warmth and cheerfulness, with big guardian badgers. Kids love to go there; it's an ideal home." Jacques, a BBC radio personality, created *Redwall* for a blind children's school in Liverpool. Throughout the series, which begins with *Redwall* (1987) and continues through *The Long Patrol* (1998), readers are reminded they must be trustworthy, speak the truth, and take a stand for what they believe in. Grade 5 and up.

Jarrell, Randall, *The Animal Family* (1965, Newbery Honor)—One of America's most outstanding poets tells the story of a hunter whose family includes a mermaid, a bear, a lynx, and a boy. The dominant themes are how to respond to loneliness, and how to create a family and hold it together. This excellent story is enhanced by Maurice Sendak's illustrations. In Jarrell's *The Bat Poet* (1963), a little brown bat discovers the world of poetry and begins to ask big questions about life. Grade 4 and up.

Kendall, Carol, *The Gammage Cup* (1959)—The Minnipins, or Small Ones, live in twelve villages in the Land Between the Mountains. They scarcely ever go outside their own village, and they have become very rigid in their beliefs and customs. Kendall's entertaining story is a satire on conformity and one of the classics in fantasy literature. Grade 5 and up.

Kennedy, Richard, *Amy's Eyes* (1985)—Amy lives in an orphanage until her sailor doll turns into a real sea captain, and Amy turns into a doll. The pair and a crew of animals set sail for adventure. Grade 2 and up.

King-Smith, Dick, *Babe: the Gallant Pig* (1985)—Most people became aware of Dick King-Smith's books when the film adaptation of *Babe* became a box-office success. He is an expert at droll stories of talking animals, and children learn quite a few facts about the animal kingdom from reading his fantasies. Children who like *Babe* will probably enjoy *The Cuckoo Child* (1993) about a farm boy who takes an ostrich egg home from his class trip to a wildlife park. In *Pretty Polly* (1992) a pet parrot tries to teach a baby chick to talk. *The Swoose* (1994) is the story of Fitzherbert, who is half goose and half swan, and his mission to cheer up Queen Victoria. Grade 2 and up.

Konigsburg, E. L., *A Proud Taste for Scarlet and Miniver* (1973)—Readers travel to heaven, where Eleanor of

Aquitaine awaits the arrival of King Henry II. Grade 5 and up.

Langton, Jane, *The Fledgling* (1980, Newbery Honor)—At Walden Pond Georgie dreams of flying. Her wish comes true when a Canadian goose befriends her. Grade 5 and up.

Laurence, Margaret, *The Olden Days Coat* (1979, re-release 1998)—A distinguished Canadian novelist tells the story of Sal, a ten-year-old who travels through time to her grandmother's past. Delightful picture book for Christmas story time. Grade 3 and up.

Lawhead, Stephen R., The Dragon King Trilogy (re-release 1996)—A coming-of-age story about Quentin, a young priest in a fantasy world. Action-adventure with strong spiritual value. The trilogy consists of *In the Hall of the Dragon King, The Warlords of Nin,* and *The Sword in the Flame.* While Lawhead's writing is uneven in quality, it will provide many preteens and teens with enjoyable, inspirational reading. Those who like his style may also enjoy *The Empyrion Saga* (science fiction) and *The Pendragon Cycle* (the legends of King Arthur with a Christian twist). Grade 9 and up.

Lindgren, Astrid, *Pippi Longstocking* (translated 1950)—Pippi is as unconventional as a child could be. She lives alone and does whatever she wants. But she has a good heart, plenty of imagination, and self-confidence. Her wild antics have made this one of the most popular children's books ever translated into English. The first in a series. Grade 3 and up.

Lowry, Lois, *The Giver* (1993, Newbery Winner)—Twelve-year-old Jonas lives in a utopian society, or so it seems until he is chosen as the new "Receiver." His task is to become a reservoir for all the memories of human-ity, and what he learns shatters his world. Read this book *with* children. It provides some excellent oppor-tunities for talking together about truth, personal responsibility, and "the culture of death"—suicide, abortion, infanticide, and euthanasia. Grade 6 and up.

Lunn, Janet, *The Root Cellar* (1985)—One of the best time-shift books, it tells the story of Rose, a thirteen-year-old orphan who leaves her wealthy grandmother's home in New York to live with relatives in rural Ontario. Rose makes "a secret garden" like the one in her favorite book, and thereby travels back to Civil War times. In the course of her adventures, she finds her roots and develops compassion. Grade 6 and up.

Macauley, David, *Why the Chicken Crossed the Road* (1987)—A chicken sets off a wild and wacky series of events in this wonderful picture book. Grade 4 and up.

MacGregor, Ellen, Miss Pickerell series—Elderly Miss Pickerell's adventures start when a rocketship lands in her cow pasture. She becomes trapped inside and takes an unexpected trip to Mars. In subsequent books, she visits space stations, lunar colonies, the Arctic, and other fascinating places. Since this series started in the early 1950s, some of the science is outdated, but the stories are still entertaining. Families can have fun comparing Miss Pickerell's scientific jaunts to those of Ms. Frizzle in The Magic School Bus series. Grade 3–6.

McCusker, Paul, Adventures in Odyssey series (Focus on the Family)—An outgrowth of the Adventures in Odyssey radio and video dramas, this series of books features the adventures and problems of three characters: Mark, who is being raised by his recently divorced mother; a tomboy named Patti; and a wise grandfather figure named Whit who owns a remarkable time-travel machine. Grade 3–6.

McKinley, Robin, *The Blue Sword* (1983, Newbery Honor)—Angharad Crewe leaves behind an easy life to become the savior of the Hillfolk. With a magical Blue Sword she leads her warrior band to victory. *The Hero and the Crown* (1985, Newbery Winner) is an epic fantasy about the adventures of Aerin, daughter of a king. Since she cannot succeed her father on the throne, she becomes a hero in her kingdom by slaying dragons with the Blue Sword. Grade 7 and up.

Masefield, John, *The Midnight Folk* (1927), *Box of Delights* (1935)—Masefield was England's poet laureate in 1930, and he wrote two wonderful stories for children. The trick is finding them since they are both out of print. Grade 4 and up.

Miller, Calvin, *The Singer* (1975)—The first of three volumes in The Singer Trilogy, a poetic retelling of the story of creation and redemption. Another imaginative work by this Baptist pastor and writer is *Walking with the Angels: The Valiant Papers and The Philippian Fragment* (1994 release of two books republished in one volume). Miller also has published The Singreale Chronicles, an interesting mix of rhyme, melodrama, humor, and philosophy. The first book in the series is *Guardians of the Singreale*. Grade 9 and up.

Myers, Bill, *The Portal* (1991)—The first in the Journeys to Farah series (Bethany). An enjoyable Christian fantasy by the creator of McGee and Me! (Focus on the Family) and Wally McDoogle (Word). Grade 4 and up.

Nolan, Dennis, *The Castle Builder* (1987)—A young boy sets out to build a giant sand castle. When he enters his castle he becomes "Sir Christopher, Builder of Castles, Tamer of Dragons, and Conqueror of the Black Knights." Danger rolls in with the rising tide. Grade 2 and up.

O'Brien, Robert C., *Mrs. Frisby and the Rats of NIMH* (1971, Newbery Winner)—Mrs. Frisby is a widow mouse who helps some intelligent lab rats from NIMH (National Institute of Mental Health) start a new society based on self-sufficiency rather than stealing. O'Brien's futuristic stories involve individual survival in what has been described as "a new Dark Ages." Grade 4 and up.

Paton, Jill Walsh, *A Chance Child* (1980)—Creep, an abused boy, escapes down an English canal and travels back in time one hundred years. He is befriended by children working in the mines and smithies whose suffering is even greater than his. Grade 5 and up.

Pinkwater, Daniel, *Ned Feldman, Space Pirate* (1994)—Ned's wild imagination turns the kitchen sink into a spaceship called the *Jolly Roger*. With Captain Lumpy Lugo at the controls, fun is the destination. In *The Blue Moose* a sophisticated and kind-hearted moose becomes headwaiter at a restaurant. K–Grade 3.

Pullman, Philip, *The Golden Compass* (U.S., 1996)—This is the first in an epic series called His Dark Materials, a fantasy inspired by Milton's *Paradise Lost*. The story continues in *The Subtle Knife*. While the books enjoy tremendous popularity with teens and have won critical acclaim, they raise many disturbing philosophical, moral, and religious questions. Parents and teachers are cautioned to read Pullman's books and be prepared to discuss the issues they raise. Grade 7 and up.

Rodgers, Mary, *Freaky Friday* (1972)—Thirteen-year-old Annabel Andrews wakes up in her mother's body. Her story is enjoyed by children who are moving into the "freaky" world of adolescence. Sequels are *A Billion for Boris* (1974) and *Summer Switch* (1982), in which Annabel's brother has his own other-body experience with his dad. Grade 5 and up.

Saint-Exupéry, Antoine de, *The Little Prince* (1943)— More popular with teens and adults than children, this is a sweet and fantastic story about a little prince who travels from his tiny world to another planet. It emphasizes the importance of responsibility and self-sacrifice in loving others, the uniqueness of every living being, and the reality of the invisible (spiritual) world. Grade 3 and up.

Salten, Felix, *Bambi* (translated from German in 1928)—Austrian writer Salten tells the story of a deer from fawn to grown buck. The animals are given human qualities and relationships. May seem too sweet and sentimental to modern children. Grade 4 and up.

Sandburg, Carl, *Rootabaga Stories* (1922)—Poet and Lincoln biographer Carl Sandburg created these funny stories with a distinctly Midwestern flavor. They feature White Horse Girl and Blue Wind Boy, Gimme the Ax, Hot Dog the Tiger, and a menagerie of entertaining characters. *Rootabaga Stories, Part One,* is available with illustrations by Maud Petersham, and *Rootabaga Stories, Part Two,* is illustrated by Michael Hague. Sandburg titled this second group of stories *Rootabaga Pigeons.* Grade 3 and up.

Selden, George (pseud. George Thompson), *The Cricket in Times Square* (1960, Newbery Honor)—The adventures of Harry the cat, Tucker the mouse, Chester the cricket, and other friends at a New York City newsstand. The first in a series of five books with fine illustrations by Garth Williams. A favorite for reading aloud. Grade 3 and up.

Sharp, Margery, *The Rescuers* (1959)—In Sharp's *Miss Bianca Stories* (1962–1970), a white mouse spans the globe to rescue those in need. Full of fun for younger children. Bianca teams up with another mouse named Bernard in *The Rescuers.* Grade 2 and up.

Siegel, Robert, *Alpha Centauri* (1980, Gold Medallion Award, *Campus Life* Merit of Excellence)—Vacationing in England, Becky and her newfound friend, Rebecca the horse, blunder into the "Eye of the Fog" and are transported through time to ancient Britain. Becky undertakes a perilous mission to save a race of benevolent centaurs. Madeleine L'Engle calls *Alpha Centauri* "absolutely fantastic! The kind of book that should be around for hundreds of years." A devout Christian and poet, Siegel has also written *The Kingdom of Wundle* (1982), a fairy tale for all ages; *Whalesong* (1981), the coming-of-age story of a humpback whale; and sequels to *Whalesong: The Ice at the End of the World* (1994) and *White Whale* (1994). Grade 6 and up.

Silverstein, Shel, *The Giving Tree* (1964)—A storybook about a boy and a tree who grow up and grow old together. The tree gives its life for the boy it loves. When read aloud by the whole family or in a classroom setting, it may provoke some differing perspectives on the nature of love. For example, does true love mean giving up everything we are to please someone else? Grade 4 and up.

Singer, Isaac Bashevis, *The Fearsome Inn* (1967, Newbery Honor), *When Schlmiel Went to Warsaw* (1968), *Naftali the Storyteller and His Horse, Sus* (1976)—Singer masterfully brings to life a society where the oral storyteller was both entertainer and philosopher. He retells Yiddish folktales, recreates the world of Jewish peasants, and draws from his own memories of growing up in Poland. Grade 2 and up.

Steig, William, *Abel's Island* (1976, Newbery Honor)—An Edwardian artist mouse has his tightly controlled human lifestyle swept away by a flood. He is marooned on an island for a year and gradually learns what it means to be a mouse. In *Doctor DeSoto* (1982, Newbery Honor), a book written for younger children, a mouse dentist goes against his better judgment to help a fox in an emergency. Grade 3 and up.

Uttley, Alison, *A Traveller in Time* (1939)—Penelope Taberner is transported back to the time of Mary,

Queen of Scots. She becomes involved in a plot to
save the queen, but knows that its outcome will be
tragic. A thought-provoking book about our inability
to change the past. Grade 5 and up.

White, John, *The Tower of Geburah* (1978)—John White
is a former associate professor of psychiatry at the
University of Manitoba and a minister who has written
several serious non-fiction books for adults. When he
ran out of Narnia books to read to his children, they
begged for more, so he started making up a similar
story for them at bedtime. He made it as much like
Narnia as he could manage. That story became *The
Tower of Geburah*, in which three children travel to another land and time. Its sequels are *The Iron Scepter*
(1981), *The Swordbearer* (1986), and *Gaal the Conqueror*
(1989). Grade 4 and up.

Wrightson, Patricia, *The Nargun and the Stars* (1974)—
Wrightson's fantasies are based on Australian myths.
They reflect the animism inherent to aboriginal be-
liefs, as well as a deep reverence for life and goodness.
Mature readers will find it interesting to contrast non-
Western fantasy with more familiar forms. Grade 5
and up.

Yolen, Jane, *The Transfigured Hart* (1975)—Richard and
Heather join to rescue a white deer from hunters and
learn his strange secret. In *The Devil's Arithmetic*
(1988), Hannah has to spend every Jewish holiday listening to her relatives tell stories. She does not appreciate hearing about the past until one evening at
Passover when she is transported to a Jewish village
in 1940s Poland. These books are suitable for grade
5 and up. *Sleeping Ugly* (1981, Grade 2 and up) is the
story of Princess Miserella, who is beautiful outside
but ugly inside, and Plain Jane, a girl with a heart of
gold and a face that matches her name. Both girls get
what they deserve. Yolen's Commander Toad series

(Grade 3 and up) is a hilarious spin-off of *Star Wars,* but Yolen's humor does not depend on familiarity with the movies. Witty, wacky, wild, and wonderful.

Yolen, winner of the World Fantasy Award, is the author of over a hundred books for adults and children, and is an expert in folklore. Fantasy writer Gene Wolf has said, "In a better world we shall hear her tales with Oscar Wilde's, Hans Christian Andersen's, and Charles Perrault's over a winter's eve of ten thousand years."

This chapter has mentioned almost one hundred writers of fantasy for children since World War I. Many of these fantasies are too mature for a very young reader, but none are too young for a very mature reader. C. S. Lewis said once, "I now enjoy the fairy tales better than I did in childhood: being now able to put more in, of course I get more out." He believed that readers who truly enjoy fantasies "for adults" are apt to enjoy fantasies "for children." Fantasies for children and those for adults have much more in common, he thought, than either has with realistic fiction.

Realistic Fiction and Biography

7 Steps in Time

Story-telling, as I see it, is a recreating of life, a breathing of life into plausible characters and of facing honestly every naturally occurring situation those characters meet.

—Ivan Southall, *Journal of Discovery: on Writing for Children*

Ivan Southall is an Australian author of strictly realistic novels for children. In a 1974 article for librarians, he told about his life as a struggling author in Australia and included a fantastic story. One evening his mother-in-law and some other relatives were playing a game that worked rather like a ouija board, and they got a message from Southall's dead father. Southall did not believe in such things, but the message gave clear directions for finding an abandoned mine nearby in the Australian bush where Chinese prospectors had left half-a-million in gold.

The family spent the next day locating the shaft, and they found what certainly looked like gold. Southall was very poor then—a failure as a family farmer and still only an amateur writer. But he decided not to take the supernatural shortcut to success. Eventually developers came and unknowingly erased every trace of the hidden gold mine. Southall never regretted his decision to ignore the spooky gold. He earned his success the way he wanted to, by writing realistic fiction. He does not pretend that his realistic fiction is true.

Readers can believe or disbelieve Southall's nonfiction account about ghosts and gold. It may be a lie. But whether Southall's farfetched story is true or not, we have to acknowledge that real life is stranger than what we call realistic fiction. As long as truth is stranger than fiction, realistic fiction does not ever get too strange.

Realistic fiction differs from fantasy in that it must stay within the bounds of what most people consider possible. It is not apt to include the views of spiritual or scientific thinkers—perspectives often included in fantasy. Realistic fiction takes the views of reality ordinarily found in school textbooks, however distorted or limited such views might be sometimes.

Realistic fiction can include as much wishful thinking or lack of awareness as any other writing of its time. For instance, as recently as 1957, a college psychology textbook entitled *Childhood and Adolescence* taught that as soon as children are old enough to read on their own, their tastes differ according to gender. Boys like adventure and heroism, they said. In contrast, girls like stories about home, school, and romance. Boys develop an interest in world events; girls limit their interest to home and neighborhood. Boys are quick to enjoy informative literature; girls prefer fiction. Furthermore, the psychologists affirmed, boys like funny stories, but girls do not.

People who were once children might well claim that the men who wrote this textbook were off into a bit of fantasy. Simple observation would have corrected them. But their point of view was acceptable enough to be considered realistic in 1957. Likewise, realistic fiction and biography is that which is in step with its time.

Authors of this fiction come from a broad spectrum of society, and their writing reflects their widely varying experiences and ideologies. There is much more variety in children's fiction today than ever before, which, with some unpleasant exceptions, is a good thing for children.

Since World War I this gigantic body of literature has consisted of works in categories we call contemporary life, animal fiction, historical fiction, adventure and mystery, humor, and biography. To narrow the scope of this chapter, we will offer recommendations in three categories: contemporary life, historical fiction, and biography. For animal fiction, adventure and mystery, and humor, refer to chapter 9, "The Kids' Hit Parade."

Before our list of recommended books, here is an introduction to the work of two contemporary authors of realistic fiction. Their books are representative of two vastly different approaches to realistic fiction.

Judy Blume

For over twenty years, Judy Blume has been considered a daring pioneer who presents the realities of growing up for children who are in fifth and sixth grades. She includes "bad words," wet dreams, masturbation, and peeking at a naked person. She often writes about wealthy New Jersey parents who are, to judge by their incredibly stupid behavior, either mentally ill or alcoholic. The materially spoiled children she describes are neurotically competitive about becoming sexually provocative and are already social climbers in elementary school. There seems to be no feeling for weather, animals, nature, or the rest of the world outside this unpleasant social environment.

Blume takes criticism of her subject matter as a prudish reluctance to be honest with children and help them toward happy sexual adjustment. A mother herself—and a product of affluent New Jersey society—she aims to guide children as well as entertain them. She happens to approve of the apparently self-centered, impersonal, shallow life-style she writes about. To a sensitive, informed adult these books are bleak stories about bleak lives, and they are depressing. But to young people they are exciting and immensely popular and are widely available in bookstores and public libraries.

Are You There God? It's Me, Margaret (1970) by Blume is often misrepresented as a story of religious tolerance. A standard guide to children's literature says, "Margaret is also confused about religion; will she be Jewish like her father or Christian like her mother? She doesn't solve all her problems but does decide that her faith is strong, that she can worship in her own way, whatever her formal affiliation." That is completely false.

In fact, Margaret's inept father has no use for the Jewish faith, and her mother hates and rejects Christianity. Margaret sees her indulgent Jewish grandmother as a bit silly and despises her old Christian grandparents, who bear about as much resemblance to Catholics or Protestants as they do to astronauts—one would have to search hard to find a more malicious caricature in children's literature.

There is no indication that Margaret considers the truth and teaching of either faith; she sees religion as a social affiliation and finds public worship a bore. She is, however, in the habit of reporting her interests to God occasionally, much as a girl of eleven jots in a diary. For example: "I can't wait until two o'clock God. That's when the dance starts. Do you think I'll get Philip Leroy for a partner? It's not so much that I like him as a person God, but as a boy he's very handsome."

Margaret stops speaking to God when she misses out on a trip to Florida. And she becomes furious at her parents and grandparents for arguing about whether she should have any religion. But when her main desire is fulfilled and she begins to menstruate, she talks to God again: "I knew you wouldn't have missed this for anything!"

One peculiar detail in this book (which is preoccupied

with menstruation), is the patently false assurance that menstruation is painless. It is common knowledge that the intense cramping pain experienced by some girls is organic, although many male doctors used to dismiss it as mental. Blume's realism sometimes ignores reality.

Blume has every right to endorse Margaret's kind of agnosticism, but it seems a shame that she has done it with disdain for the subject. And it is a shame that her book is falsely recommended as a story about tolerance and maturation.

Blume's *Forever,* for young teenage girls, describes what it is like to have casual sexual intercourse, including physical details and clever pillow talk. The accompanying risks of pregnancy, venereal disease, and prolonged emotional entanglement pose no problem for the socially successful heroine, who feels much more mature after the experience and steps into a new romance.

So long as it sells, realistic children's literature is going to continue to include drugs, divorce, suicide, gang war, crime, rape, the occult, parental adultery, deformities, unwanted pregnancies, racial prejudice, homosexuality, abortion, mental illness, and sick family relationships. It will continue to include problems of sexual awakening and religious opinion. Some of these books will be constructive and wholesome; others will seem quite unworthy.

Protests to publishers, bookstores, and libraries about specific books should not be made too hastily. Concerned parents are wise to become acquainted with similar books in order to judge which are more or less helpful and which are really pernicious. We recommend reading and discussing these books with your children, if they are going to be exposed to them anyway.

Katherine Paterson

If it is worthwhile for parents to read questionable children's books about the hard parts of life, it is even more worthwhile for them to read great children's books about the hard parts of life. And that means reading Katherine Paterson. Paterson has been described by a fellow writer as "winner of almost every imaginable award in the realm of children's literature and deserving of that recognition." She writes realistic fiction, but when her realistic characters read books, they read fantasy. She still feels that poetry and fantasy are higher forms of writing.

Paterson has always been wild about books, but she did not expect to become an author. She was born in China to missionary parents and spent part of her childhood there. She received a master's degree in English Bible in the United States, did Christian work for four years in Japan, attended theological seminary in New York, and married a Presbyterian minister. (Her book *Angels and Other Strangers* [1979] is a collection of her Christmas stories that her husband John used to read in church on Christmas Eve.) Two of the couple's four grown children are adopted from different racial backgrounds.

At the age of forty, Paterson took an adult education course that required her to write a book chapter a week. She submitted the resulting novel to different publishers for two years without success until a reader at Crowell decided it deserved the senior editor's consideration. In 1973 Crowell published *The Sign of the Chrysanthemum*, a story set in twelfth-century Japan. It was followed by two more tales about children in ancient Japan, *Of Nightingales That Weep* (1974) and *The Master Puppeteer* (1976), which won the National Book Award.

Paterson loves Lewis's Narnian Chronicles. In her *Bridge to Terabithia* (1977) she tells about what Lewis's Narnia brought to the life of a needy American boy. The book is about finding wealth in poverty, finding love in loneliness, and finding life in death and bereavement. Winner of the Newbery Medal, this book can stand as

America's finest thanks to Britain for all its wealth of children's books that we enjoy.

In 1979 Paterson's *The Great Gilly Hopkins* was a Newbery Honor Book and won numerous other major awards. It is about a lonely foster child and the difference between tough and strong. It has plenty of humor, grit, and tenderness. It is also one of the most censored children's books, due to its profanity and the brashness Gilly exhibits. Paterson responds to the criticism by affirming her deep commitment to telling true stories about real people. She see her work as "a calling from God" and believes that sugar coating her characters would be an act of disrespect for the gift God has given her. "When I wrote *Gilly Hopkins*," Paterson says, "it occurred to me to wonder if my secular publishing house would reject it because it seemed to me so blatant a rewriting of the parable of the Prodigal Son."

In 1980 Paterson's *Jacob Have I Loved* won her a second Newbery Medal. Like Paterson's other tales, it is intensely honest about flaws and hurts in family life. It tells about a sister who always works harder and always gets second-best. Life is not fair, and Paterson never pretends that it is. In all her books she shows the same healing power of love. She says her characters fall into two main categories: "the hero [who] must leave home, confront fabulous dangers, and return the victor to grant boons on his fellows," or "a wandering nobody [who] must go out from bondage through the wilderness and by the grace of God become truly someone who can give back something of what she has been given" (*A Sense of Wonder: On Reading and Writing Books for Children*, 1995).

Her stories of human redemption include *Come Sing, Jimmy Jo* (1985), a story about a boy who joins his family's bluegrass band and becomes a celebrity, and *Flip-Flop Girl* (1994), a school story about three bereft children and the importance of friendship. She has also written historical fiction set in ancient China *(The Shining Company)* and in 1800s' New England *(Jip: His Story,* about a boy growing up on a poor farm, and *Lyddie,* about a girl who goes to work in a textile mill). Her picture books are described in chapter 12.

Paterson's outstanding contribution to children's literature was acknowledged with the 1998 Hans Christian Andersen Award, a prestigious international honor. Her books have been published in twenty languages. Repeatedly, she has credited the effectiveness of her writing to her childhood immersion in Bible stories and her ongoing love for the beauty and honesty of the Scriptures.

The following lists of realistic fiction represent some of the better books available to children. They entertain without titillating, inspire without preaching, and along with truthful portrayals of life's problems, they offer a sense of meaning and hope. They have in common three characteristics that Katherine Paterson says are essential to a good book—simplicity, harmony, and illumination.

Contemporary Life

Byars, Betsy, *The Burning Questions of Bingo Brown* (1988)—Freckle-faced Bingo has lots of questions about the people around him and about life. He writes them all down in his journal and soon discovers there are always more questions than answers. An entertaining look at life's struggles and insecurities. Grade 4 and up.

Cleary, Beverly, *Ramona, the Pest* (1968), *Ramona and Her Father* (1977, Newbery Honor, Grade 1–3), *Ramona and Her Mother* (1980, National Book Award), *Ramona Quimby, Age 8* (1981, Newbery Honor), *Dear Mr. Henshaw* (1983, Newbery Winner, Grade 3–5)—Cleary presents familiar family problems with a light touch.

Cleaver, Vera and Bill, *Where the Lilies Bloom* (1965)—An

extraordinary fourteen-year-old named Mary Call Luther struggles to control and support her parentless family of four in the Smoky Mountains. Grade 5 and up.

Estes, Eleanor, *The Moffats* series—Estes, an American librarian turned writer, created the Moffat family and wrote three books about them: *The Moffats* (1941), *The Middle Moffat* (1942, Newbery Honor), and *Rufus M* (1943, Newbery Honor). They consist of simple, humorous episodes from the younger children's point of view, set in a small Connecticut town called Cranbury before and during World War I. They are among the most delightful family stories ever written and enjoyable for reading aloud. Estes won the Newbery Medal for *Ginger Pye* (1951), in which a brother and sister solve the mystery of their dog's disappearance. In *The Hundred Dresses* (1944, Newbery Honor) a Polish immigrant with only one dress to wear to school wards off her classmates' teasing with a claim to owning a vast wardrobe. Grade 2 and up.

Fleischman, Paul, *Seedfolks* (1997)—Inner city neighbors create a cooperative garden in an empty lot. A wonderful story about transcending racial, economic, and cultural barriers. Grade 6 and up.

George, Jean Craighead, *My Side of the Mountain* (1959, Newbery Honor), *Julie of the Wolves* (1994, Newbery Winner)—George does a beautiful job of connecting young readers with nature. In *My Side of the Mountain,* a young "Thoreau" makes his home in a tree. In *Julie of the Wolves,* an Eskimo girl discovers the richness of her culture when she tries to run away from it. Grade 5 and up.

Getz, David, *Thin Air* (1990)—Jacob is a sixth grader with severe asthma and allergies, but he wants to be treated just like everyone else. This entertaining and often funny story offers a great opportunity to talk with children about how to interact with those who have chronic health problems. Grade 5 and up.

Hamilton, Virginia, *M. C. Higgins, the Great* (1974, Newbery Winner)—Hamilton's maternal grandfather was born a slave and ran away from the Kentucky-Tennessee area with his mother. Her grandmother was half Cherokee. In 1975 Hamilton became the first African-American to win the Newbery Medal. She lives in Yellow Springs, Ohio, where her relatives have lived for several generations.

Hamilton has absorbed a great deal of African-American history and experience, which she transforms into literature. *Zeely* (1967, Grade 4 and up), a book about black dignity, tells the story of a child who is awed by the beauty of a neighbor who looks like a Watusi queen. *The House of Dies Drear* (1968, Grade 4 and up) is a mystery story set in a house that was once a station on the Underground Railroad. *M. C. Higgins, the Great* (1974, National Book Award as well as Newbery Winner, Grade 3 and up) is an unusual book, and one that is not extremely popular with children. M. C. Higgins, aged thirteen, lives on Sarah's Mountain and spends his time watching. The slag heap that moves toward his home poses a terrible danger to his family and makes M. C. long to move away, but moving remains a dream.

Holman, Felice, *Slake's Limbo* (1974)—Thirteen-year-old Aremis Slake, neglected and abused, finds a place of his own behind the wall of a subway tunnel. A book for mature readers. Grade 5 and up.

Hunt, Irene, *Up a Road Slowly* (1966, Newbery Winner)—When Julie's mother dies, her father sends her and her little brother to live with her strict schoolteacher aunt. A beautiful story of growing in acceptance and love. Grade 6 and up.

Konigsburg, E. L., *From the Mixed-up Files of Mrs. Basil*

E. Frankweiler (1967, Newbery Winner)—This comic drama with a touch of irony takes place inside the Metropolitan Museum of Art in New York City where two runaway children take up residence. Grade 4 and up.

Krumgold, Joseph, . . . *And Now Miguel* (1953, Newbery Winner)—A New Mexico boy longs to hear his father say that he is old enough to go to the mountains with the men to care for the sheep. Grade 5 and up.

L'Engle, Madeleine, *Meet the Austins* (1960)—The Austins are among the last intact, loyal, prosperous, and happy families in children's literature. Dr. Austin's household, overflowing with laughter and love, manages to incorporate a spoiled ten-year-old whose parents were killed in an accident. *The Moon by Night* (1963), *The Young Unicorns* (1968), and *A Ring of Endless Light* (1980) continue the story. For good or ill, this family is superior to ordinary families in culture, talent, spirit, and parental perfection—and aware of the superiority. L'Engle now regrets that she allowed her publisher to water down *Meet the Austins*, making it more sweet and pious than she had intended. She has said, "My feeling is that if a children's book isn't equally or even more enjoyed by adults then it's not worth doing." Grade 6 and up.

Little, Jean, *Mine for Keeps* (1962)—This Canadian writer was born blind. *Mine for Keeps* is a realistic account of how a young girl with cerebral palsy adjusts to family life after five years at a school for the handicapped. The sequel is *Spring Begins in March* (1966). In *Home from Far* (1965), a girl's twin brother is killed, and then foster children are brought into the home. *Take Wing* (1968) deals with mental retardation. In *Look through My Window* (1970) and *Kate* (1971), Jean Little explores growth in family relationships and self-understanding. For a deeper understanding of the visually impaired, read *Listen for the Singing* (1991) and Little's autobiography, *Stars Come Out Within* (1991). Grade 5 and up.

Mathis, Sharon Bell, *The Hundred Penny Box* (1975, Newbery Honor)—A young boy is torn between his love for his great aunt and his love for his mother, who resents having to share her home with the hundred-year-old woman. Enhanced by Leo and Diane Dillon, award-winning illustrators. Grade 2 and up.

Merrill, Jean, *The Pushcart War* (1964)—A witty satire set in New York City in 1976, in which the pushcart peddlers overthrow a truck monopoly. Grade 6 and up.

Morpurgo, Michael, *The War of Jenkins' Ear* (1995)—What would happen if Jesus came back as a British schoolboy? Toby must decide whether his new friend Christopher is what he claims—the reincarnation of Jesus Christ. Set in a 1952 prep school, this unusual story raises questions about belief and doubt, deception, and loyalty. Morpurgo leaves readers to find their own answers, so parents may want to read and discuss this provocative book with mature readers. Grade 6 and up.

Paulsen, Gary, *The Tent: A Parable in One Sitting* (1995)—Steven's father gets tired of being poor and decides to make some fast, easy money as a traveling preacher. Although Steven is embarrassed and uncomfortable about his father's con game, he is won over by their financial success and becomes part of the act. Then Steven's dad begins to pay attention to the words of Jesus in his Gideon Bible stolen from a motel. A powerful story about deception, greed, manipulation, and repentance. Grade 6 and up.

St. John, Patricia M., *Where the River Begins* (1980)—Francis, a ten-year-old caught up in gang life, turns to a Christian family for help. Other inspiring stories from this author are *The Tanglewood's Secret* (1948),

Rainbow Garden (1960), and *The Secret at Pheasant Cottage* (1978). A sampler of St. John's fiction is available in *Stories to Share: A Family Treasury of Faith* (1997, Shaw). Grade 4 and up.

Southall, Ivan, *To the Wild Sky* (1967, Book of the Year Award, Australia)—Southall writes of children in stress and danger or under specific handicaps. *Hell's End* (1963) deals with a group of children who return home from a cave exploration with their teacher and discover that their town has been flooded and deserted. *Let the Balloon Go* (1968) deals with a physically challenged child's heroic efforts at climbing a tree. Grade 5 and up.

Spinelli, Jerry, *Wringer* (1997, Newbery Honor), *Maniac Magee* (1990, Newbery Winner), *Fourth Grade Rats* (1991)—Spinelli is a master at recreating the everyday world of school children and is enjoyed especially by boys. Grade 4 and up.

Stolz, Mary, *Cider Days* (1978), *A Dog on Barkham Street* (1960), *The Noonday Friends* (1965, Newbery Honor)—Mary Stolz writes with insight and compassion about the problems of preteens, including bullies, the need for friends, irresponsibility, and parental expectations. Grade 4 and up.

Townsend, John Rowe, *Noah's Castle* (1957)—Townsend, long a children's book critic in England, decided to write some books he would like to read and has become a major writer of children's realistic fiction. In *Noah's Castle*, he tells the story of one family that disintegrates during their struggle for survival after the British economy collapses. The country's financial poverty is less than the emotional poverty of the father—who has futilely hoarded things for his own family—and his collapse is more complete than the country's. Townsend manages to write about catastrophe with courage and to describe a sick personality without rancor. The book is not a fantasy because it seems quite possible, and it is not depressing because of the goodness in some of the young characters.

Townsend's *Trouble in the Jungle* (1969) deals with slum children abandoned by adults and their skirmish with criminals. *The Intruder* (1969) tells of a boy who is mystified about his parentage after a stranger claims to be the true son of his mother and father. In *Dan Alone* (1983), Townsend tells the story of eleven-year-old Dan Lunn, who is trying to find himself in the midst of family problems. The story is set in England in 1922. Grade 4 and up.

Wrightson, Patricia, *A Race Course for Andy* (1968)—This is the story of a retarded child who believes he owns a racetrack. Wrightson is an Australian writer of great skill. Grade 4 and up.

Additional realistic stories about contemporary children are listed in chapter 8, a special section devoted to family relationships.

Historical Fiction

This type of fiction can imaginatively describe historical events or just tell stories set in some historical period. Either way, the details should be as accurate as possible. Interestingly, books originally written as contemporary fiction quickly become historical fiction to young readers, a fact which often makes their parents and teachers feel almost antique. Fifty outstanding authors of children's historical fiction follow in alphabetical order.

Armstrong, William, *Sounder* (1960, Newbery Winner)—The father in a family of black sharecroppers is jailed for stealing food for his wife and children. During his arrest the family dog is shot, and a young boy must learn how to deal with loneliness—a brief but touching story set in the nineteenth-century American South. Grade 4 and up.

Benchley, Nathaniel, *George the Drummer Boy* (1977), *Sam the Minuteman* (1969)—These stories take place at the beginning of the American Revolution. They are especially enjoyed by beginning readers. Grade 1–4.

Blos, Joan, *A Gathering of Days: A New England Girl's Journal, 1830–32* (1979, Newbery Winner, National Book Award)—The fictionalized journal of a girl coming of age in New Hampshire. *School Library Journal* commended the author for creating characters that are authentic people of their time, "old-fashioned in the best sense of the word—principled." Grade 5 and up.

Blumberg, Rhoda, *Commodore Perry in the Land of the Shogun* (1985)—A beautiful book that is both entertaining and informative. Grade 4 and up.

Brink, Carol Ryrie, *Caddie Woodlawn* (1935)—Caddie Woodlawn is set in Wisconsin in the Civil War period, but the war plays no part in the story, which is about frontier farm life. Among other adventures, high-spirited Caddie develops a friendship with some Native Americans and helps prevent an uprising. This popular book has been criticized because of Caddie's submission to a subdued feminine role as part of her maturation, and some readers object to its portrayal of Native Americans. It has also been noted that Mr. Woodlawn could not have inherited a title in England by renouncing America as the story claims. In spite of its flaws, children continue to love Caddie. Grade 4 and up.

Buck, Pearl S., *The Big Wave* (1947)—A devastating tidal wave sweeps away Jiya's family and village. His friend Kino, who lives on a mountainside, helps. Grade 5 and up.

Bulla, Clyde Robert, *A Lion to Guard Us* (1981)—Bulla

is one of the best writers of historical fiction for younger children, and his books can be enjoyed by older children who have reading difficulties. In *A Lion to Guard Us,* he tells the story of a family's journey to Jamestown. Bulla has written several other books in the same straightforward manner, including *The Secret Valley* (1993) and *The Sword in the Tree* (1962). Great for reading aloud. Grade 2–5.

Burton, Hester, *Time of Trial* (1963)—This author is known for her novels of social concern. *Time of Trial* tells of a brave seventeen-year-old girl who gets imprisoned for speaking out for social reform. Burton says that her main interest is the story of young people cast into dreadful trouble who get out of it on their own. Grade 6 and up.

Caudill, Rebecca, *Tree of Freedom* (1949, Newbery Honor)— When Stephanie's family sets out for Kentucky, each of them gets to take along one prized possession. Stephanie takes an apple seed, which sprouts into what she calls her "tree of freedom." As the Revolutionary War sweeps over the family, they discover the personal sacrifice required to keep freedom alive. Also, *The Far-Off Land* (1964). Grade 6 and up.

Collier, James Lincoln and Christopher Collier, *My Brother Sam Is Dead* (1974, Newbery Honor)—This memorable story set during the Revolutionary War can help readers understand the horrors of war and how conflicting loyalties pull families apart. Some parents object to its profanity and violence. Grade 6 and up.

Coolidge, Olivia, *Egyptian Adventure* (1954), *Roman People* (1959), *Men of Athens* (1962, Newbery Honor), and *People of Palestine* (1965)—Coolidge takes her readers to the ancient world for a look at a wide variety of social and economic classes. Grade 6 and up.

Cushman, Karen, *Catherine, Called Birdy* (1994, Newbery

Honor), *The Midwife's Apprentice* (1995, Newbery Winner), *The Ballad of Lucy Whipple* (1996)—As Cushman watched her daughter growing up, she wondered what adolescence was like for girls in other times. Her fascination with history and the feminine experience has yielded three award-winning books about strong, outgoing, independent girls: rebellious Catherine, daughter of an English knight; Alyce, an orphan in medieval England; and Lucy, a reluctant part of the California Gold Rush. Grade 6 and up.

Dalgliesh, Alice, *The Courage of Sarah Noble* (1954, Newbery Honor)—A beautiful story about an eight-year-old girl's journey with her father into the Connecticut wilderness in 1707. Although very popular, this book has been severely criticized for its portrayal of Native Americans. Dalgliesh also wrote *Thanksgiving Story* (1954, Caldecott Honor), a fictionalized account of the Plymouth Colony, as well as *The Bears on Hemlock Mountain* (1952) and *The Silver Pencil* (1944), both Newbery Honor Books. Grade 2 and up.

de Angeli, Marguerite, *The Door in the Wall* (1949, Newbery Winner)—*The New York Times* printed this in its review: "an enthralling and inspiring tale of triumph over handicap. Unusually beautiful illustrations, full of authentic detail, combine with the text to make life in England during the Middle Ages come alive." The reviewer was right! In *Thee, Hannah!* (1940), de Angeli tells the story of a strong-willed and imaginative Quaker girl living in Philadelphia just before the Civil War. *Henner's Lydia* is about a Mennonite girl. *Black Fox of Lorne* (1956, Newbery Honor) is set in medieval Scotland. Grade 3 and up.

DeJong, Meindert, *The Wheel on the School* (1955, Newbery Winner)—A group of school children try to bring the storks back to their Dutch fishing village. A good read-aloud that encourages perseverance. *The House of Sixty Fathers* (1956, Newbery Honor) is the story of Tien Pao, a Chinese boy who must make his way home from behind Japanese enemy lines. Grade 4–8.

Field, Rachel, *Calico Bush* (1931)—The story of Marguerite Ledoux, a French servant girl who settles in Maine in 1743. Grade 4 and up.

Fleischman, Paul, *Bull Run* (1993)—Sixteen characters present their unique perspectives on the first battle of the Civil War. Their stories are artfully presented to give readers a moving history lesson. Grade 5 and up.

Fleischman, Sid, *Mr. Mysterious and Company* (1962) and *By the Great Horn Spoon!* (1963)—Fleischman writes energetic tales with a generous measure of humor. *Mr. Mysterious and Company* concerns the members of the Hachette family, who give magic shows—hence the title—in small pioneer towns, working their way west. *By the Great Horn Spoon!* (1963) tells of a proper English butler who finds himself serving in the middle of the California Gold Rush. *The Whipping Boy* (1986, Newbery Winner) is set in England during the Middle Ages. Grade 4 and up.

Forbes, Esther, *Johnny Tremain* (1943, Newbery Winner)—Set in Boston during the Revolutionary War, this is the story of a young silversmith who gets involved in the rebellion by carrying messages and gathering intelligence. Forbes's excellent description gives one the feeling of being present at all events. Grade 4 and up.

Fox, Paula, *The Slave Dancer* (1973, Newbery Winner)—The story (Grade 6 and up) of an African boy who was kidnapped in 1840 and forced to work on a slave ship, exercising the sick slaves on deck. The ship is wrecked. The boy survives, but the spiritual horror of his journey is unforgettable.

One of Fox's earlier books, *How Many Miles to Babylon?* (1967, Grade 5 and up) tells of a small boy who is kidnapped by older boys and forced to assist them in their dog-stealing racket, but who lets the dogs go at night.

Gates, Doris, *Blue Willow* (1939, Newbery Honor)—A realistic look at the lives of migrant farm workers and a young girl's longing for a permanent home. Grade 4 and up.

Giff, Patricia Reilly, *Lily's Crossing* (1997, Newbery Honor)—Set in 1944 just after D-Day, this is a story about true friendship and what it can teach us about the value of honesty. The book also offers insights into dealing with separation and loss, appreciating family members, and breaking bad habits. Grade 4 and up.

Gregory, Kristiana, *Jenny of the Tetons* (1989); *Jimmy Spoon and the Pony Express* (1994); *The Stowaway: A Tale of California Pirates!* (1995), part of the Great Episodes series; *The Winter of the Red Snow: The Revolutionary War Diary of Abigail Jane Stewart* (1996), part of the Dear America series—Engaging stories with plenty of adventure and suspense. Grade 4 and up.

Hall, Donald, *Ox-Cart Man* (1979, Caldecott Winner)—A picture book presentation of early American trading. Grade 1 and up.

Hautzig, Esther, *The Endless Steppe* (1968)—Just before World War II, a Jewish family must leave their home in Poland to work in a Siberian labor camp. They survive through humor, courage, and cleverness. Grade 4 and up.

Hesse, Karen, *Out of the Dust* (1997, Newbery Winner)—A fourteen-year-old Oklahoma girl faces family tragedies and economic hardships during the dust-bowl years (Grade 7 and up). Also look for *Letters from Rifka* (1992), about a Jewish girl in 1919 Russia (Grade 6 and up).

Holm, Anne, *North to Freedom* (or *I Am David*) (1965,

translated from Danish)—The story of a boy of twelve who escapes from a Communist prison camp in Eastern Europe, which is all he has ever known, and journeys alone and ignorant through Europe to find his mother in Copenhagen. It is a heroic, emotional, and heartwarming story, one set in the recent past. Grade 5 and up.

Hunt, Irene, *Across Five Aprils* (1964, Newbery Winner)—Jethro Creighton, aged nine at the beginning of the Civil War, describes what it was like to live in that time of turmoil and grief. Also, *Trail of Apple Blossoms* (1968), a novel based on the life of Johnny Appleseed. Grade 4 and up.

Lasky, Kathryn, *A Journey to the New World: The Diary of Remember Patience Whipple* (1996) and *Dreams in the Golden Country: The Diary of Zipporah Feldman, a Jewish Immigrant Girl* (1998)—Both these books are part of Scholastic's Dear America series, a journey through America's past in the form of fictionalized diaries. *A Journey to the New World* (Grade 4 and up) is written from the viewpoint of Remember Patience, a girl aboard the Mayflower in 1620. *Dreams in the Golden Country* (Grade 4 and up) was inspired by the experiences of Lasky's immigrant grandparents. It is set in New York City in 1903. Other historical fiction by Lasky: *True North: A Novel of the Underground Railroad* (1996, Grade 6 and up, Newbery Honor); *Beyond the Divide* (1981, Grade 7 and up); *The Night Journey* (1986, National Jewish Book Award, Grade 5 and up).

Lenski, Lois, *Strawberry Girl* (1945, Newbery Winner)—Lenski started what became a series about disadvantaged regional groups with this story set in rural Florida. Other books in the series include *Boom Town Boy* (1948) and *Cotton in My Sack* (1949). In *Phebe Fairchild: Her Book* (1936, Newbery Honor), Lenski writes about a Connecticut girl of 1830. *Puritan Ad-*

venture (1944) is one of her worthwhile short novels. Grade 3 and up.

Lord, Bette Bao, *In the Year of the Boar and Jackie Robinson* (1984)—Shirley Wang moves from China to Brooklyn, New York. Although she only knows two English words when she arrives, she finds friends and the Brooklyn Dodgers. Grade 3 and up.

Lowell, Susan, *I Am Lavina Cumming* (1993)—Lavina says good-bye to her widowed father and brothers and their ranch in Arizona Territory. She is going to live with her aging aunt in Santa Cruz, California, so she can learn to be a lady. A wonderful story of courage and family relationships. Grade 4 and up.

Lowry, Lois, *Number the Stars* (1989, Newbery Winner)— Ten-year-old Annemarie and her family help Jewish friends in Nazi-occupied Denmark. Portrays deep friendship, a strong family, and heroic courage. Grade 4 and up.

MacLachlan, Patricia, *Sarah, Plain and Tall* (1985, Newbery Winner)—Sarah becomes the mail-order wife and mother to a widowed farmer and his children. The story continues in *Skylark* (1994). Grade 3 and up.

Marshall, Catherine, *Christy* (1967)—The story of a nineteen-year-old who left her comfortable home to teach in Cutter Gap's one-room schoolhouse in the Great Smokies. A book overflowing with adventures, unusual mountain customs, and Christian values. Better in every way than the television program it inspired. Grade 6 and up.

McKissack, Patricia, *A Picture of Freedom: The Diary of Clotee, a Slave Girl* (1997)—Best known for her award-winning picture books and non-fiction collaborations with her husband, Frederick, this is McKissack's first full-length work of fiction. The story was inspired by her great-great-great grandmother and enriched by the McKissacks' extensive research at several Tidewater Virginia plantations. Part of Scholastic's Dear America series. Grade 4 and up.

Manson, Christopher, *The Marvellous Blue Mouse* (1992)— Presented in illuminated manuscript style illustrations, this is the story of how the Emperor Charlemagne punished a greedy Lord Mayor. Manson attributes the tale to Notker the Stammerer, a monk of A.D. 884. Grade 2–5.

O'Dell, Scott, *Island of the Blue Dolphins* (1960, Newbery Winner)—This southern California writer was a master of historical fiction. His contribution to children's literature was honored with the Hans Christian Andersen Prize in 1962 and the creation of the coveted Scott O'Dell Award. *Island of the Blue Dolphins* is based on the real story of a twelve-year-old Native American girl. She jumps the ship that is removing her tribe from their island and swims ashore to be with her little brother, who was accidentally left behind. Wild dogs kill him, and the story becomes one of her survival, her love and care for the wounded leader dog, and their inseparable companionship. O'Dell said in an interview, *"Island of the Blue Dolphins* was a direct protest against the gun, and the killing of animals and the killing of people." Excellent selection for reading aloud. *Zia* (1976) is the sequel. Grade 3 and up.

Other outstanding O'Dell books: *The Hawk that Dare Not Hunt by Day* (reissued 1986), the story of William Tyndale and his English Bible translation; *The King's Fifth* (1966), a book following Coronado in his American expedition in search of gold; *Streams to the River, River to the Sea* (1986), the story of Sacagawea, the Native American guide for Lewis and Clark; *Carlotta* (1977), a book about a fearless girl of early California; *Sing Down the Moon* (1970, Newbery Honor), a portrayal of the Navajo people's forced migration; and *The Black Pearl* about a family of pearl divers in Baja

California (1967, ALA Best Book). Grade 5 and up.

Peck, Robert Newton, *A Day No Pigs Would Die* (1972)—A bloody and tender book about a thirteen-year-old farm boy whose simple, poverty-stricken father works himself to death as a hog butcher. It takes place in the 1920s and is written in rural Vermont vernacular, with warmth and humor. The book describes sex and death vividly but wholesomely. It should be read aloud only by those who are not ashamed to cry. There are powerful lessons here in courage, virtue, and love. *A Day No Pigs Would Die* includes the richly sensual and emotional experience of approaching maturity, the sensitive handling of religious differences, the good-natured tolerance of a little human foolishness, and the sudden awareness of the tragedy of past adultery. These qualities are the opposite of what we find in some of the most popular realistic fiction for children today such as the works of Judy Blume and Enid Blyton. Sequel, *A Part of the Sky* (1997). Grade 7 and up.

Peyton, K. M., The Flambards Quartet—In *Flambards* (1967), *The Edge of the Cloud* (1969), *Flambards in Summer* (1969), and *Flambards Divided* (1982), Peyton tells the story of a brave, resourceful young woman named Christina. The time is before and after World War I. The story includes a once-wealthy English family's decline from aristocratic living, a young man's fatal desire to be a pilot, and Christina's realistic adjustment to completely new responsibilities after the war. This series shows the immense social changes that were taking place in that tumultuous period. Grade 8 and up.

Reiss, Johanna, *The Upstairs Room* (1972) and *The Journey Back* (1976)—Eight-year-old Annie is hidden by a Dutch farm family when the Nazis invade Holland. In *The Journey Back*, her story continues. Grade 4 and up.

Ringgold, Faith, *Tar Beach* (1991) and *Aunt Harriet's Underground Railroad in the Sky* (1992)—Tar Beach is the rooftop of a 1939 Harlem apartment building where the members of an African-American family go to dream. In these picture books, eight-year-old Cassie gains an appreciation for her heritage. Grade 2–5.

Roop, Peter and Connie, *Keep the Lights Burning, Abbie* (1985)—In 1856 Abbie Burgess single-handedly kept the lights of a Maine lighthouse burning during a terrible winter storm. Her true story is sure to inspire courage. Grade 1–5

Rue, Nancy, The Christian Heritage Series (Focus on the Family)—In Series One, which begins with *The Rescue* (1995), Josiah Hutchinson, a ten-year-old boy in 1690s' Massachusetts, has a variety of adventures. Series Two is set in 1780s' Williamsburg and begins with *The Rebel* (1996). The references to Christian faith at home and in society are a subtle part of the stories. Grade 3 and up.

Schlein, Miriam, *I Sailed with Columbus* (1991)—Twelve-year-old Julio de la Vega Medina signs on as ship's boy on the *Santa Maria*. Through his eyes readers learn about the historic voyage of Columbus to America. Grade 3 and up.

Seredy, Kate, *White Stag* (1937, Newbery Winner) and *The Singing Tree* (1939)—Seredy blends folklore and history to tell stories of Hungary. Grade 4 and up.

Serraillier, Ian, *The Silver Sword* (1956)—Three Polish children journey across Europe in search of their parents, who were taken away by the Nazis. Although told calmly, it is an intensely exciting story. Grade 6 and up.

Speare, Elizabeth George, *The Witch of Blackbird Pond* (1958, Newbery Winner)—Set in a seventeenth-century Puritan community, this lively story features a witch hunt, a trial, and a girl from the Caribbean who stands up against bigotry. Another superb book by Speare is *The Bronze Bow* (1961, Newbery Winner). Set in Israel during the Roman occupation, it is the story of an orphan boy who moves from hatred to acceptance and an understanding of love. *Calico Captive* (1957) focuses on a young woman during the French and Indian War. Grade 6 and up.

For somewhat younger readers, Speare has written *The Sign of the Beaver* (1983, Newbery Honor) about a twelve-year-old boy who must survive on his own in the Maine wilderness.

Stolz, Mary, *Pangur Ban* (1988)—Inspired by a poem found in the margin of a ninth-century Irish manuscript, *Pangur Ban* deals with questions of vocation, faith, artistic talent, and responsibility. A rewarding book for family reading. Grade 7 and up.

Sutcliff, Rosemary, *Lantern Bearers* (1950, Carnegie Medal), *Eagle of the Ninth* (1954), and *The Silver Branch* (1957)—Rosemary Sutcliff stayed home from school, partly because of permanently crippling childhood arthritis. Her mother read good books to her, but she did not read for herself until she was nine. As a young adult she became a trained artist and later turned her specially-made painting desk into a full-time writing desk. It has been said that her theme is "the light and the dark." The dark is what threatens; the light is what is valued and saved. Sutcliff says her books are mostly about fighting men in a man's world. *Eagle of the Ninth* is set in the Britain of ancient Rome, as are *The Silver Branch* and *Lantern Bearers*. Other Sutcliff books include *Dawn Wind* (1961), *Warrior Scarlet* (1958), *Knight's Fee* (1960), *The Mark of the House Lord* (1965), *Song for a Dark Queen* (1978), and *Sun Horse, Moon Horse* (1978). She is considered one of the foremost writers of historical fiction for children. Grade 6 and up.

Taylor, Mildred D., *Roll of Thunder, Hear My Cry* (1976, Newbery Winner) and *Let the Circle Be Unbroken*

(1981)—Taylor presents hard truths and hopeful perspectives on being black and Southern during the Great Depression. Also *Mississippi Bridge* (1990) and *The Song of the Trees* (1975). Grade 5 and up.

Taylor, Sidney, *All-of-a-Kind Family* (1951)—Popular story of a Jewish family on New York City's Lower East Side at the turn of the century. First in a series. Grade 4 and up.

Thomas, Joyce Carol, *I Have Heard of a Land* (1998)—The story of a black woman homesteading in Oklahoma Territory. Grade 3 and up.

Uchida, Yoshiko, *Journey to Topaz* (1971)—Following the bombing of Pearl Harbor, an eleven-year-old Japanese girl and her family are sent to a relocation camp in Utah. Grade 5 and up.

Wartski, Maurene Crane, *A Boat to Nowhere* (1981)—A Vietnamese family flees their country. The grandfather's wisdom and attitude helps them survive their uprooting and difficult escape. Grade 6 and up.

Wheland, Gloria, *Hannah* (1991)—With the encouragement of a caring teacher, Hannah finds the courage to attend school in spite of her blindness. Set in Michigan in 1887. Grade 2 and up.

Wilder, Laura Ingalls, Little House books—This series begins with *Little House in the Big Woods* (1932) and concludes with *These Happy Golden Years* (1943). Based on Wilder's experiences and co-authored by her grown daughter, these books describe how the Ingalls family moved from Wisconsin to South Dakota in the late nineteenth century. Happiness for the Ingalls was not in material possessions but in everyday activities, hardships and successes, and family love. The family comes close to starvation in *The Long Winter* (1940), when blizzards, one after another, engulf the little towns on the prairie for months. When winter finally breaks and the train gets through, the family celebrates Christmas—in May. All ages; excellent selections for reading aloud.

Willard, Barbara, *Augustine Came to Kent* (1963)—In A.D. 597 a young man named Wolf journeyed from Rome to England with Augustine of Canterbury. There, in the land of Wolf's birth, he and a Saxon girl named Fritha watch as the cross takes root in English soil. Willard, a British author, also wrote *Son of Charlemagne* and *If All the Swords in England* for a Clarion/Doubleday series written to present historical events from a Christian perspective. Her best-known work for young readers is the Mantlemass series which chronicles an English family from the 1400s to the 1600s. Grade 6 and up.

Yep, Laurence, *The Star Fisher* (1991)—Fifteen-year-old Joan Lee travels with her family from Ohio to West Virginia to start a new business. Trouble starts as soon as they get off the train in a town that does not welcome Chinese-Americans. This story is based largely on experiences of the author's forebears. In *Dragonwings* (1975, Newbery Honor), Yep tells the story of a Chinese immigrant who built a flying machine in 1909, and in *Dragon's Gate* (1993, Newbery Honor) he writes about the Chinese who built the transcontinental railroad through the Sierra Mountains. Grade 5 and up.

Biographies

Samuel Johnson wrote more than two hundred years ago, "He that writes the life of another is either his friend or his enemy, and wishes either to exalt his praise or aggravate his infamy." Most biographies for children tend to the former, though the best ones avoid an over-sanctification of their subjects. Biography for children also has traditionally differed from biography for adults in that it usually leaves out scandalous, gruesome, or tragic episodes in the subject's life. In addition, biographies for children avoid documentation, and they often take greater liberties by casting facts into fictionalized dialogue. Two very loose kinds of biography are fictionalized biography and biographical fiction, the latter taking even more liberty with fact.

Biographical series are usually weak because they contain poor biographies as well as good ones. There are some notable exceptions, however. Two of the better series for beginning readers are the Harper & Row "I Can Read" history books and the Young Cromwell Biographies. The Cromwell biographies are good for older readers. The Random House Landmark Books present historical landmarks in American life and indicate reading and interest level. In upper elementary and middle school, children can enjoy the Great Lives series from Charles Scribner's Sons, exploring the world of physicians, painters, inventors, and explorers. The Harper & Row Breakthrough Books are good, emphasizing breakthroughs in human achievement. Young People's Press's Americans of Character Series, Putnam's Sports Hero Series, an American Hero series—the Horizon Caravel Books—and the American Heritage Junior Library all contain much good biography for children. One of the most inspiring series currently available is the People Who Made a Difference series published by Gareth Stevens, which includes Louis Braille, Marie Curie, Father Damien, Mahatma Gandhi, Martin Luther King, Jr., Ralph Nader, Florence Nightingale, Albert Schweitzer, Mother Teresa, Sojourner Truth, and Desmond Tutu. Biography from a distinctively Christian perspective is available in the Sower series from Mott Media.

Twenty Good Collective Biographies

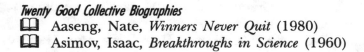

📖 Aaseng, Nate, *Winners Never Quit* (1980)
📖 Asimov, Isaac, *Breakthroughs in Science* (1960)

📖 Bontemps, Arna, *Famous Negro Athletes* (1964)
📖 Buckminster, Henrietta, *Women Who Shaped History* (1966)
📖 Daugherty, Sonia, *Ten Brave Men* (1951), *Ten Brave Women* (1953)
📖 DePauw, Linda G., *Founding Mothers: Women of America in the Revolutionary Era* (1975), *Seafaring Women* (1982)
📖 Fleming, Alice, *Doctors in Petticoats* (1964), *Great Women Teachers* (1965)
📖 Hearne, Betsy, *Seven Brave Women* (1997)
📖 Kennedy, John, *Profiles in Courage* (1964)
📖 McNeer, May and Lynd Ward, *Armed with Courage* (1957)
📖 Meltzer, Milton, *The Black Americans: A History in Their Own Words* (1964)
📖 Sinnot, Susan, *Extraordinary Hispanic Americans* (1991)
📖 Stonaker, Frances Benson, *Famous Mathematicians* (1966)
📖 Sutcliff, Rosemary, *Heroes and History* (1966)
📖 Turner, Glennette Tilley, *Take a Walk in Their Shoes* (1989)

Eighty Individual Biographies for Children

Avi, *Finding Providence: The Story of Roger Williams* (1997)—picture book.

Berk, Phyllis L., *The Duke's Command* (1966)—Biography of Handel.

Bishop, Morris, *Pascal: The Life of a Genius* (1968)

Brown, Pam, *Father Damien: The Man Who Lived and Died for the Victims of Leprosy* (1988)

Bryant, Jennifer Fisher, *Thomas Merton: Poet, Prophet, Priest* (1997, Grade 7 and up); *Lucretia Mott: A Guiding Light* (1996, Grade 5 and up), part of Eerdman's Women of Spirit series.

Bulla, Clyde, *Squanto, Friend of the White Man* (1954),

Lincoln's Birthday (1966), *Pocahontas and the Strangers* (1971) Grade 2–5.

Burch, Joann Johansen, *Fine Print: A Story about Johann Gutenberg* (1991)

Churchill, Winston, *Joan of Arc* (1969)

Coerr, Eleanor, *Sadako and the Thousand Paper Cranes* (1977)—The story of a Japanese girl who develops leukemia due to radiation poisoning. This book has comforted many families facing life-threatening childhood illnesses. Grade 3 and up.

Coles, Robert, *The Story of Ruby Bridges* (1995)

Collins, David R., *Not Only Dreamers: The Story of Martin Luther King, Sr. and Martin Luther King, Jr.* (1986)—In addition to *Not Only Dreamers* about Martin Luther King, Sr. and Jr., this Christian writer and public school teacher has written several volumes for the Sower series and strong-selling biographies of E. B. White, Beatrix Potter, Charles Dickens, and Mark Twain for Carolrhoda Books. He has also written seven presidential biographies for Garrett Educational Corporation. Sometimes editors and publishers have asked Collins to tone down the spiritual side of the subject for fear of losing public school and library sales. But Collins says, "If God and faith played an important part in a person's life, they will play an important role in my biography."

Commager, Henry Steele, *America's Robert E. Lee* (1971) Grade 5 and up.

Coolidge, Olivia, *Winston Churchill and the Story of Two World Wars* (1960, Grade 6 and up), *Tom Paine, Revolutionary* (1969), *Gandhi* (1971)

Dalgliesh, Alice, *The Columbus Story* (1955) Grade 3–5.

Daugherty, James, *Daniel Boone* (1939, first biography to win Newbery Medal, Grade 4–8), *Abraham Lincoln* (1943), *Poor Richard* (1941), *William Blake* (1960, Grade 8 and up)

D'Aulaire, Ingri and Edgar Parin, *George Washington* (1936) and *Abraham Lincoln* (1939, Caldecott Winner)—Two of the first picture book biographies. Grade 1–5.

Davidson, Margaret, *Golda Meir* (1976)

De Trevino, Elizabeth Borton, *I, Juan de Pareja* (1965, Newbery Winner)—Grade 6 and up.

Dolan, Sean, *Junipero Serra* (1991)

Forbes, Esther, *Johnny Tremain* (1944, Newbery Winner), *America's Paul Revere* (1946)—Fictionalized biography. Grade 3 and up.

Foster, Genevieve, *The World of William Penn* (1973) Grade 4 and up.

Freedman, Russell, *Lincoln: A Photobiography* (1987, Newbery winner), *Indian Chiefs* (1987), *The Wright Brothers: How They Invented the Airplane* (1991), *Eleanor Roosevelt: A Life of Discovery* (1993), *Jules Verne: Portrait of a Prophet* (1965)—Freedman brings history to life through facts, anecdotes, and carefully selected photos. Grade 5 and up.

Freeman, Douglas Southall, *Lee of Virginia* (1958)—Based on the author's Pulitzer Prize-winning four-volume biography. Grade 7 and up.

Fritz, Jean, *And Then What Happened, Paul Revere?* (1973), *Why Don't You Get a Horse, Sam Adams?* (1974), *Where Was Patrick Henry on the 29th of May?* (1975), *Will You Sign Here, John Hancock?* (1976), *What's the Big Idea, Ben Franklin?* (1976), *Can't You Make Them Behave, King George?* (1977), *The Great Little Madison* (1989), *You Want Women to Vote, Lizzie Stanton?* (1995)—Fritz is a master at making history entertaining for young readers. Her spritely biographies read like fiction, but she is committed to historical accuracy and does not invent dialogue or events (Grade 3 and up). She is also the author of some fine historical fiction including *The Cabin Faced West* (1958).

Gormley, Beatrice, *Maria Mitchell: The Soul of an Astronomer* (1995) Grade 6 and up.

Gray, Elizabeth Janet, *Young Walter Scott* (1935) Grade 6 and up.

Greenfield, Eloise, *Mary McLeod Bethune* (1977)—A tribute to a devout Christian and trailblazer in education for African-Americans. Grade 3 and up.

Jackson, Jesse, *Make a Joyful Noise Unto the Lord* (1974)—An inspiring look at the life of gospel singer Mahalia Jackson. Grade 4 and up.

Jiang, Ji-li, *Red Scarf Girl: A Memoir of the Cultural Revolution* (1997)—A story of great courage and love in the time of Mao Zedong's Cultural Revolution. Grade 5 and up.

Kent, Deborah, *Dorothy Day: Friend to the Forgotten* (1996) Grade 5 and up.

Klausner, Janet, *Sequoyah's Gift: A Portrait of the Cherokee Leader* (1993)

Knight, David C., *Isaac Newton: Mastermind of Modern Science* (1961)

Kroeber, Theodora, *Ishi, Last of His Tribe* (1964)—An exciting book about the last surviving member of the Yahi Indians, who lived in hiding at the foot of Mount Lassen, afraid of being annihilated by white men. (Kroeber was the mother of fantasy writer Ursula Le Guin.) Grade 8 and up.

Krull, Kathleen, *Wilma Unlimited: How Wilma Rudolph Became the World's Fastest Woman* (1996) K–Grade 5.

Lantier, Patricia and Beverly Birch, *Louis Braille: Bringer of Hope to the Blind* (1991)

Latham, Jean Lee, *Carry On, Mr. Bowditch* (1955)—Fictionalized biography set during the American Revolution. Grade 6 and up.

Livingston, Myra Cohn, *Let Freedom Ring: A Ballad of Martin Luther King, Jr.* (1992)

Ludwig, Charles, *Michael Faraday: Father of Electronics* (1978)

Martinze, Elizabeth Coonrod, *Sor Juana: A Trailblazing Thinker*

McGovern, Ann, *Shark Lady: True Adventures of Eugenie Clark* (1979)

Meigs, Cornelia, *Invincible Louisa: The Story of the Author of* Little Women (1968) and *Jane Addams: Pioneer for Social Justice* (1970) Grade 6 and up.

Meltzer, Milton, *Lincoln in His Own Words* (1993)—A prolific biographer who specializes in presenting the minority perspective. Several of his books are excellent sources of direct quotations from historical figures. Grade 5 and up.

Monjo, Ferdinand N., *Me and Willie and Pa* (1973, the Lincoln family), *The One Bad Thing about Father* (1987, the Roosevelt family), *Letters to Horseface* (1975, Mozart)—Monjo's speciality is biographical fiction. Grade 4 and up.

Place, Marian T., *Marcus and Narcissa Whitman: Oregon Pioneers* (1967) Grade 4 and up.

Provensen, Alice and Martin, *The Glorious Flight across the Channel with Louis Bleriot* (1983) Grade 2 and up.

Quackenbush, Robert, *Don't You Dare Shoot That Bear! A Story of Theodore Roosevelt* (1984) and *Mark Twain? What Kind of Name Is That?* (1984)—Light-hearted introductions to famous people. Fun to read aloud. Grade 1–5.

Roop, Peter and Connie, *I, Columbus: My Journal—1492–3* (1990) Grade 3 and up.

Sandburg, Carl, *Abe Lincoln Grows Up* (1928) Grade 6 and up.

Santrey, Laurence, *Young Frederick Douglass: Fight for Freedom* (1983) Grade 4 and up.

Singer, Isaac Bashevis, *A Day of Pleasure: Stories of a Boy Growing Up in Warsaw* (1968; re-released 1996) All ages.

Sis, Peter, *Starry Messenger* (1996, Caldecott Honor)—A picture book presentation of Galileo's life and work. Also, *Follow the Dream: The Story of Columbus* (1991).

Smith, E. Brooks and Robert Meredith, *Pilgrim Courage* (1962)—An adaptation of William Bradford's journal for young readers.

Sootin, Harry, *Robert Boyle: Founder of Modern Chemistry* (1962)

Stafford, Tim, *Dave Dravecky* (1992)—Part of Zondervan's Today's Heroes series. Grade 4 and up.

Stanley, Diane, and Peter Vennema, *Peter, the Great* (1986), *Shaka, King of the Zulus* (1988), *Bard of Avon: The Story of William Shakespeare* (1992), *Good Queen Bess: The Story of Elizabeth I of England* (1990), *Charles Dickens: The Man Who Had Great Expectations* (1993), *Leonardo Da Vinci* (1996)—Carefully researched picture book biographies.

Sterling, Dorothy, *Freedom Train: The Story of Harriet Tubman* (1954)

Stone, Elaine Murray, *Maximilian Kolbe: Saint of Auschwitz* (1997) Grade 3 and up.

Washington, Booker T., *Up From Slavery* (1917)

Wibberly, Leonard, Thomas Jefferson cycle (1964–1966)—One of the best biographies of Jefferson, these four volumes are done with great care and scholarship. The series begins with *Young Man from the Piedmont*. Wibberly stated in 1962, "For how can a book be educational which discourages children from reading? . . . a book which is so thin in characterization, so stilted in its prose, and is so contrived . . . that the young reader goes to it as to a penance." Also by Wibberly, *Zebulon Pike, Soldier and Explorer* (1961). Grade 4 and up.

Wilson, Janet, *The Ingenious Mr. Peale: Painter, Patriot, and Man of Science* (1996) Grade 5 and up.

Yates, Elizabeth, *Amos Fortune, Free Man* (1950, Newbery

Winner)—Yates visited the tombstone of Amos in Jaffrey, New Hampshire, and was inspired to write his biography. Amos was born a prince in Africa. He was sold in Boston, learned the tanner's trade, and eventually purchased his freedom. He spent the rest of his life buying freedom for other slaves. Yates also wrote biographies of American women of courage—Dorothy Canfield Fisher and Prudence Crandall. Grade 5 and up.

This chapter has offered only a sample of realistic fiction and biography for children in our time. Many good writers and dozens upon dozens of worthy titles were not mentioned. Young readers are in for a treat as they step through time into the world of timeless literature.

Books that Bring the Family Together

8 Roots and Wings

We all come from the past, and children ought to know what it was that went into their making, to know that life is a braided cord of humanity stretching up from time long gone, and that it cannot be defined by the span of a single journey from diaper to shroud.

—Russell Baker, *Growing Up*

To forget one's ancestors is to be a brook without a source, a tree without a root.

—Chinese Proverb

H arvey and me and Thomas J. are just like pinballs. Somebody put in a dime and punched a button and out we came, ready or not, and settled in the same groove. That's all . . ." That is how an abused girl named Carlie described herself and two other foster children to their new foster parent. "Now you don't see pinballs helping each other, do you? . . . They can't. They're just things. They hit the bumps, they go over here. They hit that light, they go over there. . . . And as soon as they get settled, somebody comes along and puts in another dime and off they go again. . . . Take a good look at a pinball machine sometime. . . . You might learn something about life" *(The Pinballs* by Betsy Byars, 1977).

While we may not feel as knocked around as Carlie, in varying degrees most of us today long for a greater

173

sense of belonging. This chapter speaks to that need by including a survey of family portraits (both factual and fictional), memoirs, poetry, and folkore.

Once upon a time there was no need to emphasize family history and folklore. It was the stuff of everyday life. Many people lived in the same close-knit community for generations, sometimes in the same house. Children grew up surrounded by relatives and neighbors who had known their family for many years. The chief entertainment was listening to stories that bound them to their forebears and their clan.

But the complexities of modern life make it hard to cultivate extended family relationships. In the race to get ahead or perhaps simply to stay afloat, it is easy for family ties to come unraveled. Throughout the twentieth century and especially since World War II, children have lived in a world dominated by rapid change. The upheaval in society, however, has not decreased children's basic need for security and nurture, personal identity, and a place in the larger context of the family and society. We can be thankful that books can help them enjoy a greater sense of kinship and heritage.

A vivid story reaches across time to connect young readers with the past. Reading about other families can help children appreciate and accept their own less-than-perfect family. Stories remind us that families are full of characters making a weird and wonderful conglomeration of virtues and vices. Stories also allow us to adopt another family, at least while we are between the covers of a book. Through reading, children can find inspiration for the families they will one day help to create.

The following list of books offers a variety of ways to explore what it means to be a family. Parents are encouraged to experience them with their children whenever possible and to talk about the thoughts and feelings they evoke. As Elizabeth Stone, a journalist and avid student of family stories, observes, "To make our own meanings out of our myriad stories is to achieve balance—at once a way to be part of and apart from our families, a way of holding on and letting go."

Fictional Family Portraits

Ackerman, Karen, *The Song and Dance Man* (1988)—A picture book about a grandfather who was a vaudeville performer. Grade 1–3.

Ayres, Katherine, *Family Tree* (1996)—Ms. Custer's sixth grade class has an assignment to discover their family history, and every subject revolves around this project. What will Tyler Stoudt do since she only has a father, and he refuses to talk about relatives? A suspenseful and deeply moving story. Grade 4 and up.

Bahr, Mary, *The Memory Box* (1995)—A diagnosis of Alzheimer's Disease prompts a boy and his grandfather to gather photos and other memorabilia of their happy times together. Grade 2 and up.

Baylor, Byrd, *The Best Town in the World* (1983)—A father shares his love of the small Texas town where he grew up. Some readers may object to a picture of boys skinny dipping. Grade 2–5.

Buck, Pearl S., *The Beech Tree* (1955)—When Mary Lou's grandfather comes to live with her family, her mother stops smiling, and the atmosphere grows tense. Mary Lou helps resolve the conflict by sharing her grandfather's story of the beech tree. Grade 2 and up.

Bunting, Eve, *A Day's Work* (1997)—Francisco and his grandfather need work, so Francisco claims they can do gardening. Their failure at the job makes for a valuable lesson in honesty. Also, *The Wednesday Surprise* (1989) and *Fly Away Home* (1991). Grade 1–3.

Burningham, John, *Granpa* (1985)—Picture book vignettes

about a little girl's relationship with her grandfather. K–Grade 2.

Cech, John, *My Grandmother's Journey* (1991)—A grandmother's story of surviving the Russian Revolution. A celebration of birth, life, and the human spirit. K–Grade 4.

Choi, Sook Nyul, *Halmoni and the Picnic* (1993)—When Yunmi's class goes on a picnic in Central Park, they invite Yunmi's recently immigrated grandmother to join them. Picture book. Grade 1–4.

Clifford, Eth, *The Remembering Box* (1985)—A nine-year-old learns about her Jewish heritage from a box of keepsakes. Grade 3 and up.

Cooney, Barbara, *Miss Rumphius* (1982, American Book Award)—Alice Rumphius, great-aunt of the story's narrator, spends her life looking for a way to make the world more beautiful. *Miss Rumphius* can help children and adults appreciate the legacy of single and childless people. Cooney made the world more beautiful by giving readers this book. In *Family Reunion* a young teen learns that a family does not have to be perfect to be worth treasuring. This book deals realistically with divorce. It contains repeated references to the biblical story of the Prodigal Son. All ages.

Creech, Sharon, *Chasing Redbird* (1997)—Zinny is not getting along with her siblings. She gets away from the conflict by restoring a historic trail. In the process she discovers some interesting things about her family. In *Walk Two Moons* (1994) a girl travels with her grandparents in search of her runaway mother. Creech's characters are quirky and unconventional, and her writing raises issues parents and teens should discuss. Grade 8 and up.

de Paola, Tomie, *Now One Foot, Now the Other* (1981)—Grandfather teaches a little boy to walk and talk. Then the grandfather has a stroke, and the grandson teaches him how to walk and talk again. In *Nana Upstairs and Nana Downstairs* (1973) de Paola tells the story of a little boy's love for his invalid great-grandmother and his grandmother, who live together. *Watch Out for the Chicken Feet in Your Soup* (1974) is about Joey and his mixed emotions about his grandmother's immigrant ways. *The Art Lesson* and *Tom* complete this group of autobiographical stories. Picture books. All ages.

Doherty, Berlie, *Granny Was a Buffer Girl* (1988)—A young woman about to leave home for college is given a send-off by three generations of her family. The gathered family tells stories as a way of saying good-bye and affirming their enduring relationships. Originally written for BBC radio. Grade 8 and up.

Dorros, Arthur, *Abuela* (1991)—Relationship between a Hispanic girl and her grandmother in New York City. K–Grade 2.

Dugan, Barbara, *Loop the Loop* (1992)—A little girl makes friends with a lively old woman in a wheelchair. Grade 2–4.

Engel, Diana, *Josephina Hates Her Name* (1989)—A little girl learns to appreciate her handed-down name. K–Grade 2.

Fakih, Kimberly Olson, *Grandpa Putter and Granny Hoe* (1992)—Grandparents compete for the affection of their twin grandchildren. Grade 2–4.

Fern, Eugene, *Pepito's Story* (1960)—Pepito loves to dance, but only his grandmother encourages his passion. Picture book. K–Grade 3.

Fleischman, Paul, *The Borning Room* (1991)—Six stories take place in the Lott home's "borning room," a place where people enter and leave the world. Set on an Ohio farm over a thirty-year period around the Civil War. Grade 5 and up.

Flourney, Valerie, *The Patchwork Quilt* (1985)—A rich portrayal of the love that holds individual members of a family together. Picture book. K–Grade 2.

Foley, Patricia, *John and the Fiddler* (1990)—When Mr. MacLoegair gives John a violin, a friendship begins that spans the generations. Grade 3–5.

Fosburgh, Lisa, *Mrs. Abercorn and the Bunce Boys* (1986)—Otis and Will Bunce do not have a dad and their mom is at work all day. The boys are on their own in getting used to their new home. Then Mrs. Abercorn, a cross, uppity neighbor, gets involved in their lives. Grade 3–6.

Fox, Mem, *Wilfrid Gordon McDonald Patridge* (1985)—Wilfrid lives next door to a home for the elderly. He makes friends with his elderly neighbors and tries to bring Miss Nancy memories to replace the ones she has lost. Also *Shoes from Grandpa* (1990). Grade 1–3.

Goffstein, M. B., *My Noah's Ark* (1978)—A ninety-year-old woman tells the story of a wooden ark and figures carved for her by her father. Picture book.

Greenfield, Eloise, *Grandpa's Face* (1988)—An African-American girl has trouble understanding her grandfather's role as an actor. Also, *Grandmama's Joy* (1984). Picture books.

Greenwald, Sheila, *Rosy Cole Discovers America!* (1992)—When Rosy's teacher assigns a family tree, Rosy decides to make up some exciting relatives. Grade 2–5.

Griffith, Helen V., *Georgia Music* (1986), *Granddaddy's Place* (1987), *Grandaddy's Stars* (1995)—Wonderful picture books about the Southern experience, these selections provide an opportunity to talk about regional speech. Grade 2–4.

Henkes, Kevin, *Sun and Spoon* (1997)—When a ten-year-old boy loses his grandmother, his world seems out of order. In his search for something to remember her by, healing comes. Grade 4 and up.

Hest, Amy, *The Crack-of-Dawn Walkers* (1984)—A brother and sister take turns walking with their grandfather. K–Grade 3.

Hiser, Bernice T., *The Adventure of Charlie and His Wheat-Straw Hat* (1986)—A handed-down story from the Civil War period, this picture book is about an eight-year-old Kentucky boy and his treasured hat made by his granny. Grade 1–3.

Hoffman, Mary, *My Grandma Has Black Hair* (1988)—A picture book that is especially meaningful for children whose grandparents are "free spirits." Grade 1–3.

Howard, Elizabeth Fitzgerald, *Aunt Flossie's Hats (and Crab Cakes Later)* (1991)—African-American girls love their visits with a story-telling great-great-aunt. Picture book. K–Grade 3.

Johnson, Dolores, *Your Dad Was Just Like You* (1993)—A grandfather helps a boy make peace with his father after the child breaks his dad's prized trophy. Grade 1–3.

Jukes, Mavis, *Blackberries in the Dark* (1994)—Austin visits his grandmother for the first time since his grandfather's death. He learns about honoring old traditions and creating new ones. Grade 1–5.

Laird, Elizabeth, *The Dust* (1992)—This novel is told from the perspective of a Kurdish girl living in Iraq. Her family has to flee to a camp in Iran. In the midst of political upheaval, Tara learns the enduring power of memory and culture. Grade 6 and up.

Levinson, Riki, *I Go with My Family to Grandma's* (1986)—Turn-of-the-century story about five families from New York City's five boroughs who meet at their grandparents' home in Manhattan. Picture book. Grade 2–4.

Locker, Thomas, *Where the River Begins* (1984), *The Mare on the Hill* (1985), *Sailing with the Wind* (1986)—Two boys gain a deeper appreciation of nature by exploring it with their grandfather. Magnificent illustrations. Grade 1 and up.

MacLachlan, Patricia, *Journey* (1991)—Journey and his

sister must live with their grandparents after their free-spirited mother leaves them. The grandfather's photographs and a stray cat help bring the family together (Grade 4 and up). *Through Grandpa's Eyes* (1979) is a picture book story of how a blind grandfather helps a boy learn to see with more than his eyes (Grade 1–4). *What You Know First* (1995, all ages) can help children deal with the sadness of moving.

Mahy, Margaret, *Dangerous Spaces* (1991)—Two cousins who do not get along learn about their family and the bond they share through an old box of stereoscopic views. Grade 3–6.

Markle, Sandra, *The Fledglings* (1992)—Kate runs away to live with her Cherokee grandfather. Grade 7 and up.

Martin, Bill and John Archambault, *Knots on a Counting Rope* (1987)—A Native American grandfather helps his blind grandson understand and value who he is. Picture book. Grade 1 and up.

Martin, Jacqueline Briggs, *Grandmother Bryant's Pocket* (1996)—Set in eighteenth-century Maine, this is the story of how a girl finds comfort after the death of her dog in a fire. PreS–Grade 3

Mathis, Sharon Bell, *The Hundred Penny Box* (1975)—Great-aunt Dew measures her years with pennies and delights her grandson with stories. Grade 2 and up.

Meyer, Carolyn, *Jubilee Journey* (1997)—Emily, a biracial teen, must come to terms with her racial identity during a visit to her African-American family in Texas. Grade 6 and up.

Miles, Miska, *Annie and the Old One* (1971)—A Navajo girl tries to prevent her grandmother's death by delaying the completion of a rug the old woman is weaving. Grade 2 and up.

Minarik, Else, *Little Bear's Visit* (1961)—Native American grandparents enrich their grandson's life. Easy-to-read. K–Grade 3.

Olson, Arielle, *Hurry Home, Grandma!* (1984)—Timothy and Melinda hope their grandmother, who is an explorer, will get home for Christmas. Picture book.

Paterson, Katherine, *Jacob Have I Loved* (1980)—Three generations live together, but not without considerable conflict and heartache. Also, *The Great Gilly Hopkins* and *Park's Quest*. Grade 6 and up.

Polacco, Patricia, *Chicken Sunday* (1992)—Three children decide to buy an Easter hat for Miss Eula, grandmother of the two boys and adopted grandmother of their neighbor, a little girl of Russian ancestry. A heartwarming story filled with friendship and faith. Also, *The Keeping Quilt* (1994) and *Thunder Cake* (1990). Picture books. All ages.

Politi, Leo, *Three Stalks of Corn* (1976)—Angelica's grandmother tells her legends about corn while Angelica cooks tortillas from corn meal and plays with corn husk dolls. The illustrations help children understand an early California Mexican community. Picture book. All ages.

Purdy, Carol, *Least of All* (1987)—In this picture book set at the turn of the century, three generations of New Englanders live together and enjoy healthy interdependent relationships. A wonderful picture book for all ages. Also, *My Little Cabbage*, a picture book about family nicknames from around the world.

Rodowsky, Colby, *Jenny and the Grand Old Great-Aunts* (1992)—A girl explores an old house and attic and conquers her fear of "ancient" relatives. Also, *Evy-Ivy-Over* (1978). Grade 1–4.

Roth, Susan and Ruth Phang, *Patchwork Tales* (1984)—A family history told with the help of quilt blocks. Includes directions for making a family memory quilt. Picture book. Also, *Another Christmas* (1992). Grade 3 and up.

Russo, Marisabina, *A Visit to Oma* (1991)—On Sundays

Celeste visits her great-grandmother. The old woman speaks a language Celeste cannot understand, so the little girl tries to imagine what Oma is saying. Picture book. K–Grade 3.

Rylant, Cynthia, *The Relatives Came* (1985, Caldecott Honor)—A delightful book about a family reunion. Also, *When I Was Young in the Mountains* (1982). Grade 1 and up.

Shub, Elizabeth, *Cutlass in the Snow* (1986)—A father and son share a family legend. Grade 1–4.

Sis, Peter, *The Three Golden Keys* (1994)—A fanciful story told by a father who wants his New York-born daughter to understand his childhood in Prague. PreS–Grade 3.

Smith, Robert Kimmel, *The War with Grandpa* (1984)—A boy dislikes having his grandfather come to live with the family. Grade 4 and up.

Stevenson, James, *Brrr!* (1991)—When Mary Ann and Louie complain about the cold weather, Grandpa tells them about the winter of 1908. One in a series of grandfather tales: *Could Be Worse* (1977), *Grandpa's Great City Tour* (1983), *Worse than Willie!* (1984), *What's under My Bed?* (1984), and *That Dreadful Day* (1985). Picture books. K–Grade 4.

Stolz, Mary, *Go Fish* (1991)—Thomas and his grandfather spend a day together, reading, fishing, and sharing stories of their African heritage. Grade 1–5.

Strete, Craig Kee, *The World in Grandfather's Hands* (1995)—When eleven-year-old Jimmy must leave his pueblo and live in the city, he is angry, lonely, and homesick. His Grandfather Whitefeather helps him hold onto the pueblo and adjust to his new home. Also *When Grandfather Journeys into Winter* (1979). Grade 3–5.

Thomas, Jane Resh, *Saying Goodbye to Grandma* (1988)—A girl goes with her family to her grandmother's

Christian funeral. Good treatment of grief and re-membrance. Grade 2–5.

Turner, Ann, *Time of the Bison* (1987)—Scar Boy hates his name until he begins to discover his special gift and place among his people. A good blending of mystery and excitement. Grade 3 and up.

Walter, Mildred Pitts, *Justin and the Best Biscuits in the World* (1986)—African-American boy learns from his grandfather what it means to be a man. Grade 3–5.

Willard, Nancy, *The Gardener's Grandchildren* (1979)—An intergenerational story with mystery, suspense, and a fascinating setting—a Scottish island. Grade 6 and up.

Yarbrough, Camille, *Cornrows* (1979)—Black children learn from their mother and grandmother about their African heritage. All ages.

Yee, Paul, *Tales from Gold Mountain: Stories of the Chinese in the New World* (1990)—This picture book beautifully illustrates the blending of folk traditions and frontier ways. Grade 3 and up.

Yep, Laurence, *Child of the Owl* (1977)—Set in San Francisco's Chinatown. A twelve-year-old girl lives with her grandmother and learns family folklore. Grade 6 and up.

Yolen, Jane, *Letting Swift River Go* (1991)—When a valley becomes the site of a new reservoir, an entire town has to relocate. A beautiful story about accepting change and moving on. Picture book. All ages.

Zolotow, Charlotte, *My Grandson Lew* (1974)—A boy and his mother call back memories of a grandfather who died when the boy was very young. Also, *This Quiet Lady* (1992). Picture books.

Memoirs

The great American novelist Willa Cather said, "Most of the material a writer works with is acquired before the age of fifteen." She also wrote, "There are only two or three human stories, and they go on repeating themselves as fiercely as if they had never happened before." There is ample evidence she was right in the abundance of autobiography and autobiographical fiction available today. Here is a sampling:

Alexander, Sue, *Sara's City* (1995)—The author recalls what it was like growing up in 1940s Chicago. An excellent portrayal of urban America as grandparents may remember it. K–Grade 3.

Anderson, Marian, *My Lord, What a Morning* (1956)—Although she grew up poor in Philadelphia, Anderson was rich in love and vocal ability. The nurture of her parents and church family helped her achieve her dream of becoming an opera singer. Grade 7 and up.

Cleary, Beverly, *A Girl from Yamhill: A Memoir* (1988)—One of the best-loved writers for children tells the story of her own childhood on a farm in Portland, Oregon. Grade 3 and up.

Dillard, Annie, *An American Childhood* (1987)—This book written for adults has been described as "a joyous ode to her own happy childhood," "by turns wry, provocative and sometimes breathtaking . . . a work marked by exquisite insight." Set in 1950s Pittsburgh. For mature readers Grade 9 and up, but portions could be read aloud to the whole family.

Dolson, Hildegarde, *We Shook the Family Tree* (1946)—A very funny story of an American novelist and short story writer's early family life.

Durrell, Gerald, *My Family and Other Animals* (1977)—This British zoologist spent five years of his boyhood with his family on the island of Corfu. Out of his love for animals he has written many enjoyable books families can share. Grade 4 and up.

Forbes, Kathryn, *Mama's Bank Account* (1943)—A bestseller that became a hit play, this book tells the author's story of growing up in San Francisco in the early 1900s. Great for family storytime or independent reading. Grade 7 and up.

Fritz, Jean, *Homesick: My Own Story* (1982) and *China Homecoming* (1985)—The child of American missionaries in China, Fritz was sent to the U.S. to attend school. A fascinating look at what "home" means to someone with roots in two countries.

Gilbreth, Frank, *Cheaper by the Dozen* (1948)—A well-meaning father attempts to run his home like an efficient factory. Twelve rambunctious children and an easy-going mother make his task hilariously challenging. Good for reading aloud to the family.

Giovanni, Nikki, *Knoxville, Tennessee* (1994)—Giovanni recalls summers spent with her grandparents, enjoying their garden and church picnics. Picture book. All ages.

Greenfield, Eloise, Lessie Jones Little, and Pattie Ridley Jones, *Childtime: A Three Generation Memoir* (1979)—A memoir about growing up black by an award-winning author, her mother, and her grandmother.

Hautzig, Esther, *The Endless Steppe: Growing Up in Siberia* (1968)—Childhood in a World War II Siberian labor camp. Grade 7 and up.

Keller, Helen, *The Story of My Life* (1954)—A narrative that highlights the importance of a mentor in a young person's life. Grade 7 and up.

Khalsa, Dayal Kaur, *Tales of a Gambling Grandma* (1986)—An unusual but worthwhile story about a Jewish grandmother who played poker to support her family. Grade 2–4.

L'Engle, Madeleine, *The Summer of the Great-Grandmother* (1974)—A gifted children's author writes lovingly and honestly about her ninety-year-old mother's last summer. Written for adults but it can be enjoyed by mature readers Grade 9 and up; also excerpts can be selected by parents for reading aloud.

Levine, Ellen, *Freedom's Children: Young Civil Rights Activists Tell Their Own Stories* (1993)—This book offers an intimate look at what it was like to grow up during some key events in the struggle for civil rights. Grade 6 and up.

Lomas Garza, Carmen, *Family Pictures/Cuadros de Familia* (1990)—A pictorial trip to a Texas border town with a talented Mexican American artist. Grade 1–5.

Sandburg, Carl, *Prairie-Town Boy* (1955)—An abridged version of *Always the Young Strangers,* an account of the childhood and teen years of this famous poet and biographer. Grade 7 and up.

Say, Allen, *Grandfather's Journey* (1993)—A grandson recounts his grandfather's travels, his life in the United States, and his return to Japan. Also, *Tree of Cranes,* Say's childhood Christmas memories. All ages.

Schwartz, Alvin, *When I Grew Up Long Ago* (1978)—An oral history collection about what it was like to be young at the turn of the century. Responses to Schwartz's interviews are arranged topically (school, recreation, work, etc.). Grade 4 and up.

Sisulu, Elinor Batezat, *The Day Gogo Went to Vote: South Africa, April 1994* (1996)—A hundred-year-old great-grandmother takes part in her country's first free election. Picture book. K–Grade 4.

Stevenson, James, *When I Was Nine* (1986) and *Higher on the Door* (1987)—Autobiography in picture book format. The author describes growing up in the 1930s. Grade 1–4.

Strait, Treva Adams, *The Price of Free Land* (1979)—The story of Nebraska homesteaders. Grade 4 and up.

Stuart, Jesse, *The Thread that Runs So True* (1949)—Getting an education was not easy for an Appalachian boy like Jesse. But at fifteen he went back to high school. Two years later he became a country school teacher. Grade 6 and up.

Sutcliff, Rosemary, *Blue Remembered Hills* (1983)—The victim of childhood arthritis, Sutcliff had an unusually secluded childhood during which she discovered her love of painting and writing. Grade 8 and up.

Taulbert, Clifton, *Once Upon a Time When We Were Colored* (1989)—Pulitzer Prize winner in which Taulbert tells how his great-aunt gave him a love for words through her letters. In his writing Taulbert clearly communicates the deep roots of his faith in God. Also, *The Last Train North* (1992) and *Watching Our Crops Come In* (1997). Written for adults but can be enjoyed by mature high school students.

Vineberg, Ethel, *Grandmother Came from Dworitz* (1987)—The author tells the story of her mother's and grandmother's youth in Russia and their family's emigration to the United States.

Wangerin, Walter, Jr., *Little Lamb, Who Made Thee? A Book about Children and Parents* (1993)—Inspirational stories and memories of growing up from a gifted Christian storyteller. Mature readers, Grade 9 and up. Some chapters are appropriate for family story time.

Wilder, Laura Ingalls, *On the Way Home* (1962)—Diary of a trip from South Dakota to Missouri in 1884 by the author of the Little House series.

Poetry

Plato claimed that poetry comes nearer to the truth than history. In exploring the thoughts, feelings, and experiences of families, this theory seems to prove correct. As the poet Robert Southey observed, "It is with words as with sunbeams—the more they are condensed, the deeper they burn." And in the light of poetry we get a clearer, more compelling vision of what it can mean to be part of a family.

Bierhorst, John, ed., *In the Trail of the Wind: American Indian Poems and Ritual Orations* (1971)—Prayers, poems, and chants from over forty languages.

Bryan, Ashley, *Walk Together Children: Black American Spirituals* (1974) and *Ashley Bryan's ABC of African American Poetry: A Jean Karl Book* (1997)

Esbensen, Barbara Juster, *Who Shrank My Grandmother's House: Poems of Discovery* (1992)

Hoberman, Mary Ann, *Fathers, Mothers, Sisters, Brothers: A Collection of Family Poems* (1991)

Janeczko, Paul B., ed., *Strings: A Gathering of Family Poems* (1984)—More than a hundred poems about family relationships.

Jones, Hettie, comp., *The Trees Stand Shining: Poetry of the North American Indians* (1971)

Lewis, Claudia, *Long Ago in Oregon* (1987)

Livingston, Myra Cohn, *Poems for Grandmothers* (1990)

Soto, Gary, *Neighborhood Odes* (1992)—Poems that picture everyday life in a Latino neighborhood.

Strickland, Dorothy S. and Michael R., eds., *Families: Poems Celebrating the African American Experience* (1994)

Folklore

The great Yiddish writer Isaac Bashevis Singer has said, "roots and folklore are almost synonymous." Within the folklore of a culture, we can find the values that have formed its people. Folk tales were shaped by the country in which they were born. Rugged lands called for people of great courage and strength, and their people spun stories to inspire these traits. In milder regions, the tales took on a gentler nature. Folklore also presents deeply held religious convictions disguised as fables, allegories, legends, epics, and morality tales.

By exposing children to a variety of folklore, we help them understand the world of stories and how characters, action, theme, and setting interact. Most folktales are fairly short and are entertaining enough to hold children's attention. These stories transport the reader to other lands and times. Yet with a little thought and discussion, the maturing child can see how the ideas and values portrayed in folktales have been absorbed and adapted by modern society. Learning about folklore also instills a sense of ethnic identity in some young people, a fact that is illustrated by the growing interest in the traditional literature of African, Asian, and Native Americans.

Unfortunately, not everything that is presented as folklore is truly a part of anyone's heritage. A case in point is Paul Bunyan, who has been portrayed in children's textbooks as a genuine folk hero. Actually, he was first introduced in 1910 by a newspaperman who claimed to have heard the tales as a young logger. Then in 1920 W. B. Laughead, a professional advertiser, put Paul Bunyan to work for the Red River Lumber Company.

Bunyan has become a part of what folklore experts prefer to call our popular American traditions. True folklore is defined as oral literature which belongs to a specific group of people, without any known author. From the perspective of academic folklorists, America is too young to have its own folklore. What we have instead is a smorgasbord of transplanted myths and legends, along with the inventions of writers. Interestingly, the fact that so many of these inventions have been used to sell products may testify to the strong currents of commercial and consumer interests in American society.

Acquainting young readers with a variety of cultures

can help them contrast their own family values with those held by others. As they read, our hope can be that they will also realize how much all human beings have in common. Most importantly, folklore emphasizes the difference between good and evil, foolishness and wisdom, actions and consequences. While helping readers to become more culturally literate, folklore also challenges them to good behavior without preaching or moralizing.

Aardema, Verna, *Behind the Back of the Mountain: Black Folktales from Southern Africa* (1973) and *Why Mosquitos Buzz in People's Ears: A West African Tale* (1975)—Picture books.

Asbjornsen, Peter Christian and Jorgen E. Moe, *East of the Sun and West of the Moon and Other Tales* (1980)—Norwegian stories. Grade 4 and up.

Bierhorst, John, *Black Rainbow: Legends of the Incas and Myths of Ancient Peru* (1976)—Grade 4 and up.

Carpenter, Frances, *Tales of a Korean Grandmother* (1972)—One in a series of ethnic "grandmother" tales. Grade 3 and up.

Carter, Dorothy, *Greedy Mariani, and Other Folktales of the Antilles* (1974)—Stories from Haiti, Jamaica, and other Caribbean islands. Grade 3 and up.

Chase, Richard, *The Jack Tales* (1943)—Stories handed down for generations in the southern Appalachia mountains. Grade 4 and up.

Chaucer, Geoffrey, *Canterbury Tales* adapted by Barbara Cohen (1988)—Grade 3 and up.

Cohn, Amy L., *From Sea to Shining Sea: A Treasury of American Folklore and Folk Songs* (1993)—An expansive collection from various cultural streams with illustrations by Caldecott award winners. All ages.

Coolidge, Olivia, *Tales of the North* (1951)—Grade 4 and up.

de Wit, Dorothy, ed., *The Talking Stone: An Anthology of Native American Tales and Legends* (1979)—Grade 3 and up.

Duong, Van Quyen and Jewell Reinhart Coburn, *Beyond the East Wind: Legends and Folktales of Vietnam* (1976)—Grade 4 and up.

Geras, Adèle, *My Grandmother's Stories: A Collection of Jewish Folk Tales* (1990)—Grade 3 and up.

Ginsburg, Mirra, *How Wilka Went to Sea, and Other Tales from West of the Urals* (1975)—Grade 3 and up.

Grimm, Jakob and Wilhelm, *The Juniper Tree and Other Tales from Grimm* ed. by Lore Segal and Maurice Sendak, trans. by Randall Jarrell (1976)—Grade 1 and up.

Hamilton, Virginia, *The People Could Fly: American Black Folktales* (1985, Grade 3 and up) and *Her Stories: African American Folktales, Fairy Tales, and True Tales* (1995)—All ages.

Haviland, Virginia, *Favorite Fairy Tales Told in India* (1973), *Favorite Fairy Tales Told in Italy* (1965), *Favorite Fairy Tales Told in Norway* (1961), *North American Legends* (1979)—Grade 2–5.

Hawthorne, Nathaniel, *A Wonder Book* (1851)—Six ancient myths retold in Hawthorne's Romantic style. Grade 4 and up.

Jaffrey, Madhur, *Seasons of Splendor: Tales, Myths and Legends of India* (1985)—Stories attached to festivals in the Hindu year. Grade 6 and up.

Joseph, Lynn, *A Wave in Her Pocket* (1991)—Joseph's aunt tells him stories of the West Indies. A combination of autobiography and fantasy. Grade 3 and up.

Lelooska, ed. by Christine Normandin, *Echoes of the Elders: The Stories and Paintings of Chief Lelooska* (1997)—Grade 3 and up.

Lester, Julius, *The Knee-High Man and Other Tales* (1972)—Black American folk literature with subtle humor accompanied by vibrant illustrations. PreS–Grade 3.

McDermott, Beverly Brodsky, *The Golem: A Jewish Legend* (1976)—Grade 4 and up.

Malcolmson, Anne, *Yankee Doodle's Cousins* (1941)—A collection of twenty-seven tall tales, legends, and stories of early America. Grade 4 and up.

Mayo, Margaret, *Magic Tales from Many Lands* (1993)—Grade 3 and up.

Reader's Digest, *American Folklore and Legend* (1978)—An anthology of popular American stories, poems, and folklore presented in an entertaining way. Grade 5 and up.

Sierra, Judy, *Nursery Tales Around the World* (1996)—Old and new tales from many cultures. A wonderful resource for parents and teachers. All ages.

Singer, Isaac Bashevis, *Naftali the Storyteller and His Horse, Sus* (1976) and *Zlateh the Goat and Other Stories* (1984)—Eastern European folktales told by a Nobel Prize winning storyteller. Grade 3 and up.

Tashjian, Virginia, *Once There Was and Was Not, Armenian Tales Retold* (1966)—Grade 2 and up.

Uchida, Yoshiko, *Sea of Gold and Other Tales from Japan* (1965) and *The Magic Listening Cap: More Folktales from Japan* (1955)—Grade 1 and up.

Untermeyer, Louis, *The World's Great Stories* (1964)—Includes Greek and Roman myths, tales of King Arthur, and the Pied Piper of Hamlin. Grade 5 and up.

Yep, Laurence, *Tongues of Jade* (1991)—A powerful collection of seventeen ancient stories brought to America by early immigrant Chinese. Grade 3 and up.

Yolen, Jane, ed., *Favorite Folktales from Around the World* (1986)—An expert in folklore gives young readers over 150 stories from forty different cultures. Grade 6 and up.

Zemach, Margot, *It Could Always Be Worse: A Yiddish Folk Tale* (1977, Caldecott Honor)—Many children will recognize this phrase often spoken by older family members. Grade 1–5.

Intergenerational Non-Fiction

Another way to explore family history and glimpse home life as previous generations experienced it is through factual books that provide windows on the past. Think of these books as an opportunity for family "show-and-tell" and, if possible, have a grandparent, great-grandparent, or other elder figure share them with young readers.

A B C: Americana from the National Gallery of Art comp. by Cynthia Elyce Rubin (1989)—Photos of antiques that provide a catalyst for exploring the past. All ages.

Allen, Thomas B., *On Granddaddy's Farm* (1989)—Picture book. PreS–Grade 3.

Bartoletti, Susan Campbell, *Growing Up in Coal Country* (1996)—First-person accounts and photographs present the life of children in turn-of-the-century Pennsylvania's coal mining communities. Grade 4 and up.

Bowyer, Carol, *The Children's Book of Houses and Homes* (1978)—A picture book of people around the world and the places they call home. Grade 4 and up.

Dowdell, Dorothy and Joseph, *The Chinese Helped Build America* (1972) and *The Japanese Helped Build America* (1970)—Very informative books for elementary and middle school children. Part of a series by Messner Publishing.

Farber, Norma, *How Does It Feel to Be Old?* (1979)—Poetic descriptions of aging with emphasis on the link with the young through genetic inheritance and memory. PreS–Grade 3.

Freedman, Russell, *Immigrant Kids* (1980)—An award-winning photo-biographer chronicles the lives of children who immigrate to America around 1900. Grade 3 and up.

Gabel, Susan, *Filling in the Blanks: A Guided Look at Growing Up Adopted* (1988)—Grade 5 and up.

Gelfand, Marilyn, *My Great-Grandpa Joe* (1986)—A photo album helps a little girl understand and appreciate her elderly relatives. Picture book. K–Grade 4.

Hilton, Suzanne, *Who Do You Think You Are? Digging for Your Family Roots* (1976)—Grade 4 and up.

Jackson, Louise A., *Grandpa Had a Windmill, Grandma Had a Churn* (1977)—Picture book about cherished belongings on a farm. All ages.

Krementz, Jill, *How It Feels to Be Adopted* (1982)—Children ages nine to sixteen relate their feelings about what it is like to be adopted. Grade 3 and up.

Leedy, Loreen, *Who's Who in My Family?* (1995)—A book about relationships within families. K–Grade 3

LeShan, Eda, *Grandparents: A Special Kind of Love* (1984)—This book offers simple, practical advice about how to relate to grandparents, who are not always easy to be with.

Muller, Jorg, *The Changing City* (1977) and *The Changing Countryside* (1977)—Visual experience of the changes that take place during a twenty-year period. Picture books.

Perl, Lila, *The Great Ancestor Hunt: The Fun of Finding Out Who You Are* (1989)—A straightforward, well-written book. Its first chapter offers a great explanation of why genealogy matters—including a reference to the Bible. Grade 3 and up.

Rosenberg, Maxine B., *Being Adopted* (1984)—A helpful book for adopted children of a different racial or cultural heritage than their adoptive parents. Grade 1–4.

Smith, MaryLou, *Grandmother's Adobe Dollhouse* (1984)—A wonderful picture book about New Mexican culture. K–Grade 3.

Wolfman, Ira, *Do People Grow on Family Trees? Genealogy for Kids and Other Beginners* (1991)—Far more than a basic how-to, this generously illustrated book contains a wealth of information about family names, immigration and naturalization, oral history, and other related topics. Grade 3 and up.

Some readers may be wondering what became of Carlie, the girl who had bounced around without ever belonging. Her story ends with her saying these encouraging words to another foster child: "As long as we are trying, Thomas J, we are not pinballs." And Thomas J replies, "Let's go home."

Animals,
Adventure,
Mystery, Humor,
and Series Books

9 The Kids' Hit Parade

> The freedom to choose one's own books is in some ways the most bracing and dramatic taste of liberty a child can know: At five or six or seven, browsing in the library or bookstore and then reading at home, the child is suddenly free to enter other worlds, spy from within on a thousand lives, leap oceans with a single bound.
> —Michelle Landsberg, *Reading for the Love of It*

For some children, reading is almost as necessary as breathing. They read widely and deeply, always eager to devour the printed page. But most children read more selectively, and their choices often disappoint parents and teachers who want them to read more enriching books. Also, there are many reluctant readers who are almost impossible to hook on books; only the most enticing bait and patient fishing will snag them.

Well-intentioned, solicitous adults often choose books for children based on their educational value or on their potential for helping children solve problems or deal with difficult experiences. (Half of the Newbery Award books of the 1970s deal with serious problems, and the trend toward this kind of fiction continues today.) Christian parents are apt to favor books that reinforce biblical worldviews. When children have freedom to select their own books, however, they are more apt to read what their friends are reading or to choose stories that are fun to read. With easy access to stories through television and videos, reading can seem like a huge effort unless it appeals strongly to a child's interests. Happily, in some exceptional books, there is mental and spiritual nourishment along with a generous serving of pleasure and amusement.

Those who are tempted to forbid fluff reading should keep in mind that the more time a youngster spends with books, the more apt that youngster is to become a lifelong reader.

The types of books described in this chapter are perennial favorites of young readers. They are grouped for easier reference, but many of the books listed cut across all four categories.

Animal Stories

This list features realistic stories about children and animals. For fantasy favorites, see chapter 6.

Anderson, C. W., *Billy and Blaze* (1936)—The first in a series of horse stories enjoyed by children of all ages.

Bagnold, Enid, *National Velvet* (1935)—Velvet Brown and her piebald horse enter a championship race. Grade 5 and up.

Baylor, Byrd, *Hawk, I'm Your Brother* (1976, Caldecott Honor)—Rudy dreams of flying over the Santos Mountains like a hawk. He captures a young bird and eventually decides to set it free. Grade 4 and up.

Boston, Lucy, *A Stranger at Green Knowe* (1961)—One of the most beautiful stories ever written, this Carnegie Award winner concerns a gorilla named Hanno and a boy named Ping—one displaced from Africa, the other from Asia—caught in a world of concrete floors. The excitement of their meeting and sharing a brief adventure together before the sad but heroic ending is unforgettable. Grade 5 and up.

Burnford, Sheila, *The Incredible Journey* (1961)—Two dogs and a cat travel 250 miles across the Canadian wilderness to their home. Some consider this book a modern classic. Grade 4 and up.

Byars, Betsy, *The Midnight Fox* (1981)—Tommy spends the summer at his aunt's and uncle's farm. He grows fond of a fox and its cub, and this puts him in conflict with his uncle, who sees the fox as a predator. Grade 4 and up.

DeJong, Meindert, *Along Came a Dog* (1958, Newbery Honor)—A dog befriends and saves the life of a crippled red hen and is itself finally accepted by the man who tried to get rid of it. DeJong's *Shadrach* (1953) is about Davie and a black rabbit. There is disappointment and anxiety, but even more joy. DeJong wrote many stories about animals and children, and *Hurry Home, Candy* (1953) about an abused dog is one of the best. Grade 4 and up.

Duffey, Betsy, *A Boy in the Doghouse* (1991)—George is training his dog. The only problem is that his dog Lucky believes he is training George. K–Grade 3.

Estes, Eleanor, *Ginger Pye* (1951, Newbery Winner)—Ginger is the smartest dog in Cranbury, Connecticut. When she vanishes, Jerry and Rachel set out to rescue their brilliant canine. Grade 3–6.

Farley, Walter, *The Black Stallion* (1944)—About as unrealistic as a wishful story can be, and about as popular as a story can be. If the book seems inept as literature, that may be because Farley was a high school student when he wrote it. He followed it with over a dozen sequels and a beautiful film by the same name. Also, *Man O' War* (1962), the story of a great racehorse. Grade 4 and up.

Flack, Marjorie, *Angus and the Ducks* (1930), *The Story about Ping* (1933)—Realistic animal stories for young children. Angus is a Scottish terrier who likes to chase ducks. Ping is a Mandarin duck who lives on China's Yangtze river.

Gardiner, John Reynolds, *Stone Fox* (1980)—Ten-year-old Willy and his dog Searchlight try to win the biggest dogsled race in the country. Grade 2 and up.

Gates, Doris, *Little Vic* (1951)—A boy becomes devoted to Little Vic, a colt sired by the greatest race horse. Grade 4 and up.

Gipson, Fred, *Old Yeller* (1956, Newbery Honor)—Travis, a fourteen-year-old boy, and his big, ugly, yellow dog must take care of the family farm in the Texas wilderness. A story filled with love, laughter, and heartache. Grade 6 and up.

Henry, Marguerite, *King of the Wind* (1948, Newbery Winner)—A classic story about a horse named Sham and his stable boy, Agba. Marguerite Henry is the best-loved author of books about horses, and many children enjoy reading and rereading all her stories. Grade 4 and up.

James, Will, *Smoky, the Cow Horse* (1926, Newbery Winner)—A cowboy story written in loping vernacular about a little range colt whose stubbornness is broken by Clint, a man who becomes his friend. Grade 5 and up.

Kjelgaard, Jim, *Big Red* (1945)—The first of three books about a boy devoted to the Irish setters that he and his father train. Kjelgaard has written several other fine animal stories. Grade 4 and up.

Knight, Eric, *Lassie Come Home* (1948)—The story of a collie dog who makes a journey from Scotland to Yorkshire, England, to rejoin her master. Grade 4 and up.

Morey, Walter, *Gentle Ben* (1976)—Fine characterization makes this story of a young Alaskan boy and his adopted bear especially satisfying. Grade 3 and up.

Mowat, Farley, *Owls in the Family* (1962)—A very funny

book about Wol and Weeps, two Saskatchewan owls who upset an entire neighborhood. Mowat tells the story of his own comical pet in *The Dog Who Wouldn't Be* (1957). Grade 4 and up.

Naylor, Phyllis Reynolds, *Shiloh* (1991, Newbery Winner)—Eleven-year-old Marty Preston rescues a young beagle from an abusive owner, but his decision to secretly keep the dog leads to lying and deception. Grade 4 and up.

North, Sterling, *Rascal: A Memoir of a Better Era* (1963)—The true story of North's friendship with a mischievous raccoon named Rascal. Grade 5 and up.

O'Brien, Jack, *Silver Chief, Dog of the North* (1933)—Jim Thorne, a Canadian Mountie, trains Silver Chief to help him in his law enforcement adventures. Grade 5 and up.

O'Hara, Mary (pseudonym for Mary Sture-Vasa), *My Friend Flicka* (1941)—This book is the first of three stories set in Wyoming on a horse ranch. Intended for adults, *My Friend Flicka* has been one of children's most beloved books for several generations. It appeals to horse-lovers, nature-lovers, and strong-willed boys and girls who find themselves in conflict with their fathers. Grade 6 and up.

Pearce, Philippa, *A Dog So Small* (1962)—One of the best writers for children in the English language explores not only our love for animals but also the relationships between three generations and the relationship of imagination to reality. Poor little Ben is promised a dog by his grandfather, but it turns out to be a flat needlework picture. Ben invents a live dog so small he can only see it with his eyes shut. While watching his dog, he is run down in the street. The story comes to a happy but not at all simplistic conclusion, which includes a real live dog. Grade 5 and up.

Rawlings, Marjorie Kinnan, *The Yearling* (1938)—Written

for adults but loved by many children, this is the story of Jody, a poor lonely boy in the Florida wilds. His love and happiness with his young pet deer Flag are shattered by the harsh realities of poverty. An extremely sad story that deals with the relationship of a boy and his father under stress. Grade 5 and up.

Rawls, Wilson, *Where the Red Fern Grows* (1961)—An exciting and bittersweet story about a boy and his two-dog hunting team. A more humorous story from Rawls is *Summer of the Monkeys* (1976). Grade 4 and up.

Rylant, Cynthia, *Every Living Thing* (1985)—A collection of short stories about relationships between people and animals. Grade 5 and up.

Steinbeck, John, *The Red Pony* (1937)—A story about a young boy and his sorrel colt. Grade 6 and up.

Street, James, *Good-bye, My Lady* (1954)—Skeeter lives on the edge of a swamp in a little cabin with his uncle. An unusual dog (African Basenji) comes into his life. After training Lady, Skeeter finds out she is a valuable dog and belongs to a kennel. He is faced with a very difficult decision. Grade 6 and up.

Terhune, Albert Peyson, *Lad: A Dog* (re-released 1993)—Over seventy years ago, Terhune wrote several books about Sunnybank and its collies. They are syrupy and rather outdated, but they are still dearly loved by many children. Also, *Best Loved Dog Stories* of Albert Payson Terhune (1987). Don't mistake the Hello Reader Lad series for the real thing. Grade 5 and up.

Adventure

Although there are aspects of the fantastic in the following adventure stories, they all reflect children's craving for challenging experiences in the real world.

Ardizzone, Edward, *Little Tim and the Brave Sea Captain*

(1936, reissued 1977)—Tim is a young stowaway on a steamship. His exciting adventures always have happy endings, and children who like the first book can go on to its sequels. K–Grade 2.

Byars, Betsy, *The Seven Treasure Hunts* (1991)—An entertaining chapter book about best friends who create a series of treasure hunts for one another. Grade 2–6.

Carlson, Natalie Savage, *The Happy Orpheline* (1957)—Twenty little girls in a dreary orphanage near Paris have amusing adventures. This book and its sequels give a slight acquaintance with France as well as a merry view of communal living. K–Grade 3.

Cleary, Beverly, *Henry Huggins* (1950)—Cleary writes humorously and unpretentiously about third grader Henry Huggins, his friends, and his dog Ribsy. Sequels to this highly improbable but very American story include *Henry and Ribsy* (1954), *Ramona the Pest* (1968), and others. Grade 3 and up.

Cross, Gillian, *The Great American Elephant Chase* (1993)—An orphan boy and a con man's daughter try to hide an elephant from a thief. *School Library Journal* describes it as "a rip-roaring romp." Grade 4 and up.

Enright, Elizabeth, *Gone-Away Lake* (1957)—Two cousins find an abandoned village at the edge of a swamp. Then they find it is not really abandoned. Grade 3 and up.

George, Jean Craighead, *My Side of the Mountain* (1959, Newbery Honor)—A New York City teen believes he can live on his own in the Catskills for a year and gets a chance to prove it. Grade 6 and up.

Houston, James, *Frozen Fire* (1977)—Two boys set out on a snowmobile to find a missing father. This exciting story set in Alaska gives insights into the Eskimo way of life. Grade 6 and up.

Irwin, Hadley, *The Original Freddie Ackerman* (1992)—Freddie refuses to spend another summer vacation with his divorced parents and respective step-families. Instead he is sent to stay with his two great-aunts on an island. What he thinks will be a boring vacation is filled with excitement. Grade 5 and up.

Mayne, William, *No More School* (1965)—Two girls keep the village school open unofficially when the teacher is ill.

Mowat, Farley, *Lost in the Barrens* (1956)—A city boy learns how to survive in Canada's far north from his Woodland Cree friend. Grade 6 and up.

O'Dell, Scott, *The Black Pearl* (1967, Newbery Honor)—A village of pearl divers compete for a treasure off the coast of Baja California. Grade 5 and up.

Ottley, Reginald, *Boy Alone* (1965), *The Roan Colt* (1967), *Rain Comes to Yamboorah* (1967)—Adventures of a young teen in the Australian Outback. Grade 5 and up.

Paulsen, Gary, *Hatchet* (1987)—When a plane crashes in the Canadian wilderness, a thirteen-year-old boy is the only survivor and the only tool he has is a hatchet. Paulsen's writing may be too raw in its realism for some families, but it is scientifically accurate and informative. Sample it before sharing with children. Also, *The River* (1991), *The Voyage of the Frog* (1989), *Dogsong* (1985, Newbery Honor). Grade 7 and up.

Ransome, Arthur, *Swallows and Amazons* (1930)—Ransome was a well-educated journalist, author, and world traveler long before he wrote and illustrated his first adventure book for children. Because Ransome himself enjoyed boats, fishing, and vacations, he wrote about children who enjoyed these same diversions. There are twelve books in all describing in accurate and convincing detail all the skills of outdoor living that time, luck, energy, and money can provide. Grade 4 and up.

Sperry, Armstrong, *Call It Courage* (1939, Newbery Winner)—Mafatu, son of a South Pacific island chief, is afraid of the ocean. Grade 4 and up.

Streatfield, Noel, *The Magic Summer* (1967)—Four children have an adventure-filled summer with their eccentric aunt in the Irish countryside. Grade 4 and up.

Taylor, Theodore, *The Cay* (1969)—Phillip is evacuated from a Dutch island off the coast of Venezuela. Nazis torpedo the boat, and the boy is marooned on an island with an old black man and a cat. An excellent book about resolving racial tensions. Grade 3 and up.

Mystery

When Kathryn Lindskoog was a fourth grader, she made a wonderful friend—Nancy Drew. She wished she could be Nancy Drew, and if she could not, she wished she could be Carolyn Keene, the woman who wrote the Nancy Drew books. She knew the stories were fictional, but she also knew there were mysteries in life and that they could be solved. And she knew she wanted to spend her life bringing out the truth and righting wrongs.

When Ranelda Hunsicker was a fourth grader, she took home a library book titled *The Secret of the Rosewood Box* by Helen Orton. In its pages history and mystery were woven together. For Hunsicker it was an intoxicating mix that kept her coming back for more. She read her way through *The Mystery of the Little Red School House*, *The Treasure in the Little Trunk*, and *The Mystery of the Chimney*. Ever since those early days of delight and discovery, she has been digging into the past and trying to solve life's puzzles.

From personal experience, the authors know that light entertainment can resonate with some of our deepest needs and desires. In mysteries a child finds reassurance that good can triumph over evil, order can come from chaos, and clear thinking can uncover hidden treasure. Here is a sampling.

Adler, David, *Cam Jansen and the Mystery of the Monkey House* (1985)—*School Library Journal* says, "The plot moves quickly and incorporates action and adventure along the way." Great for beginning or reluctant readers. Grade 2–4.

Alexander, Lloyd, *The Drackenberg Adventure* (1987)—In 1873 seventeen-year-old Vesper and her aunt and uncle attend the Diamond Jubilee of the Grand Duchess of Drackenberg. This entertaining tale offers castles, an art heist, political intrigue, and helpful gypsies. Grade 5 and up.

Brenner, Barbara, *Mystery of the Plumed Serpent* (1980)—A series of clues leads twins Elena and Michael Garcia to an ancient Mexican treasure. Grade 4 and up.

Bunting, Eve, *Jane Martin, Dog Detective* (1984)—A mystery for beginning readers. PreS–Grade 3.

Conford, Ellen, *A Case for Jenny Archer* (1988)—Reading mysteries inspires Jenny to spy on her new neighbors. She thinks they are criminals, and her efforts to uncover their dastardly deeds have surprising results. Grade 2–4.

Haas, E. A., *Incognito Mosquito, Private Insective* (1985)—The first in a series of books filled with more puns than crimes. Is it humor or mystery? Both! Grade 2–5.

Herman, Emily, *The Missing Fossil Mystery* (1996)—Liza takes her older brother Jesse's fossil to school for show-and-tell. When it disappears, she has to find it. An introduction to paleontology. Grade 1–4.

Hildick, E. W., *The Case of the Nervous Newsboy* (1976)—Jack McGurk, boy detective, is the brains of the McGurk Organization. His special training operation works so well that the paper boy being shadowed disappears. Grade 4–6.

Parish, Peggy, *Key to the Treasure* (1966)—Parish writes easy mysteries in which each chapter provides a clue and a solution. Grade 3–6.

Pinkwater, Daniel Manus, *The Snarkout Boys and the Avocado of Death* (1982), *The Muffin Fiend* (1986)—Pinkwater's zany stories and illustrations have made him a favorite with children. Grade 3 and up.

Raskin, Ellen, *The Mysterious Disappearance of Leon (I Mean Noel)* (1971), *The Tatooed Potato and Other Clues* (1977)—Raskin specializes in wit, wordplay, and nonsense. Grade 5 and up.

Sharmat, Marjorie Weinman, *Nate the Great and the Phony Clue* (1977)—Beginning readers will enjoy this story about a first-grade detective and his canine sidekick, Sludge. First in a series. Grade 1–5.

Simon, Seymour, *Einstein Anderson, Science Sleuth* (1980)—First in a series of short, amusing stories by a science writer. In each book a boy detective uses scientific principles to solve problems. Grade 3–6.

Snyder, Zilpha Keatley, *The Egypt Game* (1967, Newbery Honor)—Two eleven-year-old girls get involved in a criminal investigation as a result of their interest in Egypt. Grade 4 and up.

Sobol, Donald J., *Encyclopedia Brown, Boy Detective* (1963)—First in a series of several dozen books about the whiz-kid son of the Idaville Chief of Police. He solves the cases his dad cannot. Grade 3 and up.

Van Allsburg, Chris, *The Mysteries of Harris Burdick* (1984)—The character Burdick is a mystery writer and illustrator. She takes a publisher one page from each of her fourteen stories. When Burdick fails to return the next day as promised, readers are left to speculate on the stories suggested by her sample pages. Grade 3 and up.

Humor

Realism gives way to the ridiculous in most of the following outrageous stories. But as Solomon said, "A cheerful heart is good medicine." That proverb is true for children as well as for adults.

Aiken, Joan, *Arabel's Raven* (1974)—An amusing story about how a girl and her father care for an injured raven. Grade 3–6.

Allard, Harry, *Miss Nelson Is Missing!* (1977)—Miss Viola Swamp, one of the worst substitute teachers ever, takes over in Room 207. The children must get Miss Nelson back. The first of three in a series. K–Grade 3.

Avi, *"Who Was That Masked Man, Anyway?"* (1992)—In this trip back to 1945 a boy spends his time recreating radio dramas and spying on the family's boarder. He is sure the man is a "mad scientist." Grade 4 and up.

Barrett, Judi, *Cloudy with a Chance of Meatballs* (1978)—A picture book appropriate for all ages.

Coren, Alan, *Arthur the Kid* (1977)—A boy gets the best of a goofy outlaw gang. Grade 3–5.

Du Bois, William Pène, *The Alligator Case* (1965)—A delightful parody of the private-eye genre. Picture book.

Estes, Eleanor, the Moffat stories (1941–1943)—These old-fashioned stories still captivate children. Each chapter is complete in itself, so the books are good for short read-aloud times. Grade 3–6.

Fitzgerald, John D., *The Great Brain* (1967)—J. D. is the younger brother of "The Great Brain," otherwise known as Tom D. Fitzgerald. Based on the author's childhood, this is a funny story with a big heart. Grade 4 and up.

Fleischman, Sid, *Mr. Mysterious and Company* (1962), *Humbug Mountain* (1978), *Chancy and the Grand Rascal*

(1989)—One of the best humor writers in contemporary children's literature. Grade 4 and up.

Hurwitz, Johanna, *The Adventures of Ali Baba Bernstein* (1985)—An eight-year-old named David decides his life would be more exciting if his name were Ali Baba. Grade 2–5.

Joosee, Barbara M., *Wild Willie and King Kyle, Detectives* (1993)—The hilarious adventures of two best friends. Grade 1–4.

McCloskey, Robert, *Homer Price* (1943), *Centerburg Tales* (1951)—Today's children may enjoy the Homer Price stories best if they read them with their grandparents. They are a lot of fun and a window on what it was like to grow up in America during the 1940s and 1950s. Grade 3–6.

Manes, Stephen, *Be a Perfect Person in Just Three Days!* (1982)—Milo Crinkley tries to follow the advice in a self-help book. The results will tickle everyone's ribs. Grade 3 and up.

Park, Barbara, *Skinnybones* (1982)—Alex is a baseball player who hits more home runs with his wit than his bat. But his wisecracks get him into trouble (Grade 2–5). Also, *Junie B. Jones and a Little Monkey Business* (1993) about a little girl who thinks her new baby brother is a monkey.

Pollack, Pamela, ed., *Random House Book of Humor for Children* (1988)—A sampling of some of the best humorous literature for young readers. Most of the selections are excerpts. Grade 2 and up.

Richler, Mordecai, *Jacob Two-Two Meets the Hooded Fang* (1977)—Jacob derives his name from saying everything twice. When he insults a grownup, he is sent to Children's Prison. Grade 3–5.

Robertson, Keith, *Henry Reed, Inc.* (1948)—When Henry hears from his aunt and uncle about the research that goes on at Princeton University, he decides to set up his own research firm. Grade 5 and up.

Robinson, Barbara, *The Best Christmas Pageant Ever* (1972)—The Herdman children terrorize their school and town. In the process everyone, including those horrible Herdmans, learns a lesson. Do not save this one for Christmas. Grade 4 and up.

Yorinks, Arthur, *Oh, Brother* (1989)—Two quarrelsome twin brothers have some hilarious adventures on their way from Rotten's Home for Lost Boys to the court of the queen. All ages.

Series Books

There are two major kinds of series books: superior ones (such as the Narnian Chronicles) and inferior ones (sometimes referred to as "pulp fiction"). Literary people tend to deplore the fact that the most popular children's books in the area of contemporary life, adventure, and mystery are "pulp" series about intrepid young people such as Nancy Drew, mass-produced by "fiction-factories."

Edward Stratemeyer, the creator of Nancy Drew, was born in New Jersey in 1862 and read Horatio Alger success stories with a passion. After selling his own story of this genre, he chose his first pen name, Arthur (for author) M. (for a million copies of his future books) Winfield (for success in his chosen field). He went to work for Street and Smith, the greatest dime-novel publishers, and when Horatio Alger died, Stratemeyer had the honor of completing Alger's unfinished books.

In 1899 Stratemeyer dashed off his first three stories in the Rover Boys series, which, by 1930 when Stratemeyer died, amounted to thirty volumes and had sold five million copies. In 1906 Stratemeyer set up his Stratemeyer Syndicate, in which he wrote a few books himself and dictated outlines for hundreds and hundreds of others that he hired various writers to complete.

After his death, his daughters carried on.

Stratemeyer had invented a huge crew of imaginary authors. His chief assistant, Howard Garis, not only helped him to run the company but also wrote most of the early Tom Swift stories. When enthusiastic readers demanded details about one beloved author, May Hollis Barton, the Syndicate obligingly published a fabulous fake biography of her.

The identity of most of the real writers is still a mystery, but it may be revealed soon thanks to some recent literary detective work. According to James Keeline, a San Diego specialist in collectible children's books and an expert on the Stratemeyer Syndicate, most of the ghostwriters were journalists. "The newspaper business cultivated the right sort of writing and writers, people who were expected to produce interesting, readable material very quickly to a prescribed length." They were paid fifty to two hundred fifty dollars per book and allowed from a week to a month to complete each one. The books were full of exciting adventures from beginning to end, perfectly moral, and utterly devoid of all literary excellence, deep sensitivity, or intellectual enrichment.

They did not go unopposed. Libraries refused to carry them, which only increased sales. The chief librarian of the Boy Scouts of America wrote a tract called "Blowing Out the Boy's Brains," which swept the nation with its warning that these cheap adventure books debauch and destroy boys' imaginations by over-stimulation, just as alcohol will debauch and destroy their bodies.

Interestingly enough, when Dr. Robert A. Nisbet of Columbia University, scholar of "intellectual history" and author of many books, was asked in 1977 to list the books that had shaped his life, he named a dozen. The first three—one quarter of a list that also included Alexis de Tocqueville and William James—were the books of

Horatio Alger, the Tom Swift series by Victor Appleton, and the Boy Allies series by C. W. Hayes.

One of America's most outstanding contemporary authors, Eudora Welty, also pays tribute to the importance of series books in her childhood. On her first visit to the library, Eudora's mother told the librarian, "Let her have any book she wants, except *Elsie Dinsmore.*" When the little girl looked for Elsie, she found out it was not a single book but a whole row. And then she found other series books—Five Little Peppers, The Wizard of Oz, The Little Colonel, The Colour Fairy Books, The Camp Fire Girls. "There were many of everything, generations of everybody, instead of one," Welty recalls. "I wasn't coming to the end of reading, after all—I was saved."

After devouring all the series books she could find, Eudora noticed something strange. "I wonder whether I felt some flaw at the heart of things or whether I was just tired of not having any taste; but it seemed to me when I had finished that the last nine of those books [in the Camp Fire Girls series] weren't as good as the first one. And the same went for all series books."

The 1970s saw a tremendous new pulp novel boom first epitomized by Harlequin Books of Toronto, which published twelve new Harlequin romances every month, selling about 100 million in the United States per year. In 1983 Bantam started issuing a new series—Sweet Valley High books for girls. They are about the adventures of sixteen-year-old twin sisters Jessica and Elizabeth. There is a new title each month. Within the first five years of their release, girls bought 26 million copies of these happy books that could rightly be called bubblegum for the brain. Younger readers can enjoy similar twaddle in two spin-off series, Sweet Valley Twins and Sweet Valley Kids. No one pretends that they have depth, originality, or literary excellence. And their leading competitor, the Sweet Dreams series, is even more vacuous. These books get girls reading, and they are an escape from personal problems.

Also in the 1980s, the grandfather of all series books, the Stratemeyer Syndicate, was sold to Simon & Schuster. This publishing giant supplies today's young readers with new stories about Nancy Drew and the Hardy Boys. But parents and grandparents who pick up the new books with fond memories of their childhood heroes are in for a shock. From the covers straight through to the end of the stories, Nancy Drew is now more concerned with her appearance than she is with solving problems. Mildred Wirt Benson, who wrote the thirty original Nancy Drew books, told the *New York Times,* "I made Nancy Drew good-looking, smart, and a perfectionist. I made her a concept of the girl I'd like to be." Now instead of being wise as a fox, Nancy Drew is merely foxy. And the Hardy Boys are just another couple of hunks who deserve dates with a couple of Sweet Valley girls.

Most parents and educators could dismiss pulp series books as relatively harmless escapism. Some compared these page turners to the high-fiber, low-nutrition bulk needed in our diets. Until 1992. That is the year R. L. Stine and Scholastic, Inc. gave the world Goosebumps. The ghoulish logo titillated youngsters conditioned to crave chills and thrills by television and video games. Aimed at children aged eight to twelve, these kiddie horror stories turned out to be an incredible publishing phenomenon. In just three years Goosebumps books sold over 30 million copies. New releases skyrocketed to the bestseller lists as soon as they came out. According to *Forbes* magazine, which took note of this moneymaking phenomenon, it was the first time a children's paperback of any kind had enjoyed such success.

Soon other publishers tried to share the wealth. In 1994 Random House unveiled Supermodels of the World and Bantam Books premiered its Bloodlust and

Unicorn series. Goosebumps creator R. L. Stine started a new series called Fear Street for Simon & Schuster. Aimed at readers twelve to fifteen, its horror stories specialize in gore, violent death, hallucinations, and preternatural occurrences. One young teen described reading a Fear Street book as "really boring." But she kept reading because she wanted to know how it ended. Millions of readers get hooked this way.

The good news about Goosebumps and other disturbing fads in series fiction is that popularity can plummet as well as soar. In early 1997 Scholastic stock dropped 40 percent in value in just one day of trading. The publisher and market analyst attributed the drop to young readers' waning interest in Goosebumps. Ray Marchuk, vice president of finance and investor relations at Scholastic, said, "Times change. There are other things that attract the children's interest." For this we give thanks.

Compared to horror, glamour, and fantasy role-play series, Ann Martin's Baby-Sitters Club seems wholesome. Predating Goosebumps, this series has sold over 100 million copies. It focuses on the adventures of four middle school girls who start a baby-sitting business. Preteen girls like the easy reading and the familiar characters who share many of their interests. In an interview with Amazon.com, an on-line bookstore, Ann Martin (or was it one of her ghostwriters?) told her fans that she knew by the time she was twelve she wanted to become an author. When asked about the books she enjoyed as a child and what she reads today, Martin said, "I love horror books. But I am not much into reading books."

While Martin capitalizes on contemporary experiences, Pleasant Rowland has made a fortune on the past. An advertising expert, Rowland set out to create a product that upscale working mothers would want to buy for their daughters. She knew they were looking for quality toys and books from a catalog source and they wanted their daughters to have healthier role models than Barbie. "I began to think what I would have wanted to give a daughter," Rowland recalls. "I would want her to have a sense of the wonderful traditions of girlhood, the legacy that mothers have passed on to daughters for generations in answer to the age-old question, 'Mommy, what was it like when you were a little girl?'"

In 1986 Rowland gave mothers and daughters the American Girls books and dolls. The response was tremendous. In its first ten years, the Pleasant Company sold more than 3 million dolls and 35 million books. It started the *American Girls Magazine*, which has more subscribers than any other girls' magazine. In addition to the sweet, short, and simple storybooks that found a place in over 80 percent of school libraries, Pleasant marketed craft kits, clothing, family vacations, the American Girls Club, and a wide array of doll accessories. In 1996 the company's annual income was $187 million. In 1998 Pleasant Company was gobbled up by Mattel, the makers of Barbie.

Most educators commend the American Girls books for creating a fresh interest in American history and encouraging positive character traits, but some critics see flaws. Jeanne Brady, a professor at Penn State, calls the dolls trophy toys for rich kids. She also faults Pleasant Company for marketing nostalgia, a sentimental yearning for the past. On the other hand, parents and teachers fed up with children's products that focus on life's seamy side see the American Girls as a welcome respite. Pleasant Company offers teachers' guides to the historical periods its books and dolls represent. The stories of Felicity (1776 Virginia), Josefina (1824 New Mexico), Kirsten (1854 Minnesota), Addy (Civil War South), Samantha (1904 New York City), and Molly (WWII), are definitely formula fiction, but they can serve as stepping stones to richer reading experiences.

A trip to most local Christian bookstores makes it clear that series books are bestsellers there as well. Christian publishing companies offer a broad variety of series, most of them highly imitative of successful secular series. Usually the quality of writing is comparable, but often the plots are weighed down by preachiness and moralizing. For children who read series books to escape from responsibility and moral dilemmas, Christian series may seem like a dose of sugar-coated medicine. Other young readers will enjoy light reading woven around characters who are clearly part of their evangelical culture.

Christian publishers try to appeal to parents while satisfying children's demand for whatever is currently "cool." Often the bottom line wins as evidenced by the Spine Chillers Mysteries by Fred Katz (Word Publishing). The covers for this series reassure parents and bookstore owners that readers will "enjoy thrills and chills with the kids in this story who have fun as they demonstrate Christian character based on love for God, parents, and one another. You'll share a scare . . . but, of course, ghouls and ghosts are strictly in the imagination." On the first page of book one, a word leaps out at the reader—*goosebumps!*

It would be hard to dispute the charge that series books feed consumerism. Children often want to own every book in a series, and sometimes they want merchandise spin-offs as well. Thus, collecting series books can become more important than reading them. And series stories promote "affluenza" when their leading characters are obsessed with popularity, image, and possessions.

Rather than lecturing children about the faults of inferior series fiction, parents and teachers do well to offset brain-draining influence by reading quality books aloud and making them available for sampling. Since series are here to stay, here are some to look for in public, school, and church libraries.

Bibee, John, Home-School Detectives (InterVarsity Press)—With the growing popularity of home schooling has come a series in which home-schooled kids star. Written by the gifted creator of the earlier Spirit Flyer series. Grade 3–6.

Giff, Patricia Reilly, Kids of the Polk Street School—The children in Mrs. Rooney's classroom are always up to something, and there are twelve books to prove it! Grade 1–4.

Jackson, Dave and Neta, Trailblazer Books (Bethany)—Adventure stories centered on Christian heroes of the past, including David Livingstone, John Wesley, Amy Carmichael, William Tyndale, Harriet Tubman, Elizabeth Fry and many others. Grade 3–7.

Johnson, Lois Walfrid, Adventures of the Northwoods; Riverboat Adventures (Bethany)—Johnson has been praised for the accuracy of historical details and the quality of her writing. Grade 3–6.

Lewis, Beverly, The Cul-de-Sac Kids (Bethany)—Books for children who are ready to move from picture books to short chapter books. Each story features the amusing antics of the boys and girls who live on Blossom Hill Lane (Grade 2–5). Also, Summerhill Secrets, contemporary fiction set in Amish country. Sixteen-year-old Merry Hanson has several Amish friends. Her relationships with them help to clarify questions of faith and culture (Grade 6 and up).

Lovelace, Maud Hart, Betsy-Tacy—This series began in 1940 and its popularity has endured, thanks in large part to the devotion of grandmothers and mothers. New York columnist Anna Quindlen says, "Betsy-Tacy fans never die. They just reread." The stories are set in a little Minnesota town during the first half of the 1900s. Betsy and Tacy are five when they become best friends, and their friendship endures through ten books and *Betsy's Wedding*.

Lowry, Lois, Anatasia Krupnik—Comedy series by a Newbery winner about a fourth-grader growing up in Boston. The books follow her into junior high school.

Maifair, Linda Lee., Darcy J. Doyle, Daring Detective—The girl detective in this series has a set of wheels—on her wheelchair. Grade 3–6.

Murphy, Elspeth Campbell, Three Cousins Detective Club (Bethany)—Three super sleuth cousins solve exciting mysteries in this easy-reader series. Grade 2–6.

Myers, Bill, McGee and Me! (Focus on the Family); The Incredible Worlds of Wally McDoogle (Word); Bloodhounds, Inc. (Bethany)—Bill Myers is a talented screenwriter and film producer who infuses his stories with quick wit, high energy, hilarious antics, and Christian principles. Grade 3–6.

Nixon, Joan, Orphan Train—During the late 1800s orphaned children were sent West to find new families. Each book in this series tells the story of a boy or girl who traveled by train to a new home. The books are enhanced by a brief section of historical documents, photographs, and other background materials. Grade 3–6.

Parish, Peggy, Amelia Bedelia—There are eleven books in this series about a housekeeper who takes everything literally, including "dressing" chickens! She is loved by beginning readers.

Roddy, Lee, An American Adventure (Bethany); Ladd Family Adventures (Focus on the Family); D. J. Dillon (Chariot Victor)—Lee Roddy is the author of many successful Christian series. His books are fast paced, filled with cliffhangers, and easy to read. The children's adventures usually take place in historical settings and outdoor situations. Grade 3–6.

Rue, Nancy N., Christian Heritage (Focus on the Family) and Raise the Flag (Waterbrook Press)—Nancy Rue is a drama and English teacher. Her stories reflect her love of language and her skill in developing believable characters, dialogue, and scenes. They also encourage strong moral values. Grade 4–6.

Warner, Gertrude Chandler, The Boxcar Children—After completing a prescriptive series for a Christian publisher, Warner wanted to do something just for fun. Her fantasy was to live in a caboose or a railroad boxcar. She did the next best thing: she created The Boxcar Children series. The series is not explicitly Christian, but it reflects the author's strong Congregationalist values. (Some parents who were raised in Christian homes may remember Warner's *Peter Piper* and its sequel, *Traveling Parakeet*, written for Zondervan.) Started in 1924, The Boxcar Children retained its popularity through the years, and in 1942 Warner rewrote it with a controlled vocabulary (an approach then advocated by reading specialists). In recent years, this mystery series has become a strong seller once more, and new titles are being written and released. Grade 3–6.

Here is how one of England's most popular children's authors, Aidan Chambers, describes a child's attraction to series books. He writes in *Booktalk,*

> Suppose a child, as many do, selects a story by Enid Blyton, settles down and "reads" it, enjoys it so much that s/he goes to the shelves and finds another by the same author, "reads" it, finds another, and so on. . . . Repetitious reading of any kind of book, of any one author, is flat-earth reading. It may not know about, or worse still may not acknowledge, that the world is round, plural, disparate, many-faceted. Flat-earthers resist any invitation to explore beyond the boundaries of their familiar territory because of the fearsome dangers

they are sure lie in wait at the edge of their world. One of these dangers is called boredom, another is called difficulty. A third is fear of exhaustion (perhaps the journey round the other side—if there is another side!—will never end).

Having summed up the things that may motivate children to be "flat-earth readers," Chambers asks how we can turn their closed circle into a rising spiral of well-rounded reading experiences. The answer seems to lie in sharing reading experiences with others. When those we like and respect encourage us to read certain books, young or old, we are apt to accept the challenge. Similarly, talking with others about books can help a child understand what made a book he read appealing as well as what may have made it ultimately disappointing. Looking back on his own growth as a reader and the development of his students, Chambers writes, "It was booktalk that pumped blood into our literary veins and gave us the energy, the impetus, for exploration beyond our familiar boundaries."

Parents who want to insure more meaningful reading experiences for their children can begin by picking up their son's or daughter's favorite paperback. That has paid off for Marvin Olasky, editor of *World* magazine. "When riding on planes, as I frequently am these days, I am not reading systematic theology textbooks. . . . Instead, whenever a laptop computer cannot be used, I pull out whatever my executive secretary, Daniel Olasky, an avid twelve-year-old reader, recommends."

What does Olasky's son recommend? Brian Jacques's Redwall books, a series the editor describes as "rousing enough to engage children and clever enough to keep adults leafing through." When dad gets home, he and Daniel go for a walk and booktalk. Since Daniel is captivated by stories of battles where evil attempts to triumph over good, his father introduces him to *The Commissar Vanishes: The Falsification of Photographs and Art in Stalin's Russia.* It is a mental stretch, but one that is welcomed. And thus, book by book, the flat earth gives way to new horizons.

10 Words at Play

[A poem] may serve as a song (high or low), a mnemonic, squib, satire, advertisement, prayer, picture, noble sermon, Chinese puzzle, child's toy . . . or a balm for simple minds. . . . But the summits of poetry are mysteries.

—Ruth Pitter, *Collected Poems*

If a man were permitted to make all the ballads, he need not care who should make the laws of a nation." That overstatement by an eighteenth-century essayist (Andrew Fletcher) is about the importance of influencing people's imagination. Just as the pen is mightier than the sword, so stories do more for people than statutes, and rhymes can help children as much as rules.

Children's Poetry from the Past

The first author of a book of poems especially for children was, as mentioned in chapter 4, the Puritan minister Isaac Watts, who published *Divine Songs for Children* in 1715. His purpose was to teach Christianity to children, and he did it so beautifully that his poems were well-known by children for two centuries. His "Cradle Hymn" begins:

Hush! my dear, lie still and slumber,
Holy Angels guard thy bed!
Heavenly blessings without number,
Gently falling on thy head.

Only four years after *Divine Songs,* another book of poems for children was published in London—*Songs for the Nursery, or Mother Goose's Melodies.* There were surely earlier collections of nursery rhymes, but this is the first one on record. And not one copy is left.

A few years ago, a nostalgic English couple borrowed the equivalent of twelve thousand dollars and bought themselves a charming old thatched-roof cottage in the village of Birdbrook. As the husband repaired the stone floor, he discovered a rusty metal box under the stones. Inside were ninety-nine gold sovereigns about 150 years old, worth about seventeen thousand dollars. If anyone discovers a copy of Thomas Fleet's little *Songs for the Nursery, or Mother Goose's Melodies* (1719) he will have found a much greater treasure than a box full of gold sovereigns.

In 1744 Mary Cooper of London published at least two volumes of nursery rhymes for sixpence each, called *Tommy Thumb's Pretty Song Book* "for the Diversion of all Little Masters and Misses." They were only three inches tall and less than two inches wide, and the one remaining copy (of Volume II) is a treasure in the British Museum. The first rhyme in the book is one that knowledgeable children still say to ladybugs, in England called *ladybirds,* when they catch them and let them go unharmed. (The English name "Our Lady's bird" actually means the Virgin Mary's bug and may have been given because ladybugs aid desirable plant life.)

> Lady Bird, Lady Bird,
> Fly away home.
> Your house is on fire,
> Your children will burn.

Perhaps the first line in the oldest remaining nursery rhyme book accounts for the name and the insignia of one of today's English children's publishers. The Lady-

bird company is located in Loughborough in central
England, the city where a conference of contemporary
children's writers meets annually at the University.

Do not assume from "Lady Bird" that *Tommy Thumb's
Pretty Song Book* was all sweetness and gentility. The second rhyme is:

> Little Robin redbreast,
> Sitting on a pole,
> Niddle, Noddle,
> Went his head,
> And Poop went his Hole.

Needless to say, all coarse rhymes like that were refined
later as adult standards for children's literature became
stricter. Other familiar rhymes in that oldest collection
include "Sing a Song of Sixpence," "Little Tom Tucker,"
and "Bah, Bah Black Sheep."

John Newbery's book of nursery rhymes was published before the Revolutionary War, and the American
Isaiah Thomas pirated the edition in 1786. The toddlers
of our nation grew up on nursery rhymes from the beginning. There have been hundreds of editions of them,
large and small, some with truly beautiful illustrations.
The Annotated Mother Goose (1962) by William S. Baring-
Gould, *The Oxford Dictionary of Nursery Rhymes* (1951),
and *The Oxford Nursery Rhyme Book* (1955) by Iona and
Peter Opie are the most comprehensive contemporary
editions. For use in the home, however, the favorite edition is *A Family Book of Nursery Rhymes* (1964), also by
the Opies and illustrated by Pauline Baynes, who gave
readers the first delightful pictures of Narnia. For little
ones, try *My Very First Mother Goose* (1996) by Iona Opie
with illustrations by Rosemary Wells, one of the first
author-illustrators of board books for babies and toddlers.

Only recently have advertising jingles tended to take

the place of nursery rhymes for little children. "Mary Had a Little Lamb" is still the most famous verse of any kind in the English language.

Next came William Blake's *Songs of Innocence* in 1789, a collection of artistic poetry. Many scholars say that these poems were intended for children, and his darker *Songs of Experience*, which came five years later, for adults. Some have claimed that both volumes include good poems for children, and other readers say that all of Blake's poems are strictly for adults.

Blake was a controversial genius in his own day, and he is seen that way today as well. He saw angels and other supernatural visitors, and much of his later mystical writing is obscure. He taught his beloved wife, Catherine, to read and write, and she worked with him on his art and writing the rest of his life. They produced each of his books themselves, with personally made copper engravings of the lettering and designs and delicate watercolor shading added by hand. Each volume sold for five shillings, but they were not at all popular. Today the few that are left are almost priceless. One of the favorite poems by William Blake and one of the best suited for children is "The Lamb."

> Little Lamb, who made thee?
> Dost thou know who made thee?
>
> Gave thee life and bid thee feed
> By the stream and o'er the mead;
> Gave thee clothing of delight,
> Softest clothing, wooly, bright;
> Gave thee such a tender voice,
> Making all the vales rejoice?
>
> Little Lamb, who made thee?
> Dost thou know who made thee?

Little Lamb, I'll tell thee;
Little Lamb, I'll tell thee;

He is called by thy name,
For he calls himself a Lamb.
He is meek, and he is mild;
He became a little child.
I a child, and thou a lamb.
We are called by his name.

Little Lamb, God bless thee!
Little Lamb, God bless thee!

To turn from Blake to the next book of poetry for children is almost to turn from the sublime to the ridiculous, but sisters Ann and Jane Taylor were not writing funny verses. Their book *Original Poems for Infant Minds* (1804) was immensely popular, full of sentimental virtue and cautionary verses that warned children to behave. Children no doubt enjoyed the rhymed stories of "Meddlesome Matty" and "Dirty Jim," but the one and only poem that endures today is "Twinkle, Twinkle, Little Star."

Next came a poem for children that has remained a top seller for 150 years. On Christmas Eve in 1822, Clement C. Moore, a Bible scholar who taught Greek and Oriental Literature at an Episcopal seminary in New York, wrote a poem about Santa Claus. He spent a few hours alone in his study and then presented his family with "A Visit from St. Nicholas" or, as it is popularly called, "'Twas the Night Before Christmas." A year later he had it published in a newspaper, and soon it swept the country, permanently determining Santa's looks, personality, and *modus operandi* for American children. Moore died forty years later and is remembered today in encyclopedias for that single incredibly popular poem.

In 1845 Henrich Hoffman published a collection of

rhymed stories in Germany titled *Struwwelpeter (Slovenly Peter)*, and three years later the book was published in England for the first time. The prankish stories are not so popular as "A Visit from St. Nicholas," but the book is still being published and read.

At the time of Moore's death, a very serious, gifted, and beautiful English woman brought out a story-poem for children called *Goblin Market*. The author was Christina Rossetti, and the story told of a girl who ate enchanted fruit and almost perished by craving for more until she was saved by her loving sister. Today *Goblin Market* is interpreted by Freudians as a thinly disguised account of disappointed love, and it is enjoying revived popularity with some adult readers. Sexual symbolism aside, it seems rather sinister for children, although it is a great work of art. In 1872 Rossetti brought out her collection *Sing Song* for children, which includes delightful verses like this one:

> Mix a pancake,
> Stir a pancake,
> Pop it in the pan;
> Fry the pancake,
> Toss the pancake,—
> Catch it if you can.

This book is still a good choice for little children. Christina Rossetti was a devout Anglican who cited the King James Bible as her main source of poetic inspiration. Some critics consider her the finest female poet that England ever produced. The following lines are often quoted today, even by people who have never heard of Rossetti:

> What can I give Him,
>   Poor as I am?
> If I were a shepherd

I would give Him a lamb,
If I were a Wise Man
    I would do my part,—
But what I can I give Him,
    Give my heart.

It seems as if Rossetti's poem that begins "Minnie and Mattie / And fat little May, / Out in the country, / Spending a day" must have been the inspiration for the magnificent children's poem that e. e. cummings wrote in the mid-1950s, which begins:

maggie and milly and molly and may
went down to the beach (to play one day).

If so, we have even more to thank her for.

Shortly after Rossetti's *Sing Song*, Robert Louis Stevenson brought out what is probably the most famous poetry book for children, *A Child's Garden of Verses*. It came out in 1885 under the title *Penny Whistles*. Stevenson wrote to a friend, "I have now published, on 101 small pages, THE COMPLETE PROOF OF MR. R. L. STEVENSON'S INCAPACITY TO WRITE VERSES."

Instead he has been informally called "the poet laureate of childhood" because of this book. Verses such as "My Shadow" remain a favorite part of many adults' childhood:

I have a little shadow that goes in and out with
    me,
And what can be the use of him is more than I
    can see.
He is very, very like me from the heels up to
    the head;
And I see him jump before me, when I jump
    into my bed.

Stevenson began these verses when he was about thirty, while he was writing *Treasure Island*. He went on writing them for four years, through serious illness. Ten years after he finished them, he died of a stroke.

The next overwhelmingly popular book of poems for children came almost forty years later: *When We Were Very Young* by A. A. Milne, who also wrote *Winnie-the-Pooh*. Milne had published a little magazine verse about his son Christopher Robin, and he was urged to write more of them. After he refused, he wondered what the verses would have been like if he had agreed. So he wrote them to find out. The whimsical book was published in 1924. In 1927 he followed it with *Now We Are Six*. Both books have been reprinted hundreds of times in England and the United States.

In his autobiography Milne said,

> *When We Were Very Young* is not the work of a poet becoming playful, nor of a lover of children expressing his love, nor of a prose-writer knocking together a few jingles for the little ones; it is the work of a light-verse writer taking his job seriously even though he is taking it into the nursery. It seems that the nursery, more than any other room in the house, likes to be approached seriously.

Walter de la Mare agreed: "I know well that only the rarest kind of best in anything can be good enough for the young." His largest collection of poems for children was published in 1944—*Rhymes and Verses: Collected Poems for Children*. Some readers favor that one, and others favor an early one called *Peacock Pie* (1913). De la Mare was not only a superb verse writer like Milne, but a major poet of the twentieth century, and the only one who concentrated on children's poetry. His work is melodious, finely crafted, and often humorous.

Most people would probably name T. S. Eliot as the most prominent English poet of the twentieth century and one of the most difficult to comprehend. Relatively few people realized that he wrote a single book of children's poetry until it recently became a musical. Eliot had the nickname "Old Possum." He called his book for children *Old Possum's Book of Practical Cats* (1939). It is a zany but dignified collection of stories about cats Eliot claims to have known. All cat and light-verse lovers are happier for meeting them in this book. And children love to hear the preposterous accounts read aloud.

Eliot was an American who moved to England and became British. Two of his contemporaries who stayed in the States never wrote books for children but did make selections of their poems available to children late in their careers. These are *You Come Too* (1959) by Robert Frost and *Wind Song* (1960) by Carl Sandburg.

One of the most outstanding twentieth-century American poets for children was David McCord, who began his career with children in 1952 with his fifteenth book of verses, *Far and Few: Rhymes of the Never Was and Always Is*. David McCord was not a major poet like Eliot and Frost, but he had a superb ability to communicate the pleasures of poetry and the fascination of words. He had a marvelously lively mind, and his contribution to children's literature won him the first national award for excellence from the National Council of English Teachers.

Parents who read poetry themselves will occasionally discover in their own books wonderful poems for their children, such as the poems "anyone lived in a pretty how town" by e. e. cummings, "A Child's Christmas in Wales" by Dylan Thomas, "The Congo" by Vachel Lindsay, and "Narnian Suite" by C. S. Lewis. These four all demand to be read aloud.

Contemporary Poetry for Children

There are hundreds of good books of contemporary poetry for children available in libraries. One way to identify a family's favorite poets is to sample many of them
in an anthology.

A Few of the Best Anthologies

- Arbuthnot, May Hill, ed., *Time for Poetry* (1961)
- Bedrick, Peter, ed., *The Book of a Thousand Poems* (1986)
- Daniel, Mark, comp., *A Child's Treasury of Poems* (1986)
- De Regniers, Beatrice Shenk, et al., *Sing a Song of Popcorn: Every Child's Book of Poems* (Reissue 1988)
- Hall, Donald, ed., *The Oxford Book of Children's Verse in America* (1985)
- Kennedy, X. J., and Dorothy Kennedy, eds., *Talking Like the Rain: A Read-To-Me Book of Poems* (1992)
- Payson, Dale, comp., *The Sleepy-Time Treasury* (1975)
- Prelutsky, Jack, ed., *The Random House Book of Poetry for Children* (1983)
- Untermeyer, Louis, comp., *The Golden Treasury of Poetry* (1959)
- Whipple, Laura, ed., *Celebrating America: A Collection of Poems and Images of the American Spirit* (1994)

For a truly unusual insight into poetry-making, read *The
Bat-Poet* (1963) by Randall Jarrell and illustrated by
Maurice Sendak. It is the story of one little brown bat
who is stirred by what he sees and hears and then creates
evocative poems. "The trouble isn't making poems, the
trouble's finding somebody that will listen to them," the
little bat observes. He finds somebody. The story is wise,
whimsical, sweet, and grave.

More Than Twenty Favorite Poets and Poetry Collections

📖 Alderson, Brian, comp. and illus., *Cake and Custard* (1975)

📖 Brown, Margaret Wise, *Under the Sun and Moon and Other Poems* (1993)

📖 Cassedy, Sylvia, and Kunihiro Suetake, *Red Dragonfly on My Shoulder* (1992)

📖 de Gasztold, Carmen Bernos, *Prayers from the Ark and The Creatures Choir* (1976)

📖 de Paola, Tomie, illus., *Tomie de Paola's Book of Poems* (1976)

📖 Eliot, T. S., *Old Possum's Book of Practical Cats* (1982) illustrated by Edward Gorey; *Growltiger's Last Stand* (1987) and *Mr. Mistoffelees with Mungojerrie and Rumpleteazer* (1997), both illustrated by Errol Le Cain.

📖 Farjeon, Eleanor, *Poems for Children* (1951); *Prayer for Little Things* (1945)

📖 Field, Eugene, *The Shut-Eye Train and Other Poems of Childhood* (1991)

📖 Fleischman, Paul, *Joyful Noise: Poems for Two Voices* (1988, Newbery Winner)

📖 Frost, Robert, *Stopping by Woods on a Snowy Evening*, illustrated by Susan Jeffers (1978)

📖 Grimes, Nikki, *Come Sunday* (1996)

📖 Hopkins, Lee Bennett, comp., *Side by Side: Poems to Read Together* (1991)

📖 Hughes, Langston, *The Dream Keeper and Other Poems* (1994); *The Sweet and Sour Animal Book* (1994)

📖 Hughes, Ted, *Poetry Is* (1970)

📖 Kuskin, Karla, *Near the Window Tree* (1975)

📖 Larrick, Nancy, comp., *When the Dark Comes Dancing: A Bedtime Poetry Book* (1983); *Tambourines! Tambourines to Glory!* (1982)

📖 Livingston, Myra Cohn, *Whispers and Other Poems* (1958); *O Frabjous Day! Poetry for Holidays and Special Occasions* (1977)

📖 McCord, David, *One at a Time: Collected Poems for the Young* (1980)

📖 Merriam, Eve, *Blackberry Ink* (1985); *A Sky Full of Poems* (1986)

📖 Myers, Walter Dean, *Brown Angels: An Album of Pictures and Verse* (1993)

📖 Nye, Naomi S., ed., *This Same Sky* (1992)

📖 O'Neill, Mary, *Hailstones and Halibut Bones: Adventures in Color* (1961)

📖 Prelutsky, Jack, ed., *The Beauty of the Beast: Poems from the Animal Kingdom* (1997)

📖 Rosenberg, L., *Invisible Ladder* (1996)

📖 Sandburg, Carl, *Rainbows Are Made* (1982)

📖 Viorst, Judith, *If I Were in Charge of the World and Other Worries: Poems for Children and Their Parents* (1982)

📖 Willard, Nancy, *A Visit to William Blake's Inn: Poems for Innocent and Experienced Travelers* (1981, Newbery Winner); *The Voyage of the Ludgate Hill: Travels with Robert Louis Stevenson* (1987)

📖 Yolen, Jane, *O Jerusalem: Voices of a Sacred City* (1996); *Bird Watch* (1990)

Nonsense Books

Poetry, even when it is grave, is a kind of word play. Jokes are word play, too, and poetry, jokes, and riddles are related. Some poems are riddles, and some jokes are almost poems. They can be very sophisticated or simple enough for children. Or both. And nonsense is one of the joke forms most often written for children.

One of the earliest nonsense verses printed for children is the following nursery rhyme from *Tommy Thumb's Pretty Song Book* (1744):

Three children sliding on the Ice
  Upon a Summer's Day,
It happened that they all fell in,
  The others ran away.

Oh! had those Children been at School,
  Or sliding on dry Ground,
Ten Thousand Pounds to one Penny,
  They had not then been drown'd.

Ye Parents who have children dear,
  And eke ye that have none,
If you would keep them safe abroad,
  Pray keep them all at home.

The first great hero of nonsense in England was Edward
Lear, who was born in 1812 into a large family. Edward
was a pale, sickly child with twenty sisters and brothers.
His sister Ann, who was twenty-one when he was born,
took it upon herself to care for him from babyhood on.
When Lear was thirteen, their father was thrown into
debtors' prison, and suddenly the family was destitute.
Most of the children died in childhood or early youth,
but Edward survived. However, he always suffered from
a mild form of epilepsy, which he called "Terrible De-
mon." He learned to support himself by drawing plants,
birds, and animals in detail, and he was hired by the
Earl of Derby to live at his country estate and draw the
Earl's collection.

The stifling atmosphere in this aristocratic society
made Lear want to act silly. He did not, of course, act
that way, but he enjoyed the friendship of the Earl's little
grandchildren and started to write limericks that he illustrated with very silly sketches. Lear published his *Book
of Nonsense* in 1846 and *Nonsense Songs and Stories* in

1871. Reinhold Niebuhr said in one of his sermons that we preserve our sanity by laughing at life's surface absurdities. The Christian writer G. K. Chesterton went farther and said that nonsense is a way of looking at existence that is akin to religious humility and wonder.

The greatest master of nonsense of all time was Lear's contemporary Lewis Carroll, author of *Alice's Adventures in Wonderland* (1865). The nonsense in Alice is far less random and pointless than it seems to contemporary readers. (Some of it can be comprehended only by mathematicians!)

English children in Carroll's day all realized that when the Mad Hatter sang, "Twinkle, twinkle, little bat! / How I wonder where you're at!" it was a burlesque on Jane Taylor's five-stanza poem "The Star" from her prim and proper book *Original Poems for Infant Minds*. "The bat" probably referred to Carroll's—(Dodgson's)—fellow professor with that nickname, someone whose math lectures were often incomprehensible to students. Of course, children did not know that.

Earlier in her adventure Alice tried to recite the best-known poem in her day from Isaac Watts's *Divine Songs for Children*. It was titled "Against Idleness and Mischief":

> How doth the little busy bee
> > Improve each shining hour,
> And gather honey all the day
> From every open flower!
>
> How skillfully she builds her cell!
> > How neat she spreads the wax!
> And labours hard to store it well
> > With the sweet food she makes.

Her voice came out hoarse and strange, but less strange than the words:

How doth the little crocodile
    Improve his shining tail,
And pour the waters of the Nile
    On every golden scale!

How cheerfully he seems to grin,
    How neatly spreads his claws,
And welcomes little fishes in,
    With gently smiling jaws!

Here the safe and pious Watts poem turned into a bit of chilling savagery. Children loved the switch.

For a much broader sample of Carroll's nonsense for children, turn to *The Book of Nonsense* edited by Roger Lancelyn Green. It includes some of Carroll's letters to one of George MacDonald's daughters, and other assorted nonsense from A.D. 50 to the present.

The first children's book to hit the top of the *New York Times* bestseller list was Shel Silverstein's *A Light in the Attic* (1981). It stayed there for months, selling over a million copies in hardback. It is a collection of preposterous verses and drawings, full of funny words and freaks and horrors, wry and outrageous. And outrageously popular. To borrow Silverstein's own style:

This is a laugh-and-screamish,
Moonie-beamish, sour creamish,
Winning-teamish, stop-and-look,
Extra-squeamish kind of book.

Another best-selling creator of nonsense is Jack Prelutsky. The *Chicago Tribune* credited him with doing "almost as much as anyone to develop a living, breathing, under-twelve poetry audience." *Horn Book* described his poems as "jaunty, usually funny, often silly, sometimes gross and always childlike." Over the past thirty years, Prelutsky has given young readers more than forty books. The enthusiastic response to his *New Kid on the Block* (1984), *Something Big Has Been Here* (1990), and *The Dragons Are Singing Tonight* (1993) has prompted references to the "Rhymin' 90s."

Prelutsky, a failed illustrator who accidentally discovered his talent for verse, believes he is carrying on in the tradition of Lear, Carroll, and Hilaire Belloc. He says that writing humorous verse is hard work because every part of the poem must be exactly right for it to be funny. His favorite techniques are asking serious questions about a silly idea, finding something extraordinary in the ordinary, focusing on incongruities, exaggerating an idea until it reaches an absurd conclusion, and creating surprise endings. In addition to writing poetry, Prelutsky is an accomplished compiler of anthologies.

When Random House decided to develop Dr. Seuss's last manuscript idea, it sought the help of Prelutsky and illustrator Lane Smith. The book that resulted, *Hooray for Diffendoofer Day* (1997), has sold well, but some critics fault it for being too self-conscious. Somehow it lacks the gentle magic that was Seuss.

Parents and teachers who are tempted to avoid nonsense verse and silly rhymes in favor of more serious poetry are in danger of doing children a disservice. The foolishness of rhymes such as "Simple Simon" can help young children gain confidence about their own mental abilities and their grasp of reality. Light verse, tongue twisters, and jokes contribute to children's growing ability to see the humorous side of things—a skill they will need for life.

Over Twenty Rib-Tickling Books

📖 Belloc, Hilaire, *The Bad Child's Book of Beasts* (1896)
📖 Bodecker, N. M., *Hurry, Hurry, Mary Dear! and Other Nonsense Poems* (1976); *Let's Marry, Said the Cherry,*

and Other Nonsense Poems (1974)

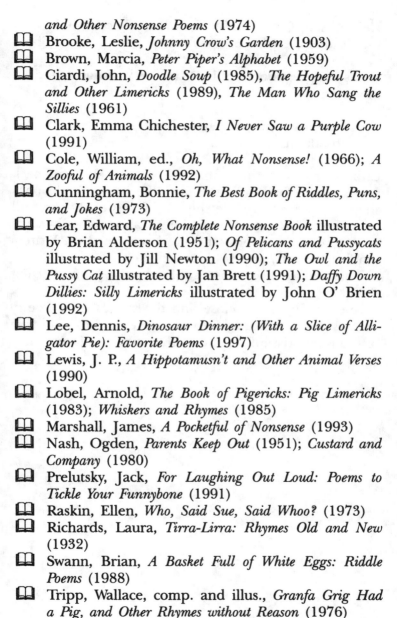

Brooke, Leslie, *Johnny Crow's Garden* (1903)

Brown, Marcia, *Peter Piper's Alphabet* (1959)

Ciardi, John, *Doodle Soup* (1985), *The Hopeful Trout and Other Limericks* (1989), *The Man Who Sang the Sillies* (1961)

Clark, Emma Chichester, *I Never Saw a Purple Cow* (1991)

Cole, William, ed., *Oh, What Nonsense!* (1966); *A Zooful of Animals* (1992)

Cunningham, Bonnie, *The Best Book of Riddles, Puns, and Jokes* (1973)

Lear, Edward, *The Complete Nonsense Book* illustrated by Brian Alderson (1951); *Of Pelicans and Pussycats* illustrated by Jill Newton (1990); *The Owl and the Pussy Cat* illustrated by Jan Brett (1991); *Daffy Down Dillies: Silly Limericks* illustrated by John O' Brien (1992)

Lee, Dennis, *Dinosaur Dinner: (With a Slice of Alligator Pie): Favorite Poems* (1997)

Lewis, J. P., *A Hippotamusn't and Other Animal Verses* (1990)

Lobel, Arnold, *The Book of Pigericks: Pig Limericks* (1983); *Whiskers and Rhymes* (1985)

Marshall, James, *A Pocketful of Nonsense* (1993)

Nash, Ogden, *Parents Keep Out* (1951); *Custard and Company* (1980)

Prelutsky, Jack, *For Laughing Out Loud: Poems to Tickle Your Funnybone* (1991)

Raskin, Ellen, *Who, Said Sue, Said Whoo?* (1973)

Richards, Laura, *Tirra-Lirra: Rhymes Old and New* (1932)

Swann, Brian, *A Basket Full of White Eggs: Riddle Poems* (1988)

Tripp, Wallace, comp. and illus., *Granfa Grig Had a Pig, and Other Rhymes without Reason* (1976)

📖 Watson, Clyde, *Father Fox's Pennyrhymes* (1971)
📖 Withers, Carl, *I Saw a Rocket Walk a Mile* (1966)

It was the great poet Emily Dickinson who gave children the lines:

> There is no frigate like a book
> To take us lands away.

Children's books sail across the oceans and sail back again. First of all, writers shape the books, and books shape the writers. People ship and transport books, and books are ships. We carry the books, and the books carry us. We read the books, and the books read us. Writers mold the books, and books mold the writers.

That sounds like nonsense. But it is a kind of living rhyme.

And so the circles close and the spirals turn. Poetry merges through fantasy into nonsense, and the flip side of nonsense is information—the subject of our next chapter.

11 Open Minds

Curiosity in children is but an appetite for knowledge. One great reason why children abandon themselves wholly to silly pursuits and trifle their time away insipidly is because they find their curiosity balked, and their inquiries neglected.

—John Locke (1632–1704)

During the 1950s a Pittsburgh girl named Annie visited the library and discovered *The Field Book of Ponds and Streams*. In it she read about a mysterious world where the fields teemed with animals and insects, a world where a curious child might find salamander larvae, tadpoles, and turtles she could carry home in a wooden bucket.

Annie wanted to write and ask the author where she, a fifth-grade student, might find a pond or stream. But she was afraid of the disappointment her ignorance might cause. So she just kept reading. Most of the books in the children's room were too vague and sentimental for her taste. Annie turned to adult books for "the true dope." What would it have been like to live in Pittsburgh when Native American children played along the banks of the rivers, when "there were no roads at all. / And the trees were very tall"? What strange places and hidden forces had created the specimens in her rock collection? How did artists depict things from real life?

"I was reading books on drawing, painting, rocks,

criminology, birds, moths, beetles, stamps, ponds and streams, medicine," Annie recalls in *An American Childhood:*

> Everywhere, things snagged me. The visible world turned me curious to books; the books propelled me reeling back to the world. . . . I opened books like jars. Here between my hands, here between some book's front and back covers, whose corners poked dents in my palm, was another map to the neighborhood I had explored all my life, and fancied I knew, a map depicting hitherto invisible landmarks. After I learned to see those, I looked around for something else. I never knew where my next revelation was coming from, but I knew it was coming—some hairpin curve, some stray bit of romance or information that would turn my life around in a twinkling.

After Annie Dillard grew up she moved to the Pacific Northwest in search of ponds and streams. And from her experiences she wrote *Pilgrim at Tinker Creek.* One of the most brilliant, disturbing, and wondrous books about nature ever written, it won the 1975 Pulitzer Prize. And it all began with her need to know about the real world.

Like Annie, today's children wonder what makes things tick. But unlike Annie, they do not have to head for the adult library collection to find answers. Today some of the best books written for children are nonfiction. Many smart adults like to use information books written for children because they are clear, direct, and beautiful.

With a wealth of children's information-filled books available and more being published each year, how can we help children find just the right book for the questions they are asking? One helpful guide is *Eyeopeners!* by Beverly Kobrin. In this substantial reference book, parents, grandparents, and other educators will find out how to fuel curiosity, how to judge a book's content and appeal, how to link facts and fiction, and how to enjoy reading-related activities. Kobrin, a California elementary-school teacher, discovered early in her career that reliance on textbooks and workbooks spelled classroom boredom. She began to gather nonfiction books on the subjects that interested her students. Their responsiveness quickly convinced her that nonfiction books supplied the information they wanted and sparked their desire to learn more.

After several years of teaching with nonfiction trade books, Kobrin was ready to compile her guide to over five hundred books. Her "Quick-Link Index" makes it easy to locate books on specific subjects. In addition to writing *Eyeopeners!* (1988), she publishes *The Kobrin Letter,* a newsletter devoted to helping parents and teachers choose and use children's books about real people, places, and things.

Kobrin's method of teaching with trade paperback books was part of an educational philosophy commonly known as "the whole language approach." Beginning in California and then spreading across the nation, schools provided students with picture books, fiction, and non-fiction instead of textbook anthologies. This trend was a great boon to children's book publishing and also made families more aware of children's literature. Unfortunately, a polarization occurred between whole-language advocates and supporters of phonics-based reading programs. In the late 1990s, in response to political and parental pressure, schools began to move back to more methodical textbook/workbook instruction. This trend, along with financial cutbacks to schools and libraries, has resulted in cutbacks by most children's book publishers. However, other innovative educational approaches are helping to keep the children's book market healthy. These include home-schooling, classical schools, and Core Knowledge schools.

Books to Build On: A Grade-by-Grade Resource Guide for Parents and Teachers (1996), edited by John Holdren and E. D. Hirsch Jr., is designed to complement the popular Core Knowledge Series *(What Your Kindergartner–Sixth Grader Needs to Know)*. It lists and briefly annotates hundreds of books about history, geography, literature, language, science, math, and the fine arts. Unlike Kobrin's work, *Books to Build On* includes fiction, nonfiction, and poetry. The emphasis, however, is on nonfiction. The book recommendations came from teachers and librarians in Core Knowledge schools, where educators and students adhere to a grade-by-grade model of specific content guidelines in every subject area. While the Core Knowledge approach to education remains highly controversial, *Books to Build On* deserves a round of applause for helping parents and teachers navigate in the ocean of information.

A more extensive bibliography of nonfiction books for children is *The New Book of Knowledge Home and School Reading and Study Guides*. Published annually, it lists more than five thousand books dealing with hundreds of topics addressed in *The New Book of Knowledge,* a popular home encyclopedia set. Guidelines for book selection were established in part by Nancy Larrick, an authority on children's literature. The book lists are not annotated, but they are grouped under fairly specific headings and described as primary (through fourth grade), intermediate (grade five through eight), or advanced (grade nine and up).

While these and other reading guides will prove helpful in homes and schools, the best guide is a child's sense of wonder. Children need the freedom to, in Jim Trelease's words, "roam and graze, encouraged but not regimented, surrounded by magazines, newspapers, and books, nurtured by parents who [are] readers." In his glowing introduction to *Eyeopeners,* Trelease continues, "Children are naturally curious about everything. Give them access to good nonfiction books, books with hearts by people with voices, and they'll read them up ravenously. And the more they read, the more they'll know."

But what about the hearts and voices of those who write children's books? It would be naive to assume that everyone in this field has the best interests of children as their primary objective. Even when they think they hold to such an objective, personal beliefs and hidden agendas can be at work. That is why children and parents need to read broadly and deeply, as well as make book discussion a habit. Such steps can give greater promise that the gold will gradually emerge from the dross and critical reading and thinking skills will develop.

In the classic *Children and Books,* May Hill Arbuthnot offers some timeless guidelines for choosing informational books:

1. Accuracy. Is there evidence of substantive research on the part of the author and illustrator?

2. Convenient presentation. How easy is it to locate information within the book?

3. Adequate treatment. Is there enough information to provide answers for a child's questions without drowning him in the subject's complexities? Are facts presented in a clear, straightforward manner? Are various viewpoints on the subject fairly represented?

4. Is the style of writing lively and engaging?

5. Are the facts well-illustrated with drawings, photographs, maps, and charts?

One of the most exciting trends in the world of nonfiction is the enhanced visual appeal of informational books. In past generations, books of facts were usually deadly dull in appearance. Now they shout from their shelves to passersby, "Look at me! Read me!" These days the full-color illustrations and dazzling design elements once restricted to picture books are just as apt to be found in instructional books about Egypt, dinosaurs, castles, snakes, and a thousand other intriguing subjects. Faced with stiff competition from electronic media and magazines, book publishers feel compelled to make their presentations as enticing as possible. Children are the beneficiaries.

Here is a small sampling from the best recent releases in the field of juvenile nonfiction.

Adkins, Jan, *Toolchest* (1973)
Aliki, *A Medieval Feast* (1983), *Corn Is Maize: The Gift of the Indians* (1976), *Mummies Made in Egypt* (1985)
Anno, Mitsumasa, *Anno's Math Games* (1997)—three volumes
Arnosky, Jim, *Drawing from Nature* (1982), *Watching Foxes* (1985), *Watching Water Birds* (1997)
Bash, Barbara, *Desert Giant: The World of the Saguaro Cactus* (1989)
Biesty, Stephen, *Incredible Cross-Sections* (1991)
Björk, Christina, *Linnea's Garden* (1987), *Linnea's Almanac* (1989)
Borland, Hal, *The Golden Circle* (1977)—a beautiful book about the changing seasons
Brandenburg, Jim, *To the Top of the World: Adventures with Arctic Wolves* (1993)
Cherry, Lynne, *A River Ran Wild: An Environmental History* (1992)
Cole, Joanna, *A Chick Hatches* (1976), *A Frog's Body* (1980), The Magic School Bus series, especially *The*

Magic School Bus Inside the Human Body (1989)—A happy marriage of fiction and non-fiction, Cole's Magic School Bus series features an oddball teacher named Ms. Frizzle. Her field trips through the waterworks, inside the earth, to the eye of a hurricane, and over the rainbow provide children with entertainment and education. K–Grade 3

Freedman, Russell, *Dinosaurs and Their Young* (1983), *Sharks* (1985), *Children of the Wild West* (1983)—A brilliant photojournalist, Freedman is best known for his biographies, but he also deserves recognition in other nonfiction areas.

Giblin, James Cross, *From Hand to Mouth: How We Invented Knives, Forks, Spoons, and Chopsticks* (1987), *The Truth about Unicorns* (1996)

Greenaway, Theresa, *Jungle* (1994)—part of the outstanding Eyewitness Books series

Greenwood, Barbara, *A Pioneer Sampler: The Daily Life of a Pioneer Family in 1840* (1994)

Hamilton, Virginia, *Many Thousand Gone: African Americans from Slavery to Freedom* (1993)

Hill, Emily, *Visual Dictionary of Ancient Civilizations* (1994)—one of several Eyewitness illustrated dictionaries

Janson, H. W., *History of Art for Young People* (5th edition, 1997)—An excellent introduction to Western art. Grade 6 and up.

Jones, Charlotte Foltz, *Mistakes That Worked* (1991)—an entertaining book about discoveries and inventions, including Silly Putty, Coca-Cola, and Post-It Notes

Krementz, Jill, *A Very Young Dancer* (1976), *A Very Young Rider* (1977), *A Very Young Circus Flyer* (1979), *A Very Young Musician* (1991), and others

Kroll, Steven, *Story of the Star-Spangled Banner* (1994)

Kurelek, William, and Margaret S. Englehart, *They Sought a New World: The Story of European Immigration to North America* (1985)

Lauber, Patricia, *Tales Mummies Tell* (1985), *Volcano: The Eruption and Healing of Mount St. Helens* (1986), *Summer of Fire: Yellowstone 1988* (1991)

Levitt, Paul, *The Weighty Word Book* (1988)

Loverance, Rowena, *Ancient Greece* (1993) and others in the See Through History series

Macaulay, David, *Cathedral: The Story of Its Construction* (1973), *City: A Story of Roman Planning and Construction* (1975), *Underground* (1976), *Castle* (1977), *Unbuilding* (1980), *Mill* (1983), *The Way Things Work* (1988), *Ship* (1993), *Pyramid* (1975)

Marshall, Ken, *Inside the Titanic* (1997)—part of Little Brown's Giant Cutaway series

Murphy, Jim, *Across America on an Emigrant Train* (1993), *The Great Fire* (1995)—story of the 1871 Chicago fire

Oard, Michael, *The Weather Book* (1996)—part of the Wonders of Creation series written from a Christian perspective and published by Master Books

Orr, Richard, and Moira Butterfield, *Nature Cross-Sections* (1995)

Parker, Steve, *Eyewitness Guide to the Natural World* (1994), *Whales and Dolphins* (1994)

Perl, Lila, *It Happened in America: True Stories from the Fifty States* (1993)

Pringle, Laurence, *Coral Reefs* (1995), *Animal Monsters: The Truth about Scary Creatures* (1997), *An Extraordinary Life: The Story of a Monarch Butterfly* (1997)

Richards, Lawrence O., *It Couldn't Just Happen: Fascinating Facts about God's World* (1994)—winner of the Gold Medallion Book Award

Romanova, Natalia, *Once There Was a Tree* (1989)

Sandler, Martin W., *The Story of American Photography: An Illustrated History for Young People* (1979)

Scholastic's *Musical Instruments* (1994)—part of the excellent Voyages of Discovery series

Schwartz, David M., *How Much Is a Million?* (1985)

Silver, Donald M., *One Small Square: Pond* (1994)—one in a series of books that explore "one small square" in the world of nature

Simon, Seymour, *Science in a Vacant Lot* (1970), *Autumn Across America* (1993), *Science Dictionary* (1994), *Earth Words: A Dictionary of the Environment* (1995), *Storms* (1989)

Spier, Peter, *We the People: The Constitution of the United States of America* (1987), *The Star-Spangled Banner* (1986)

Stanley, Jerry, *Children of the Dust Bowl: The True Story of the School at Weedpatch Camp* (1991)

Swinburne, Irene, and Laurence Swinburne, *Behind the Sealed Door: The Discovery of the Tomb and Treasures of the Tutankhamun* (1977)

Taylor, Charles, and Stephen Pople, *The Oxford Children's Book of Science* (1996)

Tunis, Edwin, *Chipmunks on the Doorstep* (1971), *The Tavern at the Ferry* (1973), *Frontier Living* (1976), *Colonial Living* (1976), *Oars, Sails, and Streams: A Picture Book of Ships* (1977), *The Young United States* (1976)

White, Ron, *How Computers Work* (1994)

Wick, Walter, *A Drop of Water: A Book of Science and Wonder* (1997)

Wolf, Bernard, *Anna's Silent World* (1977), *Connie's New Eyes* (1978)

Wroble, Lisa A., Kids Throughout History series—portrays life in Ancient Greece, the Middle Ages, the Renaissance, Colonial Times, and Pioneer Times

Books of unusual and amusing facts are gobbled up, even by immature readers. *The Guinness Book of World Records* fascinates most children sooner or later, and gifted children can get immense pleasure out of browsing in a good dictionary or encyclopedia.

Some older books of information have retained their

appeal through the years. V. M. Hillyer's *A Child's History of the World* (1924) and *A Child's Geography of the World* (1929) are quaint and engaging overviews that have been updated. They painlessly teach much to children that average high school graduates do not know.

Magazines

For information on a wide array of topics, magazines are one of the best and most engaging sources. Children who see their parents reading magazines will welcome having some of their own to enjoy. Once upon a time, the magazine choices for children were quite limited, but today there are dozens of magazines aimed at specific age groups and interests. The only problem for families is that children's magazines are not always easy to find. Most libraries subscribe to only a few magazines, and due to their lack of durability they have a relatively short shelf-life. Some large children's bookstores carry a nice assortment of magazines for browsing. But the most satisfactory way to discover which magazines parents and children will enjoy is to purchase single sample copies from the publisher. (Information on how to contact the publishers is given in appendix 4.) Some large city bookstores offer a generous selection of children's magazines for sampling.

Even the youngest "readers" can have magazines like mommy and daddy. *Babybug* (Carus Publishing Company) is a board-book magazine published every six weeks. It is designed to provide infants, toddlers, and parents with stories and poems that are fun to read aloud. For the two- to six-year-old group, the same publisher offers *Ladybug*. It features activities based on concepts such as size, color, comparison, and sequencing. These include fingerplays, action rhymes, and rebuses.

Thanks to television, most preschool children will

eagerly reach for *Sesame Street Magazine.* The lovable Muppets teach basic concepts in its pages. Six- to ten-year-olds move over to *The Electric Company,* a fun mix of learning, activities, and entertainment.

The most beloved magazine in the United States today is *Ranger Rick's Nature Magazine* (National Wildlife Federation), the only magazine to have won both the EdPress and the Golden Lamp Award (for best educational periodical). It features beautiful color photos and easy-to-read information about all kinds of animal life, conservation, the outdoors, and environmental problems. It also includes charts, maps, jokes, puzzles, projects, poems, letters, and stories. Readers from age six to twelve enjoy the playful, enthusiastic style of writing. Parents and teachers appreciate the careful research that backs up each factual article. *Your Big Backyard,* by the same publisher, is for younger readers.

Two nature magazines published in Canada have flown over the border and are now enjoyed by thousands of U.S. children. They are *Chickadee Magazine* and *Owl Magazine* (Bayard Presse Canada). In *Chickadee,* written for children ages six to nine, there is an emphasis on enjoying the outdoor world. *Owl* is for the older set, and it covers a broader range of science and nature topics. Both periodicals have wonderful photographs and are visually stimulating.

Another superb informative magazine for children is *World,* which is a little sister of *National Geographic.* Typical issues have contained lavishly illustrated articles on the details of King Tut's treasure, motocross racing, beavers and penguins, underwater music, and constellations. *World* is a winner of the Parents' Choice Golden Medal and the Golden Lamp Award for excellence in educational journalism.

Animal lovers will enjoy *Zoobooks* magazine. Each issue features a single animal through full color, glossy photographs, detailed drawings, interesting text, and activity pages.

Kids Discover presents one subject per issue and the subjects range from archaeology to earthquakes, knights and castles to the Himalayas. This magazine won the 1996 and 1997 Parents' Choice Gold Award.

Scientific thinking "with an attitude" is encouraged in *Contact Kids,* a magazine that challenges eight- to fourteen-year-olds to solve perplexing questions. Children who enjoy the Children's Television Workshop show seen on PBS will be especially attracted to this publication. Unfortunately, there are several large ads in each issue, and many of them are for candy.

Zillions, published by *Consumer Reports,* helps children understand how advertising works, how to think critically about ad claims, and how to respond intelligently to consumer enticements. This magazine won the 1993 Educational Press Golden Lamp Award.

Cobblestone and *Calliope* magazines (both by Cobblestone Publishing) have a corner on history. Both are written for children ages eight to fourteen, but *Cobblestone* deals with American history while *Calliope* covers world history. Each issue concentrates on a specific theme, so individual articles blend into an informative whole. Through essays, historical interviews, plays, biographies, recipes, photo features, poetry, activities, and puzzles, history comes alive for readers. Cobblestone Publishing offers several other magazines, including *Odyssey,* a magazine about astronomy and outer space (ages 10–16), and *Faces,* a magazine about people (ages 9–14).

Several magazines have been created specifically for use in schools. In this category the best known are *Weekly Reader* publications and *Junior Scholastic.* Since 1937 *Junior Scholastic* (Scholastic, Inc.) has brought current events, world cultures, and U.S. history into junior high/middle school classrooms. *Weekly Reader* (Xerox Education Publications) is a group of eight classroom newspapers that present current events in a grade-appropriate way. Fun as well as informative, these magazines are reasonably priced for subscription by groups of ten at the same address. *U.S. Kids* is another educational magazine about "kids doing extraordinary things, especially activities related to health, sports, the arts, interesting hobbies, the environment, and computers."

A classic contender in the risky world of juvenile periodicals is *Highlights for Children*. It has been entertaining children since 1946, and its circulation is upwards of 3 million. This general interest publication contains fiction, nonfiction, puzzles, fingerplays, and crafts for children from two to twelve. Many children's book authors first published their work in *Highlights*.

Another enduring favorite is *Jack and Jill* (Children's Better Health Institute), which has been around long enough for today's grandparents to remember enjoying it as children. Its target audience is boys and girls from seven to ten. Many of the articles and stories center on safety, exercise, and nutrition themes. *Jack and Jill* encourages its young readers to be smart and capable without being sarcastic or smug. *Children's Playmate* (for children ages six through eight), *Children's Digest* (for preteens), *Child Life* (for children ages 9-11), and *Humpty Dumpty* (for children ages four through six), and *Turtle* (for children ages three through five) are all part of the same health-oriented magazine family.

Stone Soup is a bi-monthly collection of fiction, poetry, book reviews, and art created by children (through age thirteen) for children. This magazine started in 1973 and is well-respected among educators.

Puffin Post (The Puffin Club, Penguin Books, Ltd.) is a British magazine designed to give children information about some of the authors they enjoy.

Cricket (Carus Publishing Company) includes poetry,

nonsense, information, and fiction, new and old. Established in 1973, this magazine is a high-quality general interest publication for older children. Its sister magazine, by the same publisher, is *Spider*, published for six- to nine-year-old children. Parents looking for literary and artistic excellence will be pleased with these two periodicals created by Open Court Publishing, a leader in reading programs.

Crayola Kids Magazine started in 1994 and quickly surpassed many of its competitors in circulation. Each issue of this attractive publication includes a complete children's trade paperback along with related crafts, puzzles, and activities.

American Girl is a bimonthly magazine for girls ages eight through twelve. Its popularity is derived largely from that of the American Girl book series and dolls. The magazine states that its mission is "to celebrate girls yesterday and today." A light, pleasant mix of articles, stories, profiles of female heroines, and activities fills each bimonthly issue.

For entertainment-oriented children, there is *Disney Adventures*. In less than ten years its circulation has almost reached the one million mark. Articles and stories often have adventure, science, or sports themes. Do not expect much in the way of educational content; this one is just for fun.

Since 1989 Time-Warner has published *Sports Illustrated for Kids*. Its content is divided in half between sports as played by kids and sports as played by professionals. How-to articles, interviews, and celebrity profiles, inspirational pieces, games, and puzzles fill its pages.

Moving from body to soul, there are several excellent Christian magazines now published for children and teens. Most denominations have Sunday school take-home papers. These are too numerous to mention. Instead here are a few non-denominational, general interest periodicals available by subscription.

Guideposts for Kids describes itself as a value-centered, fun to read kids' magazine for seven- to twelve-year-olds. Articles and stories are not preachy or overtly religious. Instead they address tough themes and current issues from a child's viewpoint, encouraging young readers to make positive choices. There is also a *Guideposts for Teens*.

Focus on the Family publishes four magazines for young people. *Clubhouse* is for children ages eight through twelve and has won numerous awards in Christian publishing. Its little brother is *Clubhouse Junior* for children ages four through eight. Both magazines favor fiction over nonfiction and also include games, party ideas, humor, and puzzles. In the teen category, Focus publishes *Brio* and *Breakaway*. According to *Breakaway*'s editor, "The fourteen-year-old, unchurched teen in the public school is our target," but the magazine is enjoyed by boys from eleven to eighteen attending private and home schools. *Brio* targets teen girls twelve to sixteen years old. Both magazines have a breezy, conversational style and take their cues from popular topics featured in secular magazines for this age group.

One of the finest magazines for Christian homes is *Pockets*. Its primary concern is the spiritual formation of children from six to twelve years of age. Each issue features a theme which is presented through interview articles, retold Scripture stories, personal experiences, and fiction. *Pockets* also publishes poetry, prayers, and family communication activities.

With so many quality reading materials from which to choose, children of all ages and interests can have wonderful adventures in the world of information and ideas. These reading experiences will become more meaningful when shared with an interested grownup. As the great science writer Rachel Carson said, "If a child is to keep alive his inborn sense of wonder, he needs the companionship of at least one adult who can share it, rediscovering with him the joy, excitement and mystery of the world we live in."

Picture Books and Illustrations

12 Open Eyes

And what a book it was! . . . so beautiful that Lucy stared at it for a whole minute and forgot about reading it. The paper was crisp and smooth and a nice smell came from it; and in the margins, and round the big coloured capital letters at the beginning of each spell, there were pictures . . . And the longer she read the more wonderful and more real the pictures became.

—C. S. Lewis, *The Voyage of* "The Dawn Treader"

One of the most overworked clichés is "a picture is worth a thousand words." Taken literally, the total worth of that famous quotation itself would be 0.7 percent of a snapshot. In fact, the magnificent phrase "In the beginning God created the heavens and the earth" would be worth 1 percent of somebody's sketch of that event. It is absurd to force a false competition between words and pictures.

Common sense tells us that both words and pictures are capable of ranging from sublime to wretched. Their forms and functions are obviously different. A blind person finds pictures useless and depends upon words. A color-blind person—at least 5 percent of boys are partially color-blind—misses some of the value of colored pictures. And a person suffering from aphasia, the inability to use words, may not understand words but may value pictures highly. Most people, however, find the combination of words and pictures a double delight.

Some books have no illustrations at all, some happen to have illustrations, and others depend upon their illustrations. The latter are called picture books. Book illustration is a great art form, but the custom today is that hardly any adult books have illustrations by artists. So most book illustrators have no choice but to go into books for children.

Picture Books of the Past

The first real picture book for children was translated into English in 1659. It was called *Orbis Pictus (The Visible World)* by a monk named John Amos Comenius, and was strictly informative. A contemporary equivalent is the giant *Random House Encyclopedia,* which includes eleven thousand color pictures and is very entertaining for children to browse in, although it is a sad excuse for a reference book because its scholarship is so thin and uneven. (In the same price range, *The Columbia Encyclopedia* is a superb choice for a family reference book that includes maximum worthwhile information. But it has no room for pictures.)

Between *The Visible World* and *The Random House Encyclopedia,* technology has changed picture books and illustrations radically. Color printing—in place of hand-painted water coloring—was beginning by the time Queen Victoria took the throne in 1837 and improved greatly by 1865. The first three great color picture-book artists were Walter Crane (1845–1915), Randolph Caldecott (1846–1886), and Kate Greenaway (1846–1901)— all born just as Hans Christian Andersen's *Fairy Tales* was being translated into English.

Walter Crane produced over thirty meticulously designed books for preschoolers. A master of decoration and design, he wrote:

There is at least one great advantage in designing children's books: that the imagination is singularly free, and let loose from restraints, it finds a world of its own, which may be interpreted in a spirit of playful gravity. . . . It appears to me that there is a certain receptive impressionable quality of mind, whether young or old, which we call child-like. A fresh direct vision, a quickly stimulated imagination, a love of symbolic and typical form, with a touch of poetic suggestion, a delight in frank gay colour, and a sensitiveness to the variations of line, and contrasts of form—these are some of the characteristics of the child, whether grown up or not. Happy are they who remain children in these respects through life.

Caldecott was in some ways the best artist of the three. He is remembered for the sixteen children's books he illustrated before his untimely death at the age of forty. His illustrations had more zest, humor, and energy than those of Crane and Greenaway. He often included bits of English countryside and vivid action. It is in memory of him that Americans have named their highest award for children's illustration.

Like Caldecott, Kate Greenaway produced sixteen books, and she was the most popular of the three. She owed her phenomenal success to the fine publisher Edmund Evans, an old friend of her father. He was already the successful publisher of Crane and Caldecott when she took her first collection to him.

When Evans saw her gracefully sentimental pictures of clean, happy, decorous children dressed in beautiful old-fashioned clothes from her own imagination, he immediately accepted them and soon published twenty thousand copies of her first book, *Under the Window*. That was an extremely large printing for a book that was in no way inexpensive. But it was not large enough. Before Evans could issue a second printing, copies of the first were reselling at inflated prices.

Kate Greenaway's style was sweet and serene. She was, in fact, a kind of costume designer. Clothing manufacturers used many of her original ideas, and in the U.S. a Kate Greenaway company mass produced picture-perfect dresses for little girls. Furthermore, some of her books are still in print.

In a private letter Kate Greenaway once exclaimed, "Things *are so* beautiful and wonderful, you feel there must be another life where you see more—hear more—and know more. All of it cannot die."

She wrote insignificant poems to go with her drawings, and in one of them she said, "When I am dead and all of you stand around and look upon me, my soul flown away . . . what beauteous land may I be wandering in . . . ?" She died, unmarried and childless, in 1901, the very year that Beatrix Potter, the next of the greatest picture-book artists, surprised the world with *Peter Rabbit*. Potter's life and picture books are described in chapter 5.

Crane, Caldecott, Greenaway, and Potter were all English. The most distinguished American illustrator for children up to this time was Howard Pyle, who liked to write about and draw historical romance set in England or Europe. Three of his art pupils became excellent American children's illustrators—Jessie Wilcox Smith, Maxwell Parrish, and N. C. Wyeth, the father of America's immensely popular artist Andrew Wyeth and grandfather of contemporary artist Jamie Wyeth.

Meanwhile, Arthur Rackham (1867–1934) was pursuing his career as a children's illustrator. He illustrated the original edition of *Peter Pan in Kensington Gardens* and literally dozens of other major children's books. He was a superbly gifted artist whose merging of the real with the fantastic resulted sometimes in scenes of cozy innocence and other times in grotesquely terrifying creations. He was one of the first illustrators to take advantage of the new possibilities in color halftone printing. Rackham understood the technicalities of the new process and used his colors to create profound moodiness and mystery.

Three outstanding contemporaries of Arthur Rackham were the brothers Charles and William Heath Robinson and Edmund Dulac. Fantasy and fairy tale paintings by all four of these men are still unusually rich and elegantly beautiful.

In the 1970s a San Diego publishing company named The Green Tiger Press (now an imprint of Simon & Schuster) published cards and posters of works by these four men and other early illustrators. In their catalog they said:

> The pictures in old children's books have an enormous power. Partially it originates in their importance within our history. We, in seeing them, are made to know again that glorious moment when we first entered the kingdom of books. Secondly, the pictures are magnificent. The artists, in painting and drawing for children, were cut free of earth's bonds. The medium is a liberating one, inviting those who work within it to unleash their invention, to give shape to the dreams otherwise unrealized.
>
> Yet in spite of their significance, old children's books are continually threatened with oblivion. Books themselves are fragile objects and in the hands of the most careful child they often come to harm. They are forgotten in tree houses, under the seats of rowboats, at the roots of old trees. Hundreds of thousands have been published and many of those—stories, pictures, everything—have disap-

peared, gone with the toys, the dried flowers, the small broken shoes of their owners. The relics of childhood should be treasured and preserved. Illustrated children's books are to be enormously valued. They are keys to memory, teachers of inner history, comforters, a beginning point with a path clearly marked. It is for these reasons, and for our great delight in their beauty, that the Green Tiger resolves to rescue old illustrated children's books from oblivion; not to hide them behind glass doors and display them only to antiquarians, but to reproduce, with meticulous care, the illustrations from them.

While the work of some children's illustrators is threatened with extinction, Ernest Shepard's illustrations for Milne's *Winnie-the-Pooh* are still popping up everywhere (usually colorized to make them more appealing to consumers). A cartoonist for *Punch,* Shepard illustrated all of the Pooh books. Some of his illustrations for *The Wind in the Willows* even surpass Rackham. Most of Shepard's work was pen and ink, but when he was eighty, he produced eight full-color pictures for the Golden Anniversary Edition of this famous book. Be sure to borrow that 1959 edition from the library. His daughter Mary Shepard illustrated *Mary Poppins.*

Jean de Brunhoff was a French painter who had sons four and five years old. They told their father how much they liked the story of a little elephant that their mother had made up for them. The father began to illustrate the story for his sons and soon found himself creating a large handwritten book, *The Story of Babar.* It was published right away, in 1931, and became immensely popular in England and the United States.

Jean de Brunhoff completed five more Babar books before he died in 1937, when his son Laurent was only twelve. Laurent de Brunhoff, who lives in Paris, went on with his father's series as soon as World War II ended, adding more than twenty new titles. They sell by the millions. As critic Emma Fisher observed, Babar changed from an innovation to an institution. Recently, King Babar has been accused of racism and he has often been analyzed for his political and social ideals.

Babar is also an example of the change in physical book quality. When the original set came out in the 1930s, the average life span for books was fifty years. Today Babar books are produced much more modestly, and extra touches of quality have been gradually eliminated. Worse yet, the quality of book paper has declined so in the last twenty-five years that books published today will probably turn yellow and fall apart in less than fifty years, according to the Library of Congress experts. Books printed before 1800 are much sturdier!

This is a tremendous problem for collectors and libraries. The four elements that hasten disintegration of books (besides children) are heat, fluorescent light, dampness, and air pollution. Unless some new chemical preservation methods are eventually developed, today's children's books cannot be guaranteed for future generations.

Masters of Modern Illustration

Edward Ardizzone, first winner of the Kate Greenaway Medal, was born in Vietnam in 1900 to an Italian father who was a citizen of France. However, Ardizzone was reared in England and became thoroughly British. He won the Greenaway Medal in 1956 for his book *Tim All Alone*. He began this series of books about Tim by telling and retelling them to his own children. (He became a grandfather many times over.) Although he lacked opportunity for much art training, he became a famous watercolor artist, taught art at the Royal Academy in

London, and illustrated more than 160 books.

A lover of the Authorized Version of the Bible, Ardizzone said that when he was thirteen someone gave him a pocket edition of *Pilgrim's Progress,* illustrated with tiny engravings. The vividness of Bunyan's writing and those little engravings crystallized his own desire to become an illustrator and painter. Many years later Ardizzone got to illustrate *Pilgrim's Progress* himself. He claims that children, in his opinion, have no taste in art and will enjoy both good and bad books. "All the more reason, therefore, that we should give them the best."

A more recent winner of the Kate Greenaway Medal is Pauline Baynes, who won it for the elegant children's reference book *A Dictionary of Chivalry* in 1969. This book by Grant Uden took Baynes more than two years to complete because of the wealth of detail that is typical of her delicate accuracy. Although she has illustrated dozens and dozens of books, she is best known in the United States for her illustrations of the Narnian Chronicles.

Garth Williams is one of America's most familiar illustrators. He drew the perfect pictures for *Charlotte's Web,* Laura Ingalls Wilder's Little House books, and Carlson's Orpheline stories. For all his success and honors, he never happened to win the Caldecott Medal. That is one of life's ironies. In contrast, Robert McCloskey has won the award twice and was the first artist to do so. He won it for *Make Way for Ducklings* in 1942 and then for *Time of Wonder* in 1958.

William Steig started to create storybooks when he was sixty years old. The son of two painters, he had attended City College in New York and then spent four years in art school. As soon as he graduated in 1929 he became a cartoonist for major magazines such as *The New Yorker,* and he published a dozen cartoon books for adults. "Humor is of many kinds," he said. "Mine takes life seriously." When he finally tackled books for children in

1968, Steig won the Caldecott Medal immediately for *Sylvester and the Magic Pebble*. "It feels so darn good," he said, "like being dubbed into knighthood."

Steig's 1984 book *Yellow and Pink* can be read in five minutes and enjoyed for a lifetime. In the authors' opinion, it is the wisest, wittiest, and kindest possible response to the creation-evolution controversy. Just as Gideon Bibles are placed in hotel rooms, *Yellow and Pink* should be placed in classrooms everywhere, from kindergarten through graduate school.

Richard Scarry is a picture-book creator who does not receive much praise from critics. But his merry books are so cherished by children that they often fall apart from overuse. These "educational" books are full of droll animal-people with preposterous activities and almost endless visual detail, all in good fun.

Scarry is an American who now lives in Switzerland, but wants it understood that he is loyal to his homeland and pays his full income taxes. His first and biggest success was *Best Word Book Ever* (1963), which has sold over a million copies in the United States and was published in many other countries as well. (A somewhat abridged and less durable edition is now available as *Richard Scarry's Best Little Word Book Ever* [1997, Golden].) Scarry crams as much as he can into every page; his basic motivation is fun. He has fun, children have fun, and the parents who tape the books back together have fun.

Ezra Jack Keats won the Caldecott Medal for his first book, *The Snowy Day* (1976). His warm, simple stories about black children living in the inner city take place in a moving array of colors and textures that are sheer visual delight. His book *Skates!* was so popular in Japan that it led to the opening of a roller skating rink in Tokyo, where he was the guest of honor. Later a Japanese mother wrote to tell him that her little boy so cherished his autographed copy of the book that after he was killed in a traffic accident she placed it in his coffin. Keats took that as the highest kind of tribute.

Ironically, the most popular picture book of all is ignored in all standard reference books. It is *The Poky Little Puppy* by Janette Sebring Lowry, illustrated by Gustaf Tengrenn and published by Golden Press in 1942. It has now sold over a billion copies, which reportedly makes it the best-selling book in world history.

A Master Illustrator

There is one children's artist today who is generally hailed as the greatest—Maurice Sendak. Critic John Rowe Townsend says that Sendak is not only a fine illustrator of books that do not depend upon pictures, but he is the greatest creator of picture books since color publication evolved over a century ago.

Sendak was born in Brooklyn in 1928 to parents who had come to America before World War I from small Jewish towns outside Warsaw. The father worked in New York's garment district. His three children considered him a wonderful storyteller, elaborating on tales he had heard in his own childhood. (In 1985 Sendak published *In Grandpa's House,* some of his father's story ideas with Sendak's illustrations.)

In 1950—the year that our new surge of fantasy began—Sendak was discovered by Ursula Nordstrum, children's editor at Harper & Row. In only two years he became prominent in his chosen field with *A Hole Is to Dig.* From then on he was in great demand. Among the more than fifty books he has illustrated, the Little Bear series (written by Else Minarik) is especially loved. In 1956 Sendak published the first book he had written himself, *Kenny's Window.*

Sendak is largely self-taught. He is an ardent admirer of Randolph Caldecott. Another artist who has influenced him is the mystic William Blake (1757–1827), author of "The Lamb." Sendak says he is touched by Blake's art and poetry. One of Sendak's monsters in *Where the Wild Things Are* strongly resembles the minotaur in William Blake's illustration for Dante's *Inferno*. Sendak no doubt gave us Blake's monster intentionally. He says of *Where the Wild Things Are,* "Max is my truest and therefore my dearest creation."

In his *Nutshell Library* (1962) Sendak gives children four tiny books: *Chicken Soup with Rice, One Was Johnny, Pierre,* and *Alligators All Around.* Little ones who love the size of the Beatrix Potter books will be enchanted by this even smaller collection of stories in its own case.

In 1970 Sendak became the first American artist to receive the Hans Christian Andersen Medal, an international tribute. A former art critic for the *New York Times* claimed that Sendak is "one of the most powerful men in the United States" because he "has given shape to the fantasies of millions of children—an awful responsibility." The writer must have been assuming that the peculiar potency of Sendak's work makes a deeper and more lasting impression than the rest of the images and ideas that barrage children daily.

Sendak says,

> If I have an unusual gift, it's not that I think I draw particularly better or write particularly better than other people (I've never fooled myself about that); rather, it's that I remembered things other people don't recall—the sounds and feelings and images of particular moments in childhood. It seems my child-self is still alive and active.

New Trends in Picture Books

Picture books can be beautiful, whimsical, nostalgic,

comical, or outlandish. But since the 1950s and 1960s, illustrations have become less realistic and more silly or cartoonish. The trend away from realism is one that Chris Van Allsburg laments and has tried to change. His goal is to create pictures that convince the child of the story's believability. He is convinced that creating the illusion of reality, even in the most fantastic stories, can make reading a more compelling experience.

Van Allsburg's efforts have earned him several awards and respect as one of the foremost contemporary illustrators. In 1982 he received the Caldecott Medal for *Jumanji,* and in 1986 the honor was repeated with *The Polar Express* (1985). A master of mood and mystery, his illustrations make the most of shadows, proportions, and unusual perspectives. Their dream-like quality may disturb some children, but others will be drawn to them as if to enchanted woods.

Those who prefer quirkiness and humor over mood and mystery appreciate the illustrations and storytelling of James Marshall and James Stevenson. Their books are mentioned in other chapters, but no presentation of picture books would be complete without recognition of their tremendous talent and kid appeal.

On the picture book shelves there is definitely something for everyone. And as Barbara Bader, author of *American Picturebooks from Noah's Ark to the Beast Within,* has said, "Picture books can do just about everything other kinds of books can do, and in the vibrations between words and pictures, sometimes more."

People Behind the Pictures

Children, parents, and teachers can enjoy a six-decade visit with Caldecott Medalists by reading *A Caldecott Celebration: Six Artists Share Their Paths to the Caldecott Medal* (1998). Leonard S. Marcus, a children's book historian, takes his readers into the studios of Robert McCloskey, Marcia Brown, Maurice Sendak, William Steig, Chris Van Allsburg, and David Wiesner.

Pat Cumming's *Talking with the Artists* (1992) profiles fourteen children's book illustrators. They talk about where they get their ideas, what they most enjoy drawing, and how their careers began.

For a more off-beat approach to showcasing illustrators, try *Speak! Children's Book Illustrators Brag about Their Dogs* by Michael J. Rosen.

Notable Picture Books

There are hundreds of excellent children's illustrators today, because this is an attractive field for the finest of artists. Here is a list of thirty notable picture books listed, along with the name of the illustrator, in chronological order:

Raggedy Ann and Andy (1924) Johnny Gruelle
Raggedy Ann was the name of a rag doll owned by Gruelle's only daughter, who died suddenly at the age of fourteen. He created the series of stories in memory of her. The first *Raggedy Ann Stories* appeared in 1914 and continued at a steady pace until 1937. Although his quantity seems to have interfered with the quality of his stories, Gruelle had a definite talent for playful writing and winsome illustrations. Children especially enjoy his made-up words and story games. Two of his best books are *Raggedy Ann and the Paper Dragon* and *Wooden Willie*. Look for editions with Johnny Gruelle's illustrations.

Millions of Cats (1928) Wanda Gág
An old man goes to find a cat for his wife and winds up bringing home a million felines. Newbery Honor.

The Story of Ferdinand (1936) Robert Lawson
Written by Munro Leaf, this delightful story is about a bull
who would rather smell flowers than fight in the ring.

Animals of the Bible (1937) Dorothy Lathrop
The first book to win the Caldecott Medal, its black-and-
white drawings depict some of the most unusual animals
in the Bible. The text was provided by Helen Dean Fish.
In celebration of the Caldecott's sixtieth anniversary,
HarperCollins reissued this prize winner.

Mike Mulligan and His Steam Shovel (1939) Virginia
Lee Burton
Mike and his old steam shovel, Mary Ann, dig a home
for themselves in Popperville. Also, *The Little House*
(1942, Caldecott Winner).

The Country Bunny and the Little Gold Shoes (1939)
Marjorie Flack
Writer DuBose Heyward and Flack have given children
a lovely story about a rabbit who dreams of growing up
to be an Easter Bunny. The illustrations are superb and
the country bunny has enough pluck to please most
nine-year-olds.

Madeline (1939) Ludwig Bemelmans
Madeline is the smallest of twelve little girls in a Paris
boarding school. Her adventures continue in several sequels. These cherished books teach sharing, order, love,
and courage. Bemelmans received a Caldecott Honor
Award for the first book in the series and won the Caldecott Medal for *Madeline's Rescue* (1953). Look for *Mad
about Madeline: The Complete Tales* (1993).

Curious George (1940) Hana A. Rey
The first of eight books about a monkey who is brought

to live in the city by a man in a yellow hat. Adored by most preschoolers. *The Complete Adventures of Curious George* (1995) will be treasured by Rey fans.

In My Mother's House (1941) Velino Herrera
Herrera is an acclaimed Native American mural painter. Ann Nolan Clark wrote this beautiful story about the daily life of a Pueblo Indian boy, and its universal theme is the security of a safe home and a loving family. Caldecott Honor.

The Rooster Crows (1945) Maud and Miska Petersham
This Caldecott Medal winner is a collection of American rhymes, jingles, and chants. The Petershams also created *An American ABC* (1941, Caldecott Honor), which celebrates symbols, historic places, and famous people in American history.

Stone Soup (1947) Marcia Brown
Three hungry soldiers ask for food in a French village. When the stingy peasants refuse to feed them, the soldiers make stone soup (Caldecott Honor). Brown was awarded Caldecott Medals for *Cinderella* (1954), *Once a Mouse* (1961), and *Shadow* (1983).

The Biggest Bear (1952) Lynd Ward
A charming, almost wordless book that will delight animal lovers. Caldecott Winner.

The Happy Lion (1954) Roger Duvoisin
Louise Fatio provided the text for this story about a kind lion who escapes from a French zoo.

Harold and the Purple Crayon (1955, reissued 1977) Crockett Johnson
A little boy uses his imagination and a single purple

crayon to create some amazing things. This is a great book to get kids' creative juices flowing, but you may want to cover your walls with butcher paper before reading it. Johnson also illustrated *The Carrot Seed*, a classic written by Ruth Krauss.

Crow Boy (1955) Taro Yashima
A shy little boy leaves his mountain home to attend the village school. He is soon labeled "stupid slowpoke" by the other children. It is not until sixth grade that everyone discovers Chibi's special talents. Caldecott Honor.

Chanticleer and the Fox (1958) Barbara Cooney
An adaptation of Chaucer's version of this well-known folktale about a proud rooster and a sly fox. Caldecott Winner.

Norman the Doorman (1959) Don Freeman
Freeman specializes in lovable talking animals. Best known for *Corduroy* (1968), Freeman also wrote *Fly High, Fly Low*, which was a 1959 Caldecott Honor book.

Swimmy (1964) Leo Lionni
When little Swimmy's school of fish is swallowed by a tuna, he must find a way to survive on his own (Caldecott Honor). In *Frederick* (1966) a poet mouse saves up warm words for winter. Children who enjoy Lionni's work will love *Frederick's Fables: A Treasury of Sixteen Favorite Leo Lionni Stories* (1997).

Sam, Bangs, and Moonshine (1966) Evaline Ness
Sam, the daughter of a fisherman, has a problem with the difference between reality and fantasy, or "moonshine" as her father calls it. Sam's moonshine almost causes the death of Thomas, her best friend, and her cat, Bangs. Caldecott Winner.

To Be a Slave (1969) Tom Feelings
Julius Lester drew on published and unpublished sources for personal perspectives about the experience of slavery. Tom Feelings portrayed the strength, dignity, and suffering of slaves in profound pencil drawings (Newbery Honor). Tom and Muriel Feelings gave children two fine picture books, *Moja Means One* (1972) and *Jambo Means Hello* (1973).

Frog and Toad Are Friends (1970, Caldecott Honor) Arnold Lobel
In four witty and wise books, Lobel recounts the adventures of best friends Frog and Toad. The illustrations are excellent, but the text is equally outstanding, a fact noted by the Newbery Honor award for *Frog and Toad Together* (1972). In 1981 Lobel won the Caldecott Medal for his *Fables,* a treasure of moral wisdom in a most appealing package.

The Runaway Bunny (1970) Margaret Wise Brown
A little bunny asks his mother what she would do if he ran away. For each scenario he offers, she reassures him that she would find a way to be with him. This book also provides a beautiful picture of God's steadfast love.

Look Again! (1971) Tana Hoban
Hoban's photographs and creative formats are a visual treat. Look for *Over, Under and Through and Other Spatial Concepts* (1973), *A, B, See!* (1982), *A Children's Zoo* (1985), and others.

Snow White and the Seven Dwarfs (1972) Nancy Ekholm Burkert
Poet Randall Jarrell translated this version of the Brothers Grimm story. The text is complemented by Burkert's

detailed illustrations set in medieval Europe. Caldecott Honor.

Alexander and the Terrible, Horrible, No Good, Very Bad Day (1972) Ray Cruz
Judith Viorst describes a truly awful day and the feelings it provokes in a child. Cruz's illustrations portray those feelings with a deft touch of humor. Other books about Alexander followed, and they are all available in *Absolutely Positively Alexander: The Complete Stories* (1997).

Ashanti to Zulu: African Traditions (1976) Leo and Diane Dillon
Written by Margaret Musgrove, this is a brilliant alphabet book for older children and adults (Caldecott Winner). The Dillons also won the 1976 Caldecott Medal for *Why Mosquitos Buzz in People's Ears,* a West African folktale retold by Verna Aardema, and their illustrations for *The Hundred Penny Box* (1975) by Sharon Bell Mathis helped to make it a Newbery Honor book.

Anno's Journey (1978) Mitsumasa Anno
A wordless book that can be enjoyed by all ages. It serves as a good introduction to the work of this talented Japanese artist.

The Very Hungry Caterpillar (1981) Eric Carle
Bold colorful illustrations and holes through the pages tell the story of a caterpillar's approach to snacking. Most young children find Carle's books delightful. Do not miss *Brown Bear, Brown Bear, What Do You See?* (1983), a collaboration between Carle and Bill Martin, Jr.

A Chair for My Mother (1982) Vera B. Williams
When a family loses their home in a fire, a little girl and her mother and grandmother move into an apart-

ment. Slowly they save enough coins to buy a comfortable chair. Other fine books by this author/illustrator are *Three Days on a River in a Red Canoe* and *"More More More," Said the Baby*.

Ten, Nine, Eight (1983) Molly Bang
A father and daughter share the countdown to bedtime in a quiet, pleasant way that makes going to bed a treat.

America the Beautiful (1983) Neil Waldman
A magnificent depiction of the scenes that inspired our national anthem, written by Katherine Lee Bates.

Saint George and the Dragon (1984, Caldecott Winner) Trina Schart Hyman
Retold by Margaret Hodges, this legend is a favorite with children who are fascinated by knights and the age of chivalry. Hyman has illustrated several award-winning versions of tales from the Brothers Grimm.

King Bidgood's in the Bathtub (1985) Audrey and Don Wood
A dramatic and entertaining marriage of text by Audrey (also an artist) and illustrations by Don (Caldecott Honor). Look for other books by this outstanding husband and wife team.

The Jolly Postman (1986) Janet and Allan Ahlberg
A mailman on bicycle delivers amusing mail to fairy tale characters. The pages are designed as envelopes and hold the same variety of mail that is delivered to homes today. A great way to encourage letter writing. The sequel is *The Jolly Christmas Postman* (1991).

Animalia (1987) Graeme Base
A fascinating ABC book that combines animals and al-

literative text. This best-selling English-born Australian illustrator says the work of Albrecht Durer inspired his artistic efforts. He is recognized as a virtuoso of graphic design and his books are enjoyed by all ages.

Owl Moon (1987) John Schoenherr
In this Caldecott winner written by Jane Yolen a little girl and her father go owl watching.

Mufaro's Beautiful Daughters: An African Tale (1987) John Steptoe
Mufaro has two daughters who are total opposites. Manyara is mean and greedy. Myasha is kind and generous. Caldecott Honor.

Rechenka's Eggs (1988) Patricia Polacco
A Ukrainian babushka loses her hand-painted Easter eggs when a wild goose she has rescued knocks over the egg basket. Polacco's themes reflect her family heritage (Irish and Jewish-Ukrainian) and strong character-building values.

The Mitten: A Ukrainian Folktale (1989) Jan Brett
Brett's distinctive illustrations are derived from folk motifs in clothing, architecture, and other artifacts. Some children and critics think her work is too intricate and extravagant. But millions are captivated by it.

The Art Lesson (1989) Tomie dePaola
Muralist, designer, illustrator, art teacher, anthologist, and story-teller—these all describe Tomie dePaola. *The Art Lesson* is a good introduction to his books, which could fill several library shelves. All of dePaola's illustrations are highly stylized, reflecting the influence of pre-Renaissance Italian artists and folk designs. Because of his contribution to children's religious education, his

work will be discussed in more detail in chapter 14.

Lon Po Po: A Red Riding Hood Story from China (1989, Caldecott Winner) Ed Young
A suspenseful and humorous version of this familiar tale, *Lon Po Po* stars three children who soon outwit the wolf. Young also illustrated *I Wish I Were a Butterfly* (1987) by James Howe, *The Emperor and the Kite* (1988) by Jane Yolen, and *Sadako* (1993) by Eleanor Coerr.

Black and White (1990) David Macaulay
A perplexing book at first glance, this is a masterpiece that is best enjoyed in groups where family members or students can brainstorm and pool their insights. Macauley presents four separate stories. The challenge for children (and adults!) is discovering how they are connected. Macaulay won the Caldecott Medal for this unique book, and his *Castle* and *Cathedral* are Caldecott Honor books.

Amazing Grace (1991) Caroline Binch
Written by Mary Hoffman, this is the story of a girl named Grace who wants to be Peter Pan in the class play. Her grandmother helps her keep up her confidence in spite of put-downs from classmates.

Rembrandt's Beret (1991) Stephen Alcorn
As a girl named Marie sits for her grandfather to paint her picture, he tells her about his boyhood visit to Florence's Uffizi Gallery. On that day, the old masters climbed out of their self-portraits to visit with the boy.

Three Young Pilgrims (1992) Cheryl Harness
Bartholomew, Remember, and Mary sail with their parents on the *Mayflower.* Through detailed illustrations and historical fiction, Harness chronicles their first year in the New World.

The King's Equal (1992) Vladimir Vagin
Katherine Paterson was entranced with this Russian artist's work, so she decided to write a book for him to
illustrate. The result was an original fairy tale about an
arrogant young prince who must find a bride who is his
equal in order to take the throne. When the greedy
prince finds the right woman, she challenges him to
become someone very different than he is. Paterson
and Vagin continued their collaboration with *Celia and
the Sweet, Sweet Water* (1998), a fairy tale about compassion.

Stellaluna (1993) Janell Cannon
An owl causes a little bat to be separated from her
mother. The bewildered baby settles into a bird nest.
Then one night she discovers where she really belongs.

Bub: Or, the Very Best Thing (1994) Natalie Babbit
A king and queen ask their royal counselors to help
them find the very best thing to give their son. A charming book about the importance of love.

Lilly's Purple Plastic Purse (1996) Kevin Henkes
A mouse named Lilly loves school until her wonderful
new purse gets her into trouble. *Chester's Way* features
the same mouse characters. Other fine books by this
author/illustrator are *Chrysanthemum* and *Julius, the Baby
of the World*.

Sam and the Tigers (1996) Jerry Pinkney
A retelling of one of the most controversial books in
children's literature, *Little Black Sambo* by Helen Banner-
man. Writer Julius Lester's black southern storytelling
and Jerry Pinkney's vivid illustrations combine to make
this one of the best books available about the victory of
the small and weak over the large and powerful.

My Life with the Wave (1997) Mark Buehner
This picture book is based on a story by Octavio Paz, translated and adapted by Catherine Cowan. A boy brings a wave home from his vacation. Visually and verbally rich.

Rapunzel (1997) Paul O. Zelinsky
Zelinsky drew on early French and Italian versions of this folktale to create a Caldecott Medal winner. He illustrates the elegant text with magnificent oil paintings.

Voices in the Park (1998) Anthony Browne
A multi-layered experience in a city park by the creator of the popular *Gorilla* (1985) and its sequels, *The Daydreamer* and *Changes*—all marvelous works of imagination.

Books for Babies

For generations, adults have looked for ways to make books more durable for young children. The earliest solution was cloth books that could be gently washed when they became dirty. Next came vinyl books that could be held by tiny fingers covered with peanut butter or even taken into the tub for bath time.

Then in 1979 an innovation in children's literature occurred. With the publication of *Max's First Word* by Rosemary Wells, baby board books were born. These books are made completely of laminated cardboard. Based on a 1950s concept of Dick Bruna, a Dutch poster designer, these new books for children from birth to three were small, square, chunky, colorful, and captivating.

Board books are made to be shared by adults or older siblings and infants or toddlers. They feature familiar objects and celebrate milestones in baby's development.

They picture babies and their families doing everyday things. The simple text is quickly memorized by children who have learned to talk, and the more rhythmic and repetitive it is the happier they are.

Some of the best authors and illustrators for babies:

📖 Lucy Cousins. This talented illustrator has given babies some terrific little books about animals: *Country Animals, Farm Animals, Garden Animals,* and *Pet Animals* (1991).

📖 Tana Hoban. As they look at engaging photographs, babies can answer the question, *What Is It?* (1983).

📖 Dorothy Kunhardt. *Pat the Bunny* (1940) was one of the earliest books for babies, and it is still a favorite. Spin-off books by Edith Kunhardt are *Pat the Cat* and *Pat the Puppy.* All three have things to touch, move, discover, or smell.

📖 Helen Oxenbury. Perhaps the most baby-centered of all author-illustrators, her first series of board books includes five titles: *Family, Friends, Dressing, Playing,* and *Working* (1981). Next she focused on babies' capabilities with four more titles: *I Can, I See, I Hear, I Touch* (1986). Oxenbury also wrote a series of Out and About Books (1983) for toddlers and preschoolers. It chronicles outings to birthday parties, car trips, grandparents' houses, school, and dancing class. In this same vein, she created the Very First Books series about shopping, going to the beach, and other activities of very young children.

📖 Jan Ormerod. In *Moonlight* (1982) and *Sunshine* (1982), the bedtime and morning rituals in a little girl's home are lovingly portrayed. Also look for *Bend and Stretch* (1987), *Mom's Home, Making Friends,* and *This Little Nose.*

📖 Neil Ricklen has written over twenty books for babies, including *Baby's Clothes* (1994) and *Baby's Home*.

📖 Rosemary Wells. The adventures of baby rabbit Max and his bossy big sister, Ruby, continue in *Max's Bath, Max's Bedtime, Max's Birthday, Max's Breakfast, Max's New Suit, Max's Ride,* and *Max's Toys*.

Many favorite picture books have been released in board book editions. Parents should look at these carefully to make sure they actually reflect babies' and toddlers' interests rather than publishers' marketing strategy. A good rule to remember is, the younger the child, the simpler the pictures and concepts.

In addition to books that babies can hold, chew, and throw, parents should also have on hand a book of fingerplays and songs. Two favorites are Tom Glazer's *Eye Winker, Tom Tinker, Chin Chopper* (1992) and *Singing Bee! A Collection of Children's Songs* (1982) compiled by Jane Hart.

Picture Strip Books

Maurice Sendak's *In the Night Kitchen* is the nocturnal fantasy of a black-haired boy named Mickey, who ends up safely back in bed in the final comic-strip panel. (This book is disliked by some people because it pictures Mickey nude. But the illustration is not suggestive or vulgar.) Sendak's creation of Mickey was much influenced by the great forerunner of Walt Disney, Winston McCay, who created *Little Nemo* comic strips. (McCay's Little Nemo was a black-haired boy with nocturnal fantasy adventures like Mickey's—only Nemo's were sixty years earlier.)

Older children enjoy the familiar comic book format in Hergé's *Tintin*. The title character is a boy reporter who has adventures around the world. His traveling companions are Captain Haddock and Professor Calculus.

To be honest about picture books and illustrations for children, one has to admit that ordinary comics are the most popular picture books of all. The very year that gave us *Alice's Adventures in Wonderland,* 1865, marked the beginning of comic strips and comic books, for "Max and Moritz" by Wilhelm Busch appeared in Germany in that year. "The Yellow Kid" first appeared in the *New York World* on February 16, 1896. But it was not until 1907 that America got its first really successful comic strip, "Mutt and Jeff." These first comic strips were printed in black and white. Then in 1933 comics took on color. Since then, comic strips have become a staple of America's reading diet. About twelve million drawings have been done for comic strips. They have produced such fictitious celebrities as Little Orphan Annie, Barnie Google, the Katzenjammer Kids, Blondie, Superman, Donald Duck, Batman, and, in 1950, the "Peanuts" children.

Between 1963 and 1969 alone, 36 million copies of eighteen different "Peanuts" books were printed. There were also two books by Robert Short, *The Gospel According to Peanuts* and *The Parables of Peanuts,* pointing out how these strips reflect Christian beliefs and values. Here is how their creator, Charles M. Schultz, sums up his artistic philosophy: "If you do not say anything in a cartoon, you might as well not draw it at all. . . . So I contend that a cartoonist must be given a chance to do his own preaching."

The best picture books and comics illuminate truth for anyone with the eyes and heart of a child. And, as the greatest Teacher said, that is the doorway to heaven.

Talking Books
and Multimedia
Resources

13 Open Ears

"Grandmother dear, what big ears you have!"
"The better to hear you with, my child!"
    —"Little Red Riding Hood," *Perrault's Fairy Tales*

Reading silently is one thing. Reading aloud is another. Listening to someone read aloud is quite different again. And listening to a recording of someone else reading is a different thing altogether. It puts more people and more technology between the book and the listener. The live reader is the middleman between the author and the audience. The recorded reader becomes a plastic middleman, but a very valuable one.

What a wonder it is when the author of a beloved book tells us the story in a recording. Charles Dickens and Mark Twain used to add to their income by reading or reciting their works to crowded theaters full of enthusiastic listeners. They were superb readers and entertainers. But there was no way to record their voices.

Vachel Lindsay, who lived from 1879 to 1931, used to travel about the American Midwest giving readings of his poetry when recording was still a crude art. There is one weak, scratchy sounding album of his old reading performances—hearing it makes clear why he was in demand. His bold, rhythmic, explosive rendition makes his poems come alive as he intended. Once we have heard his oral version, the printed poems take on more of his tone and pacing.

James Weldon Johnson, whose life began a few years before Lindsay's and ended a few years after, was a teacher, lawyer, musician, American Consul in South America, and secretary of the National Association for the Advancement of Colored People. He is remembered primarily now for *God's Trombones* (1927), a series of poems in the tradition of vigorous African-American sermons, rich in imagery. He was a magnificent reader and recorded these brilliantly on 78-rpm records. Today they are available on cassettes. Children will especially enjoy the poem-sermon "The Creation."

Carl Sandburg made many recordings, including his book *Rootabaga Stories,* which comes in three albums. In at least one family, the children listened to his rolling renditions so often that as young adults they would still quote whole passages back and forth when something set them off. Sandburg also recorded his short stories for children, "The Five Marvelous Pretzels" and "The Three Nice Mice Brothers," along with a collection of his children's poems, which begins with his explanation of what poetry is. His Peter Potato Blossom Wishes says, "And you have to listen close up with your ears and be nice when you are listening." No one can read Sandburg better than Sandburg.

Across the Atlantic, no one could read Dylan Thomas better than Thomas himself. His "Child's Christmas in Wales," "Reminiscences of Childhood," "The Visit to Grandpa's," and "Quite Early One Morning" bring his childhood alive. They are fascinating, especially if one gets a printed version to understand better the humor and beauty in the waterfalls of words that seem to thunder from him.

Frank O'Connor's two short stories about his Irish childhood, told in his own clear Irish brogue, "My Oedipus Complex" and "The Drunkard," might be enjoyed by older children as well as parents (who will want to

listen to them first because families vary in their standards of propriety). The latter tells how the bored little
boy samples and drinks his father's two pints of ale after
a neighbor's funeral and becomes sick, disgracing himself and his father. Thus he accidentally achieves his
heart's desire—to save his parents from one of his "tee-
totalling" father's drinking sprees. Both stories are told
with tenderness and good humor.

J. R. R. Tolkien was not always easy to understand in
personal conversation because he would drop his voice
low, or get excited and run his words together. But he
had a flair for drama. Fortunately, there is an album
available on which he reads the riddle chapter from *The
Hobbit*. The title of the album is *J. R. R. Tolkien Reads
and Sings His* The Hobbit *and* The Fellowship of the
Ring.

Once one has fallen in love with *Old Possum's Book
of Practical Cats* with its droll illustrations, what better
pleasure than to hear these story-poems read aloud in
a very dignified British style by T. S. Eliot himself.
One cannot hear his eyes twinkling, but one is sure
they are.

Ogden Nash's humor is farther beyond the comprehension of children, but there are probably some of his
preposterous verses that they would enjoy hearing him
read with his proper Boston accent. He recorded an entire
album of them.

Many of these audio classics were lost to listeners
when phonograph records were replaced by cassettes
and compact discs, but in recent years major publishers
have vied with each other for the right to reissue
authors' readings of their own works. A case in point is
E. B. White's *Charlotte's Web,* which cost Bantam hundreds of thousands of dollars. If the price seems high,
consider that audiobooks earn publishers well over a billion dollars a year.

An Audiobook Sampler

Most of the following companies offer tapes for purchase or rental, and catalogs are available upon request. (Information on how to contact the companies is given in appendix 4.)

- American Bible Society
  A Few Who Dared to Trust God, six hours of Bible stories from the *Contemporary English Version* recorded on five cassettes and narrated by outstanding actors, including Julie Harris, Clifton Davis, and Ken Howard. ABA offers other excellent audio and video Scripture presentations and Bible software.

- Audio Book Contractors
  The Queen's Museum and Other Fanciful Tales by Frank R. Stockton

- Books in Motion

- Books on Tape
  Claiming the world's largest selection of unabridged audiobooks, Books on Tape offers a fairly substantial list of children's classics. Here is a sampling from their catalog:
  The Adventures of Tom Sawyer by Mark Twain
  Alice's Adventures in Wonderland and through the Looking-Glass by Lewis Carroll
  Anne of Green Gables by Lucy Maud Montgomery
  Black Beauty by Anna Sewell
  The Boxcar Children by Gertrude Chandler Warner
  Call It Courage by Armstrong Sperry
  Cinderella, Rumpelstiltskin and Other Stories by Charles Perrault and the Brothers Grimm

Just So Stories and *The Jungle Book* by Rudyard
   Kipling
Heidi by Johanna Spyri
The Little Princess and *Little Lord Fauntleroy* by
   Frances Hodgson Burnett
Little Women by Louisa May Alcott
The Merry Adventures of Robin Hood by Howard Pyle
My Friend Flicka by Mary O'Hara
Peter Pan by J. M. Barrie
The Princess and Curdie and *The Princess and the Gob-
   lin* by George MacDonald
Ramona Quimby series by Beverly Cleary
The Swiss Family Robinson by Johann David Wyss
The Ugly Duckling and Other Stories by Hans Chris-
   tian Andersen
Where the Red Fern Grows by Wilson Rawls
White Fang by Jack London
Wrinkle in Time series read by the author, Madeleine
   L'Engle
Winnie-the-Pooh by A. A. Milne, performed by
   Charles Kuralt (a Grammy Award nominee)
The Wizard of Oz by L. Frank Baum

◆ Caedmon Records offers a literary subscription plan
   with age-appropriate recordings from a list of core
   resources. Among their finest selections are:
   Animal Stories by Walter de la Mare, narrated by
      Lynn Redgrave
   Arthur's Christmas Cookies by Lillian Hoban
   The Emperor's New Clothes and Other Tales by Hans
      Christian Andersen, narrated by Sir Michael
      Redgrave
   Zlateh the Goat and Other Stories by Isaac Bashevis
      Singer

◆ Folkways specializes in children's songs and literature.

Spanish translations of numerous recordings are available.

◆ Listening Library
This company specializes in audiobooks for children, producing nearly one-third of the 1998 American Library Association's Notable Recordings for Children award winners. Some large bookstores and children's bookstores sell Listening Library audiobooks, but for a complete listing of tapes for rent or purchase contact the company. Here are a few of the many titles available:

The Boggart and the Monster by Susan Cooper

The Castle in the Attic and *The Battle for the Castle* by Elizabeth Winthrop, read by the author

Children of Christmas and *Every Living Thing* by Cynthia Rylant

Chuck and Danielle by Peter Dickinson

The Farthest-Away Mountain and *The Fairy Rebel* by Lynne Reid Banks

From the Mixed-Up Files of Mrs. Basil E. Frankweiler and *The View from Saturday* by E. L. Konigsburg

Knee Knock Rise by Natalie Babbitt

Mick Harte Was Here by Barbara Park (winner of the 1998 Benjamin Franklin Award for children's audiobook)

Out of the Dust by Karen Hesse

The Polar Express by Chris Van Allsburg

Rascal by Sterling North

Redwall by Brian Jacques, read by the author (winner of the 1998 Audie Award for Best Children's Title)

Shadow of a Bull by Maia Wojciechowska

The Sign of the Beaver by Elizabeth George Speare

Three Terrible Trins by Dick King-Smith

◆ Recorded Books offers a wide variety of children's titles including:

A Gathering of Days by Joan W. Blos
Lyddie by Katherine Paterson
Nightjohn by Gary Paulsen
Number the Stars by Lois Lowry
On to Oregon! by Honoré Morrow
The Slave Dancer by Paula Fox

◆ Spoken Arts
   Sir Percival and the Fisher King, Arthurian legends
   performed by Odds Bodkin

As you and your children explore the world of audiobooks, keep a list of favorite narrators and look for their work.

Books on Film

Since the advent of motion pictures, many children's books have been adapted for the big screen. Film versions of books tend to change the stories, replacing complex characters with one-dimensional stereotypes, rich language with coarse or trite dialogue, and multi-layered themes with simplistic scenarios. Another drawback is that videos do not allow children and parents to enjoy illustrations in the actual books or to read along with the narrator as they can with audiobooks. Worst of all, seeing a film can lead children to think they already know the story and do not need to read the book.

It is almost always better for families to share a great book before seeing it presented on film. This allows children to experience their own rich mental pictures unhindered by moviemakers' images, and it encourages them to watch films with a more critical eye. Usually children who read a book and then see the movie come away somewhat disappointed and are thus drawn back to the pleasures of reading. Sometimes, however, reluctant readers can be drawn to books by enjoying a movie adaptation. (*You Can Use Television to Stimulate Your Child's Reading Habits* by the International Reading Association offers tips that also apply to videos. For more information on obtaining their free guide, see appendix 4.)

Here is a sampling of outstanding children's books available on video. Appendix 4 provides phone numbers of film producers and distributors who sell directly to the public. Catalogs from most of these companies are available upon request.

Alice in Wonderland (distributed by Fusion Video)—Lou Bunin's *Alice in Wonderland* is more faithful to Lewis Carroll's classic than the Disney version. It stars Carol Marsh as Alice and the Wonderland characters are portrayed by stop action puppets.

The Amazing Bone and Other Stories (Children's Circle Home Video)—The stories in this award-winning animated collection are *The Amazing Bone* by William Steig, *John Brown, Rose and the Midnight Cat* by Jenny Wagner, *A Picture for Harold's Room* by Crocket Johnson, and *The Trip* by Ezra Jack Keats.

Anne of Green Gables and *Anne of Avonlea* (available in most video stores)—A Canadian mini-series of much better quality than the Disney Channel TV series. Based on the novels of Lucy Maud Montgomery.

Arthur (PBS; distributed by The Video Catalog)—Marc Brown's stories about a young bespectacled aardvark as seen on television. Each video features two shows.

Babar (Family Home Entertainment)—Brunhoff's Babar comes to life through animation. Some brief cartoon violence is offset by stories that encourage doing right, loving others, and being responsible.

Babe (available in most video stores)—Animatronics is the key to believable talking animals, but the real magic is in the story of a farmer's special bond with his sheepherding pig. Based on a wonderful children's book by fantasy writer Dick King-Smith.

The Berenstain Bears series (Random House Home Video)—These stories are based on the best-selling books of Stan and Jan Berenstain. The Bear family works together to find solutions to common problems. The resulting domestic dramas have been called contemporary "morality plays."

The Best Christmas Pageant Ever (Regency; distributed by Christian Book Distributors)—The horrible Herdman kids take over the Christmas pageant. Based on Barbara Robinson's bestseller.

Caddie Woodlawn (Bridgestone)—Caddie is a ten-year-old Wisconsin pioneer who prefers tomboy adventures to "lady-like" pursuits. A live-action movie based on the book by Carol Ryrie Brink.

Captains Courageous (MGM/UA, available in most video stores)—A feature film presentation of Rudyard Kipling's classic story. Brilliant acting, but too intense for young children.

Carnival of the Animals (Twin Tower)—A winning combination of animation, live action filmed at the world-famous San Diego Zoo, rhymes by Ogden Nash, and classic music.

Cigars of the Pharaoh (SONY Wonder)—Part of the low-violence animated Adventures of Tintin series. If your children enjoy this one, look for *Secret of the Unicorn*.

The Chronicles of Narnia (Wonderworks/Public Media, distributed by Vision Video)—Live-action presentations of four of C. S. Lewis's classic children's fantasies: *The Lion, the Witch and the Wardrobe, Prince Caspian, The Voyage of* "The Dawn Treader," and *The Silver Chair.* Enjoyable but not equal to the animatronics children are accustomed to in theater productions. A cartoonish version of *The Lion, the Witch and the Wardrobe* was produced by Children's Television Work-

shop. It is fairly faithful to the text, but the animation
fails to capture the wonder of Narnia.

Clifford series (Family Home Entertainment)—Clifford
the Big Red Dog teaches young children the alphabet,
numbers, opposites, shapes, and more.

Coot Club and The Big Six (distributed by Fusion Video)—
Live-action adaptations of Arthur Ransome's Swallows
and Amazons. Filmed in England.

Corduroy and Other Bear Stories (Children's Circle Home
Videos)—This award-winning video features a live-
action version of Don Freeman's book Corduroy, "Pan-
ama" by European storyteller Janosch, and Blueberries
for Sal by Robert McCloskey.

The Country Mouse and the City Mouse: A Christmas Tale
(Random House Home Video)—A contemporary ad-
aptation of Aesop's fable by animator Michael Sporn.
Noted for his tender portrayal of storybook charac-
ters, Sporn has done several other outstanding chil-
dren's videos including Trinka Hakes Noble's The Day
Jimmy's Boa Ate the Wash (Children's Circle Home Vid-
eos), Ira Sleeps Over by Bernard Waber (Family Home
Entertainment), Mike Mulligan and His Steam Shovel by
Virginia Lee Burton, The Red Shoes by Hans Christian
Andersen, and Robert Louis Stevenson's A Child's Garden of Verses (Family Home Entertainment).

Dangerous Journey (Moody, distributed by Vision Video)—
Nine episodes on one tape present Bunyan's Pilgrim's
Progress. Based on the book adaptation titled Danger-
ous Journey.

Doctor De Soto and Other Stories (Children's Circle Home
Videos)—The most honored release by Children's Circle Home Videos. The title story by William Steig was
nominated for an Academy Award for Best Animated
Short Film. It also features Patrick by Quentin Blake,
Curious George Rides a Bike by H. A. Rey, and The Hat
by Tomi Ungerer.

The Elephant's Child (Random House Home Video)—
Rabbit Ears Productions has given children a classic
adaptation of Rudyard Kipling's beloved story. Jack
Nicholson narrates and the music is by Bobby McFer-
rin. The same talented people teamed up to create
How the Rhinocerous Got His Skin.

The Ezra Jack Keats Library (Children's Circle Home Videos)—This video features *The Snowy Day, A Whistle for
Willie, Peter's Chair, A Letter to Amy, Pet Show,* and *Trip.*
Following the stories, Ezra Jack Keats invites viewers
into his studio for a brief visit.

Faerie Tale Theatre series by Shelley Duvall (FoxVideo,
available in most video stores)—Duvall has given children some dazzling contemporary portrayals of classic
fairy tales. The whole family can enjoy the witty script-
ing, magnificent sets, and celebrity casting.

Follow the Drinking Gourd (Rabbit Ears/BMG Kids)—Morgan Freeman narrates this animated story about the
Underground Railroad.

Harold and the Purple Crayon and Other Harold Stories
(Children's Circle Home Video)—An excellent animated version of three Crockett Johnson stories.

Jacob Have I Loved (Public Media Video, WonderWorks)—
Katherine Paterson's superb novel about the conflict
and rivalry between teenage twin sisters.

Johnny Appleseed (Rabbit Ears/BMG Kids)—Garrison Keil-
lor tells the story of John Chapman, the man who
planted apple seeds and hope across America.

Little Women (available in most video stores)—Try the
1933 black and white movie and then compare the
1994 major motion picture release. Families who enjoy
discussing film-making and acting will find both viewing experiences interesting and enjoyable. To see the
setting for Alcott's classic, the latest release is prefer-
able.

Madeline (Children's Circle Home Video)—Ludwig Bemelmans' cherished books are presented through animation. Children may find it interesting to compare these videos with the 1998 major motion picture release, and the books.

Martin the Cobbler (Billy Budd Video, distributed by Vision Video)—A high-quality clay animation version of Leo Tolstoy's short story "Where Love Is." Billy Budd Video has produced another Tolstoy story in *Michael the Visitor.* They also offer claymation films of *God's Trombones, The Velveteen Rabbit, The Little Prince,* and *Rip Van Winkle.*

The Marzipan Pig (Family Home Entertainment)—Some film critics consider this the finest children's video ever made. It is an animated adaptation of a book by Russell Hoban.

Maurice Sendak's Really Rosie (Children's Circle Home Videos)—Rosie directs her own make-believe movie starring the neighborhood kids. The characters are taken from Sendak's *The Nutshell Library* and *The Sign on Rosie's Door.* A major award-winner! For more imaginative stories from this author/illustrator, watch *The Maurice Sendak Library* (Children's Circle Home Videos), featuring *Where the Wild Things Are, In the Night Kitchen,* and several short poems from *The Nutshell Library.*

McGee and Me! series (Tyndale House Publishers; available in most Christian bookstores or from Christian Book Distributors)—Nick creates a cartoon character called McGee, a quirky character with a mission. For an entertaining presentation of Christian values without sermonizing, this series is hard to beat. The success of the twelve McGee and Me! videos enabled their creators, George Taweel and Rob Loos, to start their own company (Taweel-Loos & Company Video). Look for their sequel called *Secret Adventure: Spin.*

More Stories for the Very Young (Children's Circle Home

Video)—Two- to four-year-olds will enjoy this animated presentation of *The Little Red Hen* by Paul Galdone, *Petunia* by Roger Duvoisin, and *Not So Fast, Songololo* by Niki Daly.

Noah's Ark (Hi-Tops Video; distributed by Vision Video)—James Earl Jones narrates this animated film based on Peter Spier's book.

Pollyanna (BBC; distributed by Vision Video)—Far superior to the Disney version of this children's classic.

Ramona series (Lorimar Home Video/Warner Home Video)—Canadian productions of Beverly Cleary's beloved stories about Ramona Quimby.

Richard Scarry's Best Neighborhood, Ever! and *Richard Scarry's Busiest Neighborhood, Ever!* (Phillips Interactive Media)—Interactive videos for the preschool set featuring the work of a beloved children's book illustrator.

The Robert McCloskey Library (Children's Circle Home Video)—Released in 1991, the fiftieth anniversary of McCloskey's *Make Way for Ducklings*, this animated video includes *Blueberries for Sal, Time of Wonder, Burt Dow: Deep-Water Man,* and *Lentil.*

Sarah Plain and Tall (Hallmark Hall of Fame/Vision Video)—Glenn Close plays the part of a mail-order bride who wins a place in the hearts of a widowed farmer and his children. Based on the story written by Patricia MacLachlan.

The Secret Garden (1987 Hallmark Hall of Fame adaptation and 1993 major motion picture, both available in most video stores)—Two fine adaptations of Frances Hodgson Burnett's classic.

The Secret of NIMH (MGM/UA, available in most video stores)—This animated feature-length version of Robert O'Brien's book is a great film for the whole family.

The Snowman (Children's Circle Home Video)—An ani-

mated version of Raymond Brigg's book about a little
boy and his snowman and their flight around the
world.

Tell Me Why series (Prism Entertainment/Paramount)—
Eighteen tapes based on the best-selling book series
by Arkady Leokum. On each video, children ask questions about a specific subject (space, weather, plants,
gems, medicine) and get fascinating answers. Some of
the answers given will conflict with Christian parents'
beliefs, but the series provides a wealth of information
and opportunities to talk with children about other
viewpoints.

Treasures of the Snow (Children's Media Productions/Vi-
sion Video)—Patricia St. John's story of forgiveness
and reconciliation is presented in live action and
filmed on location in the Swiss Alps. *Tanglewood's Secret*
by St. John is also available on video.

The Velveteen Rabbit (Rabbit Ears)—Meryl Streep narrates
an animated presentation of Margery Williams's classic
about a stuffed rabbit who is made "real" by love.

Where's Spot? (King Rollo Films, Ltd., available from
Movies Unlimited)—A perfect animated presentation
of author Eric Carle's book. Others in this series are
Spot Goes to a Party and *Spot Goes to the Farm.*

The Wind in the Willows (four volumes, HBO video)—
Kenneth Grahame's classic comes to life through
elaborate model animation.

Families interested in securing video presentations of
some of the best children's books should contact *Reading
Rainbow.* Since 1983 this PBS program has done an outstanding job of showcasing literature for children ages
five through eight. It is extremely faithful to the real texts
and illustrations. More recently a PBS show called *Wish-
bone* has introduced children of all ages to literary classics in an imaginative and effective way. Another PBS

program, *WonderWorks*, presents dramatic adaptations of children's classics for viewers from eight to eighty, but their productions are uneven in quality. Many *Wonder-Works* films are available in video stores and public libraries.

The American Library Association (ALA) offers guidelines for selecting children's videos and, in cooperation with the Carnegie Corporation, gives awards to top videos each year. It has also produced a video called *Choosing the Best in Children's Video*, hosted by Christopher Reeve. Many libraries have a copy, or it may be purchased by sending one dollar to the ALA. (For information on how to contact the ALA, and for further sources of help in choosing videos, see appendix 4.)

Computer Software

David Macaulay, best-selling author/illustrator of *The Way Things Work*, wrote in *School Library Journal* (May 1995) about the way CD-ROMs ought to work. He said, "I'd want the same things I'd want in a book. I'd want good content, and I'd want to be lured into the information in a clear and logical way." Following is a listing of software packages that have been honored by parents, teachers, and librarians as meeting those criteria.

Reference Software

📖 *The Amazing Expedition CD-Rom Bible* by Mary Hollingsworth—More than fifty stories from the *New Living Bible* version, along with games and activities, timeline, and historical background. Other enjoyable Bible software packages are available from Christian bookstores and Christian Book Distributors mail-order service.

📖 DK's *My First Incredible Amazing Dictionary*—K–Grade 2.

📖 DK's *Eyewitness Encyclopedia*—Grade 3–6.

📖 *Microsoft Bookshelf*—Features a dictionary, Internet directory, world atlas, thesaurus, world almanac, dictionary of quotations, and rudimentary encyclopedia. Grade 3 and up.

📖 *World Book Multimedia Encyclopedia*—Grade 2 and up.

📖 *Encyclopedia Americana*—Grade 9 and up.

Literature-Based Software

📖 *Aesop's The Tortoise and the Hare*—part of Broderbund Software's excellent Living Book series of interactive storybooks, Winner of the *Newsweek* Editor's Choice Award. PreS–Grade 3.

📖 *Alien Tales*—In this game show format, children compete against alien plagiarists who claim to have written children's classics. If kids do not know the answers to game questions, they can consult the CD's 450 book excerpts, plot summaries, and author biographies. In the process, they sample some great literature and get practice in reading comprehension. Grade 4 and up.

📖 *Anno's Learning Games*—based on the book, *Anno's Math Games*. Grade 1–5.

📖 *Arthur's Birthday, Arthur's Reading Race* (winner of the *Newsweek* Editor's Choice Award) and *Arthur's Teacher Trouble*—based on the books by Marc Brown. Grade 1–4.

📖 *The Berenstain Bears Collection*—based on the stories of Stan and Jan Berenstain. PreS–Grade 3.

📖 *The Cat in the Hat, Dr. Seuss's ABC* (winner of the *Newsweek* Editor's Choice Award), and *Green Eggs and Ham*—Living Books series. PreS–Grade 2.

📖 *If You Give a Mouse a Cookie*—based on the book by Laura Numeroff. PreS–Grade 2.

📖 *Just Grandma and Me*—based on the book by Mercer

Mayer, Living Books series. Winner of the *Newsweek* Editor's Choice Award. PreS–Grade 3.

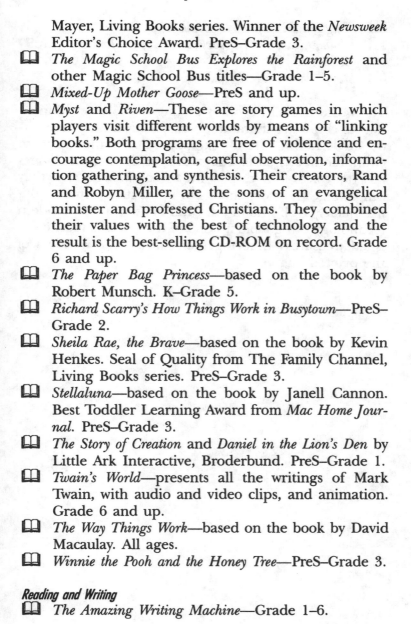 *The Magic School Bus Explores the Rainforest* and other Magic School Bus titles—Grade 1–5.

Mixed-Up Mother Goose—PreS and up.

Myst and *Riven*—These are story games in which players visit different worlds by means of "linking books." Both programs are free of violence and encourage contemplation, careful observation, information gathering, and synthesis. Their creators, Rand and Robyn Miller, are the sons of an evangelical minister and professed Christians. They combined their values with the best of technology and the result is the best-selling CD-ROM on record. Grade 6 and up.

The Paper Bag Princess—based on the book by Robert Munsch. K–Grade 5.

Richard Scarry's How Things Work in Busytown—PreS–Grade 2.

Sheila Rae, the Brave—based on the book by Kevin Henkes. Seal of Quality from The Family Channel, Living Books series. PreS–Grade 3.

Stellaluna—based on the book by Janell Cannon. Best Toddler Learning Award from *Mac Home Journal*. PreS–Grade 3.

The Story of Creation and *Daniel in the Lion's Den* by Little Ark Interactive, Broderbund. PreS–Grade 1.

Twain's World—presents all the writings of Mark Twain, with audio and video clips, and animation. Grade 6 and up.

The Way Things Work—based on the book by David Macaulay. All ages.

Winnie the Pooh and the Honey Tree—PreS–Grade 3.

Reading and Writing

The Amazing Writing Machine—Grade 1–6.

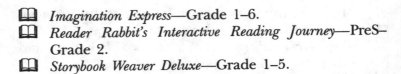

- 📖 *Imagination Express*—Grade 1–6.
- 📖 *Reader Rabbit's Interactive Reading Journey*—PreS– Grade 2.
- 📖 *Storybook Weaver Deluxe*—Grade 1–5.

The world of multimedia is adding a whole new dimension to children's literature. Now youngsters can see Little Red Riding Hood skipping down the path to Grandmother's house. They can hear the Big Bad Wolf's falsetto voice as it drips with poison honey. And they can change the story thanks to interactive software. But like that sly Wolf who hid in Grandmother's bed, modern technology can gobble up one of the family's most cherished treasures—time together sharing the wonders of the printed page.

Christian Nurture   **14 Open Hearts**
and Values

> Remember these commands and cherish them. . . .
> Teach them to your children. Talk about them
> when you are at home and when you are away,
> when you are resting and when you are working.
> —Deuteronomy 11:18-19

A Protestant geography book of 1818 included this kind of information about foreign countries:

Q. What do the I-tal-i-ans wor-ship?
A. They wor-ship i-dols and a piece of bread.
Q. Would not God be ang-ry that I-tal-i-ans wor-ship i-dols and a piece of bread?
A. God is ang-ry.

In the late 1950s and into the 1960s, children were getting similar instruction from *Pete and Penny Play and Pray.* The catechistic style was replaced by a children's story, but the intent was the same. One of the little children listening to *Pete and Penny Play and Pray* at bedtime was Franky Schaeffer, son of conservative Presbyterian missionaries to Switzerland. He recalls this devotional book's portrayal of a Catholic boy named Antonio who thought he was praying to God when he was worshipping an idol. Rather than learning what his parents hoped he would from Pete and Penny, Franky became fascinated by ritual, incense, icons, candles, and contemplative worship. Today he is a devout member of the Greek Orthodox Church.

For centuries homes and schools have tried to impart religious values to children in the heart of their general education and entertainment. That is a fine ideal. But all too often the education or entertainment has been diminished by the well-intentioned but misguided and second-rate Christian nurture. There is, however, one Book in which artistic expression, human drama, and spiritual values are divinely fused.

The Best Storybook of All

Obviously the basic book for Christian training in the home is the Bible. But how can the very young or older people with limited ability profit from such extremely varied and inexhaustibly rich and complex literature?

First, there are predigested bits of Scripture that are always available for very young children. The dozens of inexpensive Arch books, often written in rhyme, with vividly colored pictures of varying quality, are generally beloved by preschoolers. Tens of millions have been published so far. They are lively, brief, simple, and interesting.

There are also dozens and dozens of Bible story picture books available, some telling only one story and others telling many. *The Bible in Pictures for Little Eyes* by Kenneth Taylor contains 184 illustrated one-paragraph accounts of events in the Old and New Testaments, each with three questions. For many years this was the most popular survey of the entire Bible for children near kindergarten age. Today its quaint and sentimental illustrations delight some little eyes, but most children are attracted to more contemporary artwork. In 1990, Dr. Taylor and Gil Beers teamed up to create *The Bible for Children* for more sophisticated youngsters.

Jesus, the Friend of Children (1976, Gold Medallion) is one of the large picture books illustrated by the famous team Richard and Frances Hook. It includes almost fifty brief stories of Jesus' life, each faced by a full-color picture. It is handsome and impressive, but now it can only be found in libraries and used book stores. Fortunately, the Hooks' wonderful artwork is available in *McGee's Favorite Bible Stories* (adapted from *The Book for Children*) by Kenneth Taylor. This large volume features three hundred stories from the Old and New Testaments.

Needless to say, countless picture books with Bible texts, often from the King James Version, come and go through the years. One of those that is very beautiful is *And It Came to Pass* (1971), the Christmas story retold by Jean Slaughter and illustrated by Caldecott winner Leonard Weisgard.

There are plenty of children's Bibles to choose from. Some are merely adult Bibles with illustrations. Others omit the parts of the Bible that will not be meaningful to children and try to simplify the vocabulary and ideas, often adding colored illustrations. Prominent examples are the *Contemporary English Version Illustrated Bible for Children, The New Living Translation Children's Bible,* Golden Press's handsome *Children's Bible,* Catherine Vos's *The Child's Story Bible,* Pearl Buck's literary *The Story Bible,* Concordia's *Holy Bible for Children,* Word's large *Children's New Testament,* the *NIV Children's Bible,* Walter Wangerin's *The Book of God for Children,* and *A Child's Bible* from Paulist Press, in two sturdy paperback volumes full of colored illustrations.

There are so many good Bible versions today that it is hard to go wrong. But two should not be overlooked. First is the *Good News Bible: Today's English Version* (1976). It is one of the simplest translations in standard English, full of easy introductions, outlines, definitions, maps, and other aids, as well as appropriate line illustrations by Annie Vallotton. This gifted Swiss illustrator is an excellent Bible storyteller, and children can enjoy her *Story Line* presentations on video cassettes (available from American Bible Society).

The *New Living Translation* is one of the newest; the King James (or Authorized) Bible is the oldest still in use. Many uninformed people have thought the King James was the original version of the Word of God, instead of one translation among many. Admittedly, the Authorized Version is no longer our most accurate version; there are definite minor errors in it. And it is written in the archaic English that Shakespeare used; therefore, many of the correct passages are misunderstood by today's readers. For meaning, it would be a shame to limit oneself to the Authorized Version. But for beauty it is a shame to ignore it. Its eloquence and stately cadences are almost unrivaled in English literature. Countless children have read it, scarcely knowing what it meant but captivated by the vigor, poetry, and mystery of it all. Since the Holy Book of Christianity in its 1611 version is one of the greatest works of literature of all time, Christian families might as well use this treasure occasionally and enjoy this part of our cultural heritage.

Faith and Fiction

It is said that for over two centuries most homes in England had two books if no others—the King James Bible and *Pilgrim's Progress,* two of the finest works of English literature. The first was perfected by a committee of brilliant scholars; the second was composed by John Bunyan, a poor uneducated country man in his jail cell. (For more about Bunyan, see chapter 5.) The story of Christian's pilgrimage marked a major turning point in Christian nurture.

When Bunyan wrote *Pilgrim's Progress* in 1678, devout Protestants had a deep distrust of fiction. America's leading Puritan minister, Cotton Mather, called it "Satan's library," and England's Richard Baxter confessed that as an adolescent he was "extremely bewitched with a Love of Romances, Fables and old Tales."

In *Sighs from Hell: or The Groans of a Damned Soul*, Bunyan wrote about his sinful youth:

> The Scriptures, thought I, what are they? a dead letter, a little Ink and Paper, of three or four Shillings price. . . . Give me a Ballad, a Newsbook, George on Horseback, or Bevis of Southampton [a chapbook adventure story about a brave knight who married a Saracen princess]. Give me some book that teaches curious Arts, but for the holy Scriptures I cared not.

He deeply regretted his prodigal years, but his youthful fondness for imaginative tales no doubt contributed to the writing of *Pilgrim's Progress*. In Bunyan's allegory, Sir Bevis of the chapbook was transformed into the pilgrim Christian, who must also face enemies and danger to reach his goal.

It took great courage to publish this imaginative work, but after much soul-searching its author decided that it would be a means of presenting the gospel to those who would never read a theological work. He was right. For over three centuries, *Pilgrim's Progress* has been read by more people in more languages than any book other than the Bible.

Unfortunately, *Pilgrim's Progress* seems to have become a classic in Mark Twain's sense of the word—"A book which people praise and don't read." Even people who despise the Christian teaching in it readily agree that it is one of the great works of English literature. But the handsomest current edition, illustrated by Caldecott-winning artist Robert Lawson and first published by Lippincott in 1939, turns out not to be the real *Pilgrim's Progress* at all. It is an extensive revision, produced by Mary Godolphin in 1884. She not only cut the story down to one-fifth of its length—which might be all right—but she reworded every sentence. She left the language almost as old-fashioned as ever, but changed *burden* to *load*, *wilderness* to *wild waste*, *trembled* to *shook*, *children* to *sweet babes*—and so on. The entire book was changed to words of one syllable! In the first sentence alone she took out *walking, reading, lighted, certain*, and more.

Furthermore, in this 1884 edition the publisher announced proudly that he was selling *Robinson Crusoe, The Swiss Family Robinson*, and *Aesop's Fables* in the same uniform one-syllable style. Since Bunyan's flowing prose is utterly superb—except when he stops to preach a bit—all children who read this choppy version, the one most apt to be in public libraries, are getting only a staccato abbreviation of the story.

Little Pilgrim's Progress by Helen L. Taylor sells in many Christian bookstores as an easy-to-read version, but it is not that at all. Taylor has changed Pilgrim from the married father of four children, who repents his adult sins, to a sweet little boy whose mother is dead. She has changed Pilgrim's wife Christiana, who had four growing sons, into a sweet little orphan girl with a baby sister and two brothers to care for. All the rest of the story has to be changed accordingly.

Whatever the merits of Taylor's *Little Pilgrim's Progress*, it is no closer to the real thing than Mary Godolphin's rewriting was. Who knows how many people read one or the other and think they have read Bunyan's masterpiece. Parents who want to introduce children to Bunyan's classic are advised to choose *Dangerous Journey* (Eerdmans, 1985), edited by Oliver Hunkin and well illustrated by Alan Perry. It is faithful to the original story and its language.

When children are mature enough to enjoy *Pilgrim's Progress* as it was originally written, families may want to invest in the edition annotated by Warren Wiersbe (Moody Press, 1980).

Some non-Christians claim that children enjoy the story as a literal journey and no more, missing all the Christian allegory. That seems highly questionable, since Bunyan makes his allegory so vivid and pointed.

One problem for children reading *Pilgrim's Progress* could be Bunyan's conviction that only a very few Christians get to the Celestial City and that danger of falling into hell stretches clear up to the gate of heaven. There is a strong element of narrowness and terror in the book along with its heroism, humor, and pleasures. Parents who feel that the life view is a bit too negative can explain to their children that Bunyan was severely persecuted for his religion and that in his day sincere believers tended to be more intolerant of other believers.

We may not agree with Bunyan that a Christian is very apt to fall from the grace of God, but we can all identify with many of Pilgrim's follies and triumphs and learn with him and Christiana. One verse seems worth memorizing:

> He that is down need fear no fall,
> He that is low no pride,
> He that is humble ever shall
> Have God to be his guide.

C. S. Lewis gave a talk on BBC radio near the end of his life paying tribute to *Pilgrim's Progress*. He ended with this sentence:

> But most, I fancy, have discovered that to be born is to be exposed to delights and miseries greater

than imagination could have anticipated; that the choice of ways at any cross-road may be more important than we think; and that short cuts may lead to very nasty places.

Today someone could end a talk about Lewis's own Chronicles of Narnia with the very same sentence. Like *Pilgrim's Progress,* these stories warn about short cuts, stress the importance of choices, and portray the delights and miseries of life with extreme clarity. The Narnian Chronicles have already been described in the chapter on contemporary fantasy, but they are more than fantasy. They are Christian fantasy. They are not real allegory, like *Pilgrim's Progress,* but they teach Christian truth just as strongly in their own way. Much children's literature is highly moral, inspiring, and uplifting; but the stories of Narnia are also imbued with Christian theology. It would be hard to think of a more successful blending of entertainment with Christian teaching. Lewis would be unhappy if parents ever spoiled the stories for children by turning them into Bible lessons. He meant for Narnia to work its own work in readers' imaginations.

Unfortunately, some people find it hard to trust that children can derive appropriate nurture without underlining the moral of a story. They look for fiction that leaves little to the imagination, or they add their own instructive comments to the author's creation. The deluge of "problem" novels in the 1970s and 1980s and the character-building anthologies published during the 1990s demonstrate the ongoing conviction that children's stories should teach fairly obvious lessons.

This philosophy irks many writers, especially those with a strong commitment to maintaining the integrity of a story. Natalie Babbitt, author of *Tuck Everlasting,* gave young readers an outstanding novel about death and immortality, and she is a firm believer that books should expand our vision of life and human nature. But she has no tolerance for stories with obvious lessons. "I was mostly good when I was a child," she recalled in an American Library Association presentation,

> But when my mother read *The Water Babies* aloud, it had a negative effect. I don't recall ever disliking a character in a book as much as I disliked Mrs. Doasyouwouldbedoneby. I think that may have been during the same period when I was spanked six times in a single week for a rich variety of crimes. Messages can backfire.

This is a cautionary tale that wise parents will heed. But it does not mean that families cannot benefit from books such as William Bennett's *Tales of Virtue* (1993) and *The Moral Compass* (1995), Colin Greer and Herbert Kohl's *A Call to Character* (1995), William Kilpatrick's *Books that Build Character* (1994), or Jill and Stuart Briscoe's *The Family Book of Christian Values* (1995). Still, rather than reaching for these anthologies at bedtime or story hour, adults with children's best interests at heart will use them as reference guides. These collections of enriching children's literature can point parents and teachers to picture books and novels that offer delight as well as edification. Many children's classics can be used creatively and effectively in family devotions. For example, to explain God's relentless love to little ones, a minister used *The Runaway Bunny* picture book. Like a stained glass window scene, it illuminated a biblical truth for children who might have been less captivated by the familiar story of the lost sheep.

Most children love family traditions. Books can be one of the best parts of family traditions. One Methodist minister began his Christmas meditation in a national magazine with the sentence, "It is not Christmas in our house without reading Barbara Robinson's *The Best Christmas Pageant Ever*" (Avon, 1979).

For families who like traditional devotional materials, the most enduringly popular books are probably *Little Visits with God* and *More Little Visits with God* by Jahamann and Simon. There are many similar books with simple anecdotes illustrating moral or theological points. Some children enjoy these, and others find them too pious or boring.

One of the loveliest of the countless prayer books for children is *Moments with God,* published by Regina.

Agnes Sanford wrote a pair of unusual but endearing books for children, *Let's Believe* and *A Pasture for Peterkin* (written in the 1950s and now out of print). Their clear teaching about how inner thought and prayer life affect outer circumstances was bold indeed. The rather sweet old-fashioned approach was balanced with strong faith and briskly practical psychology, so the two books spoke to parents as well as children. It is worth the effort of searching out these buried treasures.

Stories of courage in the face of danger have always attracted children. One of the best books in this category was Myrna Grant's *Vanya* (1975, out of print), the story of a young Soviet soldier, and this was followed by several books about Ivan, including *Ivan and the Secret Suitcase.* Today's young readers can find similar stories of faith under fire in Dave and Neta Jackson's Trailblazer Books (Bethany House).

In the 1950s and 1960s, children enjoyed *Peter Piper, Missionary Parakeet* by Gertrude Warner (author of The Boxcar Children series), which describes the amusing true adventures of an unusual bird. Next came the evocative little fantasy *Semo: A Dolphin's Search for Christ* (1977) by S. G. Harrell. Semo was a dolphin who lived at the time of Christ, and he played a loving part in the lives of both Peter and Christ. (Madeleine L'Engle's *A*

Ring of Endless Light is another spiritual story about dolphins.) Now children can read *The Crippled Lamb* (1994, Gold Medallion) by Max Lucado, a tender tale about Joshua, a little lamb with black spots and a limp. He realizes his worth when he gets to keep the baby Jesus warm. But the most moving Christian animal story of all—one that can bring tears to the eyes of almost everyone—is the story "Robin Redbreast" by Selma Lagerlöf, Swedish poet and novelist. She was the first woman to win the Nobel Prize for literature.

The holidays, especially Christmas, are celebrated in a wide variety of children's books. Just as selecting the right gifts for our children takes time, finding just the right books for the seasons of our lives requires some shopping and comparing. A case in point is *One Wintry Night* (1994) by Ruth Bell Graham. It is a beautiful picture book by one of America's finest Christian women, and it has been a bestseller. But a reviewer in *School Library Journal* described it as "written in an earnest, instructive, and sometimes cloying tone . . . less than compelling because it tries too hard to do too much." On the other hand, Nonny Hogrogian's *The First Christmas* (1995) was described by the same critic as a work where "narrative, gospel, and art create a whole that is inspired in its simplicity and beauty." Whether or not one agrees with these assessments, we can agree on the importance of choosing books that clearly and simply beckon children to the life of faith.

In the world of picture books, Tomie dePaola and Tasha Tudor are two award-winning illustrators with a special interest in spiritual themes. Author-illustrator dePaola seriously considered becoming a Benedictine monk, but he decided his place of service was in the larger world. He believes he is being true to the gift God gave him by drawing his pictures. In *Noah and the Ark* (1983), *David and Goliath* (1984), *Tomie dePaola's Book of Bible Stories* (1990), *The Miracles of Jesus* (1987), and *The Parables of Jesus* (1987) he presents favorite stories from the Scriptures. *Francis the Poor Man of Assisi* (1982) is an inspirational biography presented with beauty and respect. A Renaissance French folktale about a young juggler named Giovanni is retold in *The Clown of God* (1978). This book is perhaps dePaola's best tribute to the life of faith. He has also written about *Patrick: Patron Saint of Ireland* (1992) and *Christopher: The Holy Giant* (1995). His love of the Christmas season and its true meaning is reflected in *The Christmas Pageant* (1978), *The Friendly Beasts* (1981), *The Story of the Three Wise Kings* (1983), and *An Early American Christmas* (1987).

Tasha Tudor's illustrations evoke a simpler time in America, and their old fashioned charm is a nice complement to selections from the Bible. *And It Was So: Words from the Scripture* (re-released, 1996), *Give Us This Day: The Lord's Prayer* (1987, re-released 1992), and *The Lord Is My Shepherd: The Twenty-Third Psalm* (1980, re-released, 1999) depict treasured passages from the Bible. Tudor has also compiled and illustrated *First Prayers* (1952), *More Prayers* (1967), *First Graces* (1955), and other inspirational anthologies. In all her books she emphasizes the importance of intimate family relationships, integrity and hard work, and delight in God's creation. Some critics think her books are too sentimental and nostalgic, but children and adults continue to appreciate her work and the values behind it.

Scott O'Dell, winner of both the Newbery Award and the Hans Christian Anderson Award, ardently admires William Tyndale for sacrificing his life to give England the Bible in English. Tyndale's translation, for which he died at the stake in 1536, is the basis of our King James Version. In 1975 O'Dell published *The Hawk That Dare Not Hunt by Day,* a novel based upon Tyndale's life. O'Dell did research for two years, visiting England and the continent more than once in preparation for this story, which is rich in historical details about smuggling, sea life, and the Black Death.

Of course children move into adult literature as soon as they are ready. Much standard fare, such as Catherine Marshall's *Christy*, is easily read by mature twelve-year-olds. Other family favorites are *Robinson Crusoe* by Daniel Defoe, *Ben Hur* by Lew Wallace, *The Robe* by Lloyd Douglas, and *In His Steps* by Charles Sheldon.

In addition, there are dozens of books especially for young Christian readers—adventure tales, animal parables, family stories, missionary stories, and tales set out in the country or back in the past that are printed in inexpensive editions. These range from the good quality of Patricia St. John's stories to humble but happy Archie comic books.

It seems to be extremely difficult for highly competent writers to produce distinctly Christian fiction of great merit. The more doctrine the book includes, the lower it usually ranks as literature. The finer the writing, the less specific doctrine one is apt to find. C. S. Lewis urged authors not to force specific morals and doctrine into their fiction. It will not ring true, he advised, unless it is inevitable.

Nonfiction author John White was inspired by C. S. Lewis's Narnian Chronicles to write his own fantasies of the imaginary world of Anthropos (see chapter 6). The Spirit Flyer series by John Bibee also features vivid tales of spiritual power and spiritual warfare, subtly packed with Bible truth.

Artistic merit aside, popular series of Christian adventure books continue to entertain and inspire many young readers. Parents and grandparents who grew up with Paul Hutchen's Sugar Creek Gang, Mary Christian's Goosehill Gang, Paul White's worthy Jungle Doctor books, and the Danny Orlis series by Bernard Palmer can share these stories with today's young readers. (See chapter 9 for more Christian series books.)

In the Lindskoog home there is a little paperback with brittle pages, musty and browning, but the print is still clear. *The Austin Boys Adrift* by Ken Anderson was presented to a boy named John in 1944. At the end, two too-perfect Austin boys have suddenly become international heroes and have also led tough anti-religious Lieutenant Wilson to the Lord. Tim has miraculously survived a burst appendix, followed by a successful enemy aircraft attack, a crash at sea, several days on a raft without food and water, a violent storm, and belated surgery. Jim speaks to Tim at the end of the story:

> "You know the Lord really does things for a fellow. I wish every fellow in the world had Him for a friend . . . It makes life lots more fun, doesn't it, Tim?"
>
> "It sure does, Jim."
>
> Then, looking silently at each other for a moment as they gripped each other's hands, Jim and Tim Austin said that as long as they lived they were going to seek God's will in everything, for they had learned beyond a doubt that God leads those who put their trust in Him.

Actually, this is poor prose. But at least one boy who received it for Christmas came to love great literature anyway—and to believe the basic message that the Austin boys share with Bunyan's Pilgrim: "God leads those who put their trust in Him."

There is a store sticker in the front of that old paperback book. It says, "Christian Reading in Christian Homes." It is an old ideal and a good one.

The following books are recommended to parents who

are interested in growing young Christians.

Bible Stories

A for the Ark (1952) by Roger Duvoisin—A biblically accurate picture book.

The Beginner's Bible (1989) adapted by Karen Henley.

The Blessing of the Lord: Stories from the Old and New Testaments (1997) retold by Gary D. Schmidt, illustrated by Dennis Nolan—Each of the twenty-five stories is "set in a moment of crisis when human frailty comes face to face with God." Grade 6 and up.

The Book of Adam to Moses (1992)—stories from the five books of Moses translated by Lore Segal and illustrated by Leonard Baskin.

Brian Wildsmith's Illustrated Bible Stories (1969)—text by Philip Turner. Also *A Christmas Story* (1989) and *Joseph* (1997).

Catherine Marshall's Story Bible (1982)—with illustrations by Swiss children.

The Children's Bible in 365 Stories (1985) by Mary Batchelor, illustrated by John Haysom—PreS–Grade 4.

David's Songs: His Psalms and Their Story (1992) compiled by Colin Eisler, illustrated by Jerry Pinkney—Grade 3 and up.

I Am Joseph (1980) by Barbara Cohen—Grade 6 and up.

In the Beginning of the World (1982) by Masahiro Kasuya

In the Beginning There Was No Sky (1986) by Walter Wangerin, Jr., illustrated by Joe Boddy—Retells the story of creation with emphasis upon God's love for the listening child.

Jonah and the Great Fish (1984), *Noah and the Great Flood* (1977) illustrated by Warwick Hutton.

Ladder of Angels (1979) by Madeleine L'Engle—Stories from the Old Testament illustrated with children's art work. Also *The Glorious Impossible* (1990), which describes the life of Jesus Christ with scenes from fourteenth century Italian artist Giotto.

Look What You've Done Now, Moses (1984), *Abram, Abram, Where Are You Going?* by Fredrick and Patricia McKissack, illustrated by Joe Boddy—Excellent for beginning readers. PreS–Grade 3.

Marian's Big Book of Bible Stories (re-released, 1988) by Marian M. Schoolland—A favorite for over thirty years. Also *Leading Little Ones to God: A Child's Book of Bible Teachings* (1962; re-released, 1995, Gold Medallion). PreS–Grade 3.

Mary and Martha (1995) by Marty Rhodes Figley, illustrated by Cat Bowman Smith—PreS–Grade 3.

The Mighty Ones: Great Men and Women of Early Bible Days by Meindert De Jong.

Noah's Ark (1977), *The Book of Jonah* (1985) by Peter Spier—Picture books for all ages.

The Precious Pearl (1986) by Nick Butterworth, illustrated by Mike Inkpen—Part of a series on the parables of Jesus. PreS–Grade 2.

Read-Aloud Bible Stories, Volume One (1982, Gold Medallion), *Volume Two* (1985) by Ella Lindvall, illustrated by Kent Puckett.

The Seven Days of Creation by Leonard Everett Fisher (1981)—A picture book for all ages.

The Shepherd's Song: The Twenty-Third Psalm (1993) illustrated by Julia Miner.

Stories from the Bible (1971) retold by Alvin Tresselt, illustrated by Lynd Ward.

Stories that Jesus Told: The Parables Retold for Children (1995) by Patricia St. John, illustrated by Tony Morris—Grade 2 and up.

To Everything There Is a Season, from Ecclesiastes, illustrated by Leo and Diane Dillon.

The United Bible Societies' Scripture Comic Book series—Stories from the Old and New Testament are vividly illustrated for children and teens. Available in

English and Spanish from the American Bible Society.
The Wicked City (1972) by Isaac Bashevis Singer, illustrated by Leonard Everett Fisher.
Women of the Bible (1998) by Carol Armstrong—A picture book for all ages.

Bible Study
The All Time Awesome Bible Search (1991) by Sandy Silverthorne.
The Ancient World of the Bible (1994) by Malcolm Day—excellent illustrations, maps, and a timeline complement the thought-provoking text on the Old Testament. Grade 3 and up.
The Baker Bible Dictionary for Kids (1997) by Daryl J. Lucas, Bruce Barton, and James C. Galvin—One of the most complete and easy-to-use reference books for children. Grade 3 and up.
Bible Animals (1992) by Bruce Barton, James C. Galvin, and others—Part of The Bible Discovery Collection from Tyndale. Full color illustrations and fascinating text convey much more than zoology. Grade 3 and up.
Bible History Atlas (1982) by F. F. Bruce.
Bible Lands (1991, DK Eyewitness series) by Jonathan N. Tubbs.
How Our Bible Came to Us: The Story of the Book that Changed the World (1985) by Meryl Doney—Grade 3 and up.
I Want to Know Series: I Want to Know More about the Bible, About God, About Jesus, About Prayer (1998) by Rick Osborne and K. Christie Bowler—Four volumes. Grade 2–5.
The International Children's Bible Handbook (1997, Gold Medallion) by Lawrence Richards.
Jerusalem, Shining Still (1987) by Karla Kuskin, illustrated by David Frampton.

Jesus, the Man Who Changed History (1997) by Meryl Doney—Grade 3 and up.

Plants of the Bible, Trees of the Bible, Birds of the Bible, Animals of the Bible (1978) by Vic Mitchell—K–Grade 5.

Tell Me the Truth (1997) by Joni Eareckson Tada, illustrated by Ron DiCianni—A picture book presentation of seven biblical truths children need in order to grow up confident and secure.

What the Bible Is All About for Young Explorers (1987, Gold Medallion) by Frances Blakenbaker.

The World of the Bible for Young Readers (1988) by Yair Hoffman—Written from a Jewish perspective, this illustrated book covers the history of Israel during its first two thousand years. It includes legends. Grade 6 and up.

Prayer and Family Devotions

Amazing Grace: The Story of the Hymn (1997) by Linda Granfield, illustrated by Janet Wilson—If hymns are part of a child's worship experience, it can be enjoyable to hear about the people who wrote them and the situations that inspired them.

Anytime Prayers (1994) by Madeleine L'Engle, illustrated by photographer Maria Rooney.

Big Thoughts for Little People (1971) and *Giant Steps for Little People* (1985) by Kenneth Taylor—PreS–Grade 3.

A Child's Book of Prayers (1985) illustrated by Michael Hague.

The Creation (1994) by James Weldon Johnson, illustrated by James E. Ransome—A magnificent story poem. Grade 6 and up.

Do You See Me God? (1990, Gold Medallion) by Elspeth Campbell Murphy—PreS–Grade 1.

Does God Know How to Tie Shoes? (1993) by Nancy White Carlstrom, illustrated by Lori McElrath-Eslick—PreS–Grade 3.

God Cares series (1983–84) by Elspeth Campbell Murphy—PreS–Grade 3.

God, I've Gotta Talk to You (1974) by Ann Jennings and Walter Wangerin.

Is Anybody Listening When I Pray? (1980) by Phoebe Cranor—This book is written more to parents than children, but its twenty chapters are excellent resources for family devotions. Grade 5 and up, adaptable to the needs of younger children.

Just in Case You Ever Wonder (1992, Gold Medallion), *Tell Me the Story* (1992, Gold Medallion), and *Tell Me the Secrets* (1993) by Max Lucado, illustrated by Ron DiCianni.

Let's-Talk-About-It series by Lois Walfrid Johnson—Each book in this series features twenty-five short stories about children making tough decisions. The stories are followed by questions that help readers decide how they would respond. Titles in the series: *Secrets of the Best Choice, Thanks for Being My Friend, You Are Wonderfully Made, You're Worth More than You Think.* Grade 3–6.

The Lion Book of Children's Prayers (1977) edited by Mary Batchelor—Also released in the U.S. as *The Doubleday Book of Children's Prayers* (1997).

Listen to the Animals and *Animals that Show and Tell* by William L. Coleman—Family devotional books that celebrate the Creator and His creation (Grade 3 and up). This author has written many other enjoyable and informative children's books.

My Heart, Christ's Home (1997) by Robert Boyd Munger and Carolyn Nystrom—A picture book adaptation of the Christian classic.

Nobody Else Will Listen (1973) by Marjorie Holmes—Grade 6 and up.

The One Year Book of Devotions for Kids (1993–97)—The first two volumes of this three-volume set draw material from the Children's Bible Hour radio broadcast. The third is by Jill Briscoe. Grade 3 and up.

Parables from Nature: Earthly Stories with a Heavenly Meaning (1954) by John Calvin Reid—Grade 1–5.

Paw Paw Chuck's Big Ideas in the Bible (1995, Gold Medallion) by Chuck Swindoll—A storytelling grandfather puts biblical principles in easy reach of young children.

Prayer for a Child (1944, Caldecott Winner) by Rachel Field, illustrated by Elizabeth Orton Jones.

Someday . . . Heaven (1993), *Somewhere Angels* (1994), and *Someone Awesome* (1995) by Larry Libby—Picture books for all ages.

Songs of the Sun (1952) by Francis of Assisi, illustrated by Elizabeth Orton Jones.

Story Sunday: Christian Fairy Tales for Young and Old Alike (1978) by John R. Aurelio—Fables and parables that highlight Christian truth or morals in an entertaining way. Also, *Mosquitoes in Paradise* and *Gather Round.*

The Sunday Morning Fun Book (1995) by Annette LaPlaca, illustrated by David LaPlaca.

A View from the Zoo (1987) and *It's a Jungle Out There* (1996) by Gary Richmond—A former zookeeper combines critters, comedy, and Christian principles.

What Is A Christian? (1992) by Carolyn Nystrom—Part of the Children's Bible Basics series. Also, *What Happens When We Die?* (Gold Medallion). K–Grade 4.

When the Aardvark Parked on the Ark (1984) by Calvin Miller—Playful poetry on biblical themes. Grade 3 and up.

Who Am I? (1992) by Katherine Paterson—Also, *Images of God: Views of the Invisible* (1997) by Katherine and John Paterson. Grade 5 and up.

Biography

The Boy Who Sailed 'Round the World Alone (1985) by Robin Lee Graham—Grade 5 and up.

Destination: Moon (1990, Gold Medallion) by James Irwin

God's Troubadour (1957) by Sophie Jewett—story of St. Francis illustrated by Giotto.

The Good Man of Assisi (re-released, 1998) by Mary Coker Joslin—a biography of St. Francis.

Her Own Way: The Story of Lottie Moon by Helen Monsell

Hero Tales: A Family Treasury of True Stories from the Lives of Christian Heroes (1996–97) by Dave and Neta Jackson—Two volumes of biographical vignettes especially appropriate for family devotions. Grade 4–8.

John Wesley (1951) by May McNeer, illustrated by Lynd Ward—Grade 4 and up.

The Life and Times of Mother Theresa (1997) by Tanya Rice.

Maximillian Kolbe: Saint of Auschwitz (1997) by Elaine Murray Stone—Grade 3 and up.

Martin Luther: Hero of Faith (1962) by Frederick Nohl—Grade 6 and up.

Mother Cabrini: Missionary to the World (re-released, 1997) by Frances Parkinson Keyes.

Night Preacher (1969) by Louise A. Vernon.

Roots Deep and Strong: Great Men and Women of the Church (1995) by Mary E. Penrose. Grade 4 and up.

Saint Patrick (1998) by Ann Tompert—a picture book based on Patrick's confession and letters.

Sor Juana: A Trailblazing Thinker (1994) by Elizabeth Coonrod Martinez. Grade 5 and up.

St. Francis (1996) by Brian Wildsmith—Grade 4–7.

St. Valentine (1992) by Robert Sabuda—Picture book.

Squanto and the First Thanksgiving (1983) by Joyce K. Kessel—K–Grade 3.

They Dared to Cross Frontiers (1975) by Faye De Beck Flynt—Stories about brave American Christians, including John Woolman, Frederick Douglass, John Eliot, Sequoyah, Mary McLeod Bethune, and Martin Luther King, Jr.

Thomas Merton: Poet, Prophet, Priest (1997) by Jennifer Fisher Bryant—Grade 7 and up.

Holidays

Amahl and the Night Visitors (1986) by Gian Carlo Menotti.

The Animals' Christmas and Other Stories (1997) by Avril Rowlands—Grade 2–5.

Baby Jesus Like My Brother (1995) by Margery Wheeler Brown, illustrated by George Ford—A little girl helps her younger brother understand what Christmas is all about. PreS–Grade 3.

Branta and the Golden Stone (1993) by Walter Wangerin, illustrated by Deborah Healy—A Christmas book for the whole family.

The Candymaker's Gift (1996) by Helen Haidle—A similar picture book is *The Legend of the Candy Cane* (1997) by Lori Walburg.

The Cat Who Knew the Meaning of Christmas (1996) by Marion Chapman Gremmels, illustrated by Dave LaFleur.

Christ in Christmas: A Family Advent Celebration (1989) and *Christ in Easter: A Family Celebration of Holy Week* (1990)—These NavPress anthologies provide hymns, poems, Scriptures, activities, and weekly devotionals by evangelical leaders.

Christmas in the Barn (1949) by Margaret Wise Brown, illustrated by Barbara Cooney.

The Christmas Miracle of Jonathan Toomey (1995) by Susan Woyciechowski, illustrated by P. J. Lynch.

Easter Bunny, Are You for Real? (re-release, 1998) by Harold Myra, illustrated by Jane Kurisu—Also, *Santa, Are You for Real?* (1977) and *Halloween, Is It for Real?* (1982). K–Grade 4.

Easter: The King James Version (1989) illustrated by Jan Pienkowski.

The Easter Story (1990) by Carol Heyer.

Elijah's Angel: A Story for Chanukah and Christmas (1992) by Michael J. Rosen, illustrated by Aminah Brenda and Lynn Robinson—Elijah is a woodcarver, preacher, and friend of a Jewish boy who visits his shop. Their friendship is tested when Christmas arrives. A marvelous picture book for the whole family.

He Is Risen (1985) by Elizabeth Winthrop—The story of the resurrection told simply with lavish illustrations.

I Am Christmas (1995) by Nancy White Carlstrom, illustrated by Lori McElrath-Eslick—A picture book for all ages.

A Midnight Clear: Twelve Stories for the Christmas Season (1995) by Katherine Paterson—Grade 5 and up.

My Son, My Savior (1997) by Calvin Miller, illustrated by Ron DiCianni—A beautiful presentation of the Christmas story for the whole family.

Once Upon a Pony: A Mountain Christmas (1994) by Nancy Ward Balderose—A young boy and girl set out to deliver a load of coal to their church before the Christmas Eve service. Their encounters on the way are a vivid lesson in compassion. K–Grade 3.

Silent Night: Its Story and Song (1997) by Margaret Hodges, illustrated by Tim Ladwig.

Song of the Morning (1997) and *Star of Wonder* (1997) compiled by Pat Alexander—Outstanding collections of Christmas and Easter stories for family and classroom reading. Alexander, former editorial director of Lion Publishing, has also compiled *A Feast of Good Stories* (1997). All three volumes reflect a Christian worldview.

Tell Me a Story at Christmas: Heartwarming Stories from around the World (1996) edited by Kathryn Deering.

Religious Fiction

Many of the novels and picture books listed in other chapters have strongly Christian themes. Parents are encouraged to use books from both secular and religious publishers in nurturing their children's spiritual development. A variety of Christian series books are mentioned in chapter 9. Here are some more suggestions:

Adventures in the Big Thicket (1990) and *Treasure in an Oatmeal Box* (1990, Gold Medallion) by Ken Gire.

The Bronze Bow (1961, Newbery Winner) by Elizabeth Speare.

Ears and the Secret Song (1995) by Meryl Doney, illustrated by William Geldart—Also, *The Very Worried Sparrow* (1978) illustrated by Gillian Gaze.

The Gifts of the Child Christ: And Other Stories and Fairy Tales (re-release, 1996) by George MacDonald, edited by Glenn E. Sadler.

It's the Truth, Christopher (1984) by Patricia McKissack—K–Grade 3.

Marty Makes a Difference by Joseph D. Trimble—When a boy's church is burned down, he is hurt and confused but determined to help with rebuilding (K–Grade 5). Another similar book with a strong message is *When Our Church Building Burned Down* (1986) by Martha Whitmore Hickman.

One Small Lost Sheep (1997) by Claudia Mills, illustrated by Walter Lyon Krudop—A picture book for all ages.

Potter (1986, Gold Medallion) by Walter Wangerin.

The Shoemaker's Dream (1982) by Mildred Schell, illustrated by Masahiro Kasuya—Martin dreams that Jesus will visit him the next day. He has several visitors but is disappointed that none of them is Jesus. Then he makes a wonderful discovery. Based on the story by Leo Tolstoy. PreS–Grade 3.

Sir Gibbie (1992, Gold Medallion) by George MacDonald, edited by Kathryn Lindskoog.

Stories to Share: A Family Treasury of Faith (1997) by Patricia St. John—This Christian author has given young readers several excellent novels, including *Star of Light, The Tanglewood's Secret, Rainbow Garden, Treasures of the Snow,* and *Where the River Begins.* Grade 3 and up.

A Tale of Three Trees (1989) by Angela Elwell Hunt, illustrated by Tim Jonke—This adaptation of an old folktale has been a bestseller ever since its release. It is one the whole family can enjoy.

Tales of the Kingdom (1983, Gold Medallion) and *Tales of the Resistance* (1986) by David and Karen Mains—Christian fantasies that are ideal for reading aloud. Grade 3–5.

Yellow and Pink by William Steig—A picture book for all ages about creation.

Over seventy years ago, Carolyn Sherwin Bailey offered parents a book called *Stories Children Need.* (Interestingly, it was published by Milton Bradley, now famous for children's games.) She introduced her character-building anthology with these words: "The powers of imagination . . . may build the house of the child's spirit as high as a tower or they may tear it down to its foundations, leaving the soul bare. . . . Every story which a child hears becomes a part of his mental and spiritual life."

In pursuing character for ourselves and for our children, Bethel College professor Daniel Taylor has said we need to think more in terms of stories:

> We live in stories the way fish live in water, breathing them in and out, buoyed up by them, taking from them our sustenance. . . . We are characters making choices over time—and living with the consequences—and that is the essence of story both in literature and in life.

Books are a realm of adventure for people who cannot

go out to find all the adventure they hunger for in travel and activity. Books are a source of security and tradition for people who cannot get all the stability and safety they hunger for in our confused and upset society. Books can help us escape from either worry or indifference into reality.

The best thing about loving books is that they so often lead us on into more love of people, love of beauty, love of goodness, and love of God.

The Literature of
Daily Living

15 Telling Our
Stories

My story is important not because it is mine . . .
but because if I tell it anything like right, the
chances are you will recognize that in many ways
it is yours. Maybe nothing is more important
than that we keep track . . . of these stories of
who we are and where we have come from and
the people we have met along the way because
it is precisely through these stories in all their
particularity . . . that God makes himself known
to each of us most powerfully and personally . . .
to lose track of our stories is to be profoundly
impoverished not only humanly but spiritually.
—Frederick Buechner, *Telling Secrets*

If you'd not be forgotten as soon as you are
    dead and rotten,
Either write things worth reading, or do
    things worth writing.
—Benjamin Franklin, *Poor Richard's Almanac*

We're looking for people to write children's books,"
the ad says:

We need writers. There are over 150 publishers of
books for children and more than 250 magazines,
all of which have a need for writers. . . . Have you

ever read a children's story and said "I can do better than that?" Have you ever deplored the lack of good new literature for young readers? . . . The market is enormous. Editors and publishers of children's literature are searching for talented writers. . . . Last year, more than 30 million children's books were published, producing total sales of over 170 million dollars!

But the enthusiastic company that is urging people to become writers for children is actually a correspondence school. It wants to teach basic writing techniques to would-be writers for a price. It may offer very good instruction. But, contrary to the ad's claim, there is no shortage of writers for children.

Quite the contrary—editors and publishers are already besieged with truckloads of manuscripts they cannot use. Many publishers return about a hundred manuscripts a week. Some publishers no longer return unsolicited manuscripts because their staff is so overloaded. They hardly ever accept one that comes in uninvited.

Editors are always on the lookout for phenomenally good writers—or writers whose sales might be phenomenal. But they groan as they plow through the ordinary material that pours in all year long. One editor claimed that she received several amateurishly written stories about twins every month. Blond twins.

Aspiring writers should always take heart, however, when they remember that both Dr. Seuss and Richard Adams had their first books—which were far from trite—rejected by many, many publishers before they were accepted and became immensely popular. Editors do guess wrong about some children's books.

Very few writers of children's literature who get published can support themselves with their craft. Many of the best had the privilege of an expensive university education; many have been aided by financial support from spouses or inheritance; and most have to write after regular work hours—which leaves little time for anything else. For parents, that is not easy.

But all parents can become successful authors at home, where their stories matter most. As journalist and family folklorist Elizabeth Stone writes, "Our lives are shaped not just by our families, but by the stories they tell. Tales of our parents' and grandparents' lives, whether happy or not, form in us a sense of ourselves— of who we are, or should be" (*Black Sheep and Kissing Cousins: How Our Family Stories Shape Us*). These stories give children a sense of their family's uniqueness and the common bonds shared by its members. Family stories also can convey deeply held family values as expressed in actual life choices rather than in the abstract, and they can help children learn to deal with failure and flaws in themselves and in others.

According to those at Reading Is Fundamental, a national nonprofit organization devoted to encouraging young readers and their families,

> Telling stories to children, as well as reading aloud, helps develop skills and motivates children to read on their own. Some of the best-loved children's books began as stories told to young listeners.
>
> What makes storytelling so appealing? Anyone can tell stories, *anywhere, anytime*. Stories are free for the asking. Their only cost is something we all can afford to give our children: our time.

This chapter provides an array of ideas about how one can easily create family stories that will be a joy through the years, perhaps for generations to come.

Many mothers start to fill in a baby book for their

child but get bogged down as the months and years fly by. Alas, when did baby cut his molars, and what was baby's second present from Santa, and when did baby first go to the barber shop? The book is apt to go totally blank long before its subject gets to the university degrees, civic honors, and military exploits section sometimes found at the end.

Nevertheless, a baby book can be a good help at first, especially if the parent adds funny stories about baby and relatives and illustrates them with photographs, special greeting cards, or little smudges of the strained beets that baby threw on the wall. Later that grown-up person will marvel at these proofs that he was ever such a funny little animal and so loved. One family even taped in their sliver of pink soap with four small clear tooth marks, a memento of the day their toddler checked to see if pink soap tastes like candy. Silly as all that sounds, it is a rare child who does not take special pleasure in looking at "my baby book" later. It makes a child feel special.

What children seem to enjoy most is a simple collection of many of the funny or quaint things that they said in their early years. They still enjoy these collections when they are adults. Because such a collection will probably range from age one to about age eight, the parent is wise to begin with a loose-leaf notebook that includes a pocket where scraps of paper can be tucked temporarily. If parents usually carry paper and pen when going out, as many do, and if there are plenty of pens and pads around the house, they can often scribble down amusing sayings at the time, with the date if possible. These can be tucked into the notebook's pocket later and eventually copied onto the pages. The first sayings can be mere baby talk, and the later ones will include all kinds of linguistic and psychological subtleties.

Here are just a few from two very ordinary little boys:

"The Lord is my shepherd, I shall not want
    him."
"I brush my teeth so I won't get academies."
"Dad, if Hawaii is part of the United States, how
    did it get so far away?"
"After infinity comes trinity."
"Dad, your hair has a hole in the middle."
"I don't want this piece of bread. This piece is
    the knee."

Drawings, notes, and letters by the children provide
samples of their growth and personality well worth sav-
ing. They can be stashed in a special drawer or, if time
allows, arranged in a scrapbook. One grandmother offered to take all these pictures and memorabilia and
combine them into a "This Is Your Life" book for her
grandchildren. The pictures were used to illustrate the
story-commentary she wrote.

Descriptions of family trips and special times or
celebrations can also be a pleasure to read later, especially if feelings are emphasized instead of a list of
details.

And photo albums, of course, the picture books of
family life, never lose their interest. Slides and home
movies from parents' and grandparents' childhood help
today's child connect with the past. Videotapes offer a
wealth of memories, and families who own cassette recorders can create their own collection of audiobooks.
One family asked their two grandmothers to tell tales
from their childhood, youth, and child-rearing years on
cassette tape for permanent enjoyment. One of these
grandmothers amplified her tale with a special Swedish
hymn from her childhood. She sang and played it on
the piano, with descriptions of a turn-of-the-century
Christmas in Minnesota and the snowy, early-morning
sled trip to church, where this hymn was always sung

in excited reverence as her own father played the organ.

Some families make up stories by taking turns being the storyteller, going around in a circle and cutting off each speaker every three minutes. Then the next family member continues until a set time when the story has to end. Such stories do not need to be silly, but they are apt to turn out that way before they are over. It is a pleasure to have recordings of children's voices in activities such as these in later years when everything has changed. We cannot stop that change; nor should we try. But we can keep mementos so the past is never lost to us.

Another possibility is having a "radio show," with each family member reading a bit of literature that he or she especially likes. Participants can also interview each other, inquiring about friends, hobbies, pets, opinions, accomplishments, or frustrations, as if they were really on a radio show. Some children—and parents—like to invent commercials to go between interviews.

A more imaginative kind of "radio program" would be spontaneous dramatizations, setting up a situation such as a family receiving a telegram announcing that an unknown great-uncle has died and left them a million dollars. Or, for more structure, each family member can take the part of a character in a simple story they all know, such as "Goldilocks and the Three Bears," and act it out spontaneously, with or without a narrator. This can also be done with short Bible stories.

While not all of us are gifted with dramatic flair, every family interchange from breakfast conversations to bedtime prayers is laden with character and meaning. The secret is capturing it. A word fitly spoken, Solomon said, is like apples of gold in a silver setting. There is really no shortage of those golden apples. Our world is full of words of wisdom, humor, beauty, and love if we but listen.

All in the Family

For help in identifying, recording, and presenting family stories refer to the following helpful resources:

📖 Zondervan's Family Share Together series (four volumes) by Deborah and Gregg Lewis: *Did I Ever Tell You About When Your Parents Were Children?*, *Did I Ever Tell You About When You Were Little?*, *Did I Ever Tell You How Our Family Got Started?*, and *Did I Ever Tell You About When Your Grandparents Were Young?* These little books are easy to carry along on family outings. Keep one of them handy to encourage family storytelling on trips, vacations, and quiet evenings at home.

📖 *Families Writing* (Writer's Digest Books, 1989) by Peter R. Stillman. The best single source of suggestions for family writing activities. Highly recommended for every home library.

📖 *A Family Remembers: How to Create a Family Memoir Using Video and Tape Recorders* (International Self-Counsel Press, 1993).

📖 *The Family Storytelling Handbook* (Macmillan, 1987) by Anne Pellowski, illustrated by Lynn Sweat. Explains how to use stories, anecdotes, rhymes, handkerchiefs, paper, and other objects to enrich your family traditions.

📖 *Family Storytelling: Sharing Stories and Reading Happily Ever After* (1989). A helpful pamphlet presented by Reading Is Fundamental.

📖 *Family Tales, Family Wisdom: How to Gather the Stories of a Lifetime and Share Them with Your Family* (William Morrow, 1991) by Dr. Robert U. Akeret with Daniel Klein. A psychologist presents a strong case for collecting "elder tales" from senior family members and using them as a source of family bonding and enrichment.

📖 *Tell Me a Story: Stories for Your Grandchildren and the Art of Telling Them* (Doubleday, 1984) by Charlie and Martha Shedd. Offers models and practical advice.

📖 *Writing from Within: A Unique Guide to Writing Your Life's Stories* (Hunter House, 1990) by Bernard Selling. Tap your own memory for material as well as gathering and recording the memoirs of relatives. Additional help in memoir writing is available from *How to Write the Story of Your Life* (Writer's Digest Books, 1984) by Frank P. Thomas.

📖 "Writing the Past: Poetry, Memory, and History" from *English Journal* (April 1991). Contains several articles about helping children write autobiography, biography, memoir, and poetry based on personal memories.

Some children take an interest in writing diaries. This gives some sustained writing practice, which is worthwhile. Besides that, it helps children become more aware of how a year passes and how they spend their time, money, and energy. They like to put a part of their lives into book form, wondering what will happen on all the blank pages to come. These diaries should be secret, if they are to be at all exciting.

One of the most moving books of our century happens to be a child's diary. It is the story of Anne Frank, a Jewish girl in Holland who was hiding from the Nazis with her family. The Nazis destroyed Anne Frank, but they did not find her diary. It is ours to read today with smiles and tears.

Journals are generally much more creative and enriching than diaries. They, too, are usually private; however, there could be a family journal for members who are close and supportive. A large loose-leaf notebook would allow members to draw, write, or type on their own sheets of three-hole paper, then date and include them, day by day or week by week. All members could examine and think about the contributions of the other members. Everyone could put in fears, hopes, joys, interests, responses, discoveries, ideas, poems, stories, dreams, songs, prayers, and letters to oneself or to the rest of the family.

Just as an in-depth private journal can put an individual more in touch with his or her inner self and capacities, so a family journal might put a family more in touch with itself. The story it gradually told would be the inner story of a group of unique, growing people. Just making this book together could influence that story. Here the humblest contribution is as valuable as the most artistic. A truly skillful sonnet by one member is no "better" than an awkward bit of verse with misspelled words.

One September an English teacher asked her young teenage students to write on the old topic "What I Did Last Summer." (She believed it was a good old topic.) A girl named Janet told about being the only survivor of an August traffic accident that killed her father and brother. She said that she would not have shared her sorrow if she had not been asked to write the paper, and that writing about it helped. She ended by deciding that the summer of her childhood was suddenly over.

Each one of us will someday reflect upon how we spent the summer of our lives. There is no more fascinating and profound story. It began "Once upon a time," and it will eventually end beyond all imagining.

Appendix One

Further Recommended Reading for Parents and Teachers

Bodger, Joan. *How the Heather Looks: A Joyous Journey to the British Sources of Children's Books*. New York: Viking, 1959.

Cullinan, Bernice E. *Literature and the Child*. New York: Harcourt Brace Jovanovich, 1981.

Egoff, Sheila, G. T. Stubbs, and L. F. Ashley, eds. *Only Connect: Readings on Children's Literature*. Oxford: Oxford University Press, 1996.

Gilbar, Steven. *The Open Door: When Writers First Learned to Read*. Boston: Godine, 1989.

Hearne, Betsy. *Choosing Books for Children*. New York: Delacorte, 1990.

Holdren, John, and E. D. Hirsch, Jr. *Books to Build On*. New York: Delta, Bantam Doubleday Dell, 1996.

Hopkins, Lee Bennett. *Books Are by People* (1969), *More Books by More People* (1974). New York: Citation.

Hydrick, Janie. *Parent's Guide to Literacy for the 21st Century*. Urbana, IL: National Council of Teachers of English, 1996.

Johnson, Edna, Evelyn R. Sickels, and Frances Clarke Sayers. *Anthology of Children's Literature, Fourth Edition*. Boston: Houghton Mifflin, 1970.

Kobrin, Beverly. *Eyeopeners! How to Choose and Use Children's Books about Real People, Places, and Things*. New York: Viking Penguin, 1988.

Kropp, Paul. *Raising a Reader: Make Your Child a Reader for Life*. New York: Doubleday, 1996.

Lamne, Linda Leonard. *Raising Readers: A Guide to Sharing Literature with Young Children*. New York: Walker & Company, 1980.

Landsberg, Michele. *Reading for the Love of It: Best Books for Young Readers*. New York: Prentice Hall, 1987.

MacAlpine, Loretta. *Inside KidVid: The Essential Parents' Guide to Video*. Penguin, 1995.

Newbery and Caldecott Medal Books 1956–1965 with Acceptance Papers, Biographies of the Award Winners and Evaluating Articles by Elizabeth

H. Gross, Carolyn Horovitz, and Norma R. Fryatt.
*Newbery and Caldecott Medal Books 1976–1985 with Acceptance Papers
by the Award Winners, Biographical Notes, and Evaluating Essays.*
*Once Upon a Time . . . Celebrating the Magic of Children's Books in Honor
of the Twentieth Anniversary Of READING IS FUNDAMENTAL.* New
York: G. P. Putnam's and Sons, 1986.

Paterson, Katherine. *A Sense of Wonder: On Reading and Writing Books for
Children.* New York: Plume, 1995. (Combines two previously published books, *Gates of Excellence* and *The Spying Heart,* in one volume.)

Pearl, Patricia. *Children's Religious Books: An Annotated Bibliography.*
New York: Garland Publishing, 1988.

Reasoner, Charles. *Releasing Children to Literature* (1976), *Where the
Readers Are* (1972), *When Children Read* (1975), *Bringing Children
and Books Together* (1979). New York: Dell.

Thomas, Virginia Coff, and Betty Davis Miller. *Children's Literature
for All God's Children.* Atlanta: John Knox, 1986.

Tomlinson, Carl M. *Essentials of Children's Literature.* New York: Allyn
& Bacon, 1996.

Townsend, John Rowe. *Written for Children.* Rev. ed. Philadelphia:
Lippincott, 1974.

Trelease, Jim. *The New Read-Aloud Handbook.* New York: Penguin
Books, 1989.

Walsh, Frances. *That Eager Zest.* Philadelphia: Lippincott, 1961.

Wintle, Justin, and Emma Fisher. *The Pied Pipers: Interviews with Influential Creators of Children's Literature.* New York: Paddington
Press, 1974. (Twenty-two interviews, two letters.)

Zinsser, William, ed. *Worlds of Childhood: The Art and Craft of Writing
for Children.* Boston: Houghton Mifflin, 1990. (Contributions by
Jean Fritz, Maurice Sendak, Jill Krementz, Jack Prelutsky, Rosemary Wells, and Katherine Paterson.)

For current reviews of children's books, check with your local public
library for the following publications.

Horn Book magazine (Park Square Building, 31st Street and James
Avenue, Boston, MA 02116, 1-800-325-1170). The emphasis in
this bi-monthly periodical is literary quality. Website: *www.hbook.com*

Parents Choice (Box 185, Waban, MA 02168).

School Library Journal

Other helpful resources are listed in appendix 4.

Appendix Two

Major Awards in Children's Literature

Most parents and teachers are familiar with two children's book awards, the **Newbery Medal** and the **Caldecott Medal.** But over the years many other awards have been created to honor books in other countries and in special categories. Here are some of the major honors currently being given.

Aesop Prize conferred by the American Folklore Society for most outstanding children's and young adult books incorporating folklore.

The **Hans Christian Andersen Award** is often referred to as the little Nobel prize. It was established in 1956 by the International Board on Books for Young People and is awarded every two years to living authors who have made an important international contribution by their complete work rather than a single book. Five different countries are represented on the selection committee, and since 1966 they also award medals to illustrators.

Mildred L. Batchelder Award for the best children's book first published in a foreign language and subsequently translated into English for publication in the U.S.

Boston Globe-Horn Award.

Bratislava Golden Apple Award for books in English.

Children's Book Award of the National Association of Multicultural Education.

Mr. Christie Award for Best Canadian Children's Book.

Margaret A. Edwards Award for Oustanding Literature for Young Adults.

Gold Medallion Award presented by the Evangelical Publishers Association for excellence in Christian publishing. The entries are submitted by publishers and the judges are primarily Christian retailers.

Coretta Scott King Awards for children's books that promote racial equality.

Scott O'Dell Award for Children's and Young Adult Historical Fiction.

Pura Belpre Award which honors Latino writers and illustrators.

UNICEF award which is presented at the premier event in children's book publishing—Italy's Bologna Book Fair at which over 4,000 publishers from over 80 countries are represented.

Laura Ingalls Wilder Medal given to a U.S. author or illustrator whose books have made a lasting contribution to literature for children.

National Book Awards. From 1969 through 1983 children's books were honored at the U.S. National Book Awards' annual convention. During that fourteen-year period, the following children's books received awards:

1969—*Journey from Peppermint Street* by Meindert De Jong

1970—*A Day of Pleasure: Stories of a Boy Growing Up in Warsaw* by Isaac Bashevis Singer

1971—*The Marvelous Misadventures of Sebastian* by Lloyd Alexander

1972—*The Slightly Irregular Fire Engine or the Hithering Dithering Djinn* by Donald Bartheleme

1973—*The Farthest Shore* by Ursula K. LeGuin

1974—*The Court of the Stone Children* by Eleanor Cameron

1975—*M. C. Higgins the Great* by Virginia Hamilton

1976—*Bert Breen's Barn* by Walter D. Edmonds

1977—*The Master Puppeteer* by Katherine Paterson

1978—*The View from the Oak: The Private World of Other Creatures* by Herbert and Judith Kohl

1979—*The Great Gilly Hopkins* by Katherine Paterson

1980—*A Gathering of Days: A New England Girl's Journals 1830–1832* by Joan W. Blos; *A Swiftly Tilting Planet* by Madeleine L'Engle

1981—*The Night Swimmers* by Betsy Byars; *Ramona and Her Mother* by Beverly Cleary; *Oh, Boy! Babies!* by Alison Cragin Herzig and Jane Lawrence Mali

1982—*A Penguin Year* by Susan Bonners; *Words by Heart* by Ouida Sebestyen; *Outside Over There* by Maurice Sendak; *Noah's Ark* by Peter Spier

1983—*Miss Rumphius* by Barbara Cooney; *A Place Apart* by Paula Fox; *A House Is a House for Me* by Mary Ann Hoberman; *Homesick* by Jean Fritz; *Doctor De Soto* by William Steig; *Marked by Fire* by Joyce Carol Thomas

"And the Winners Are . . ."

There are numerous ways to find out which children's books and authors win annual awards. Perhaps the easiest of all is to visit the public library and talk with the children's reference librarian. Many libraries provide cumulative lists of Newbery and Caldecott winners. Other resources are listed in appendix 4.

Appendix Three

Great Thoughts about Books for Children

"Books are the food of youth." Cicero

"For my part I do not write for children, but for the childlike, whether five or fifty or seventy-five."—George MacDonald, author of *The Princess and the Goblin*

"One talks about writing for children—this is all piffle. There's no such thing as writing for children."—Richard Adams, author of *Watership Down*

"I write for the child I was. If you write for the child that was in your own mind there's no division between that child and yourself now, so it should be valid for both."—Lucy Boston, author of *The Children of Green Knowe*

"Like any good writer, I write to amuse myself, not some imaginary audience, and I rather suspect that it is a great help if one has managed never really to grow up. Some writers, I have noticed, have a tendency to write down to children. That way lies disaster."—E. B. White, author of *Charlotte's Web*

"I never write for children. It's just that what I have to say is often too difficult for adults to understand."—Madeleine L'Engle, author of *A Wrinkle in Time*

"To grow up surrounded by books of fantasy, fairy tales, myths means to grow up with an awareness of mystery and wonder, and to be unafraid of those marvels beyond the limited realm of fact."—Madeleine L'Engle

"The only trouble I have is in battening down my imagination and fantasy life, even at my advanced age. It's the same problem I had as a child, only now nobody's going to hit me over the head for it.

They're going to pay me an advance instead."—Maurice Sendak, author of *Where the Wild Things Are*

"I don't think you ever do get inside another child's mind, but you do get inside the child in yourself. There's a certain unresolved child in every adult."—Charlotte Zolotow, author of *Big Sister and Little Sister*

"I would much rather speak to the growing adult in the child than speak to the child where he is at a given moment. . . . I believe growing up is what it's all about. . . . There are a great many writers for children, who are perhaps more interested in recapturing their own childhood; whereas I am trying to come to terms with my adult-hood. . . . The kids sense this too, that I speak to the child as a growing person."—Lloyd Alexander, author of the *Prydain Chronicles*

"Children read books, not reviews. They do not give a hoot about the critics."—Isaac Bashevis Singer, author of *Fearsome Inn*

"Perhaps it is only in childhood that books have any deep influence on our lives. In later life we admire, we are entertained, we may modify some views we already hold, but we are more likely to find in books merely a confirmation of what is in our minds already. . . . What do we ever get nowadays from reading to equal the excitement and the revelation in those first fourteen years?"—Graham Greene

"No kind of writing lodges itself so deeply in our memory, echoing there for the rest of our lives, as the books that we met in our childhood, and when we grow up and read them to our own children they are the oldest of old friends."—William Zinsser

"Children are people. They're just smaller and less experienced. They are not taken in by the smug playfulness of those who write down to them as if they were dull-witted and slightly deaf."—Hugh Lofting, author of *Doctor Dolittle*

"People always ask children's book authors where they get their ideas, as though they pull them off a coat rack. They have to come from within yourself. If I write something that I feel is outside of myself, a story for kiddies, I'll throw it in the garbage."—Arnold Lobel, author of *Frog and Toad*

"I'm trying to write for my readers the best story, the truest story of which I am capable. . . . We know that those of us who write for children are called, not to do something to a child, but to be some-one for a child."—Katherine Paterson, author of *Bridge to Terabithia*

"I am called to listen to the sound of my own heart—to write the story within myself that demands to be told at that particular point in my life. And if I do this faithfully, clothing that idea in the flesh of human experience and setting it in a true place, the sound from my heart will resound in the reader's heart."—Katherine Paterson

"The gift of creative reading, like all natural gifts, must be nourished or it will atrophy. And you nourish it, in much the same way you nourish the gift of writing—you read, think, talk, look, listen, hate, fear, love, weep—and bring all of your life like a sieve to what you read. That which is not worthy of your gift will quickly pass through, but the gold remains."—Katherine Paterson

"Blessings be the inventor of the alphabet, pen and printing press! Life would be—to me in all events—a terrible thing without books."—Lucy Maud Montgomery, author of *Anne of Green Gables*

"A book is a garden carried in the pocket."—Chinese proverb

"If you are tired of the real landscape look at it in a mirror. By putting bread, gold, horse, apple, or the very roads into a myth, we do not retreat from reality: we rediscover it. As long as the story lingers in our mind, the real things are more themselves."—C. S. Lewis, author of *The Lion, the Witch and the Wardrobe*

"I now enjoy fairy tales better than I did in childhood: being now able to put more in, of course I get more out."—C. S. Lewis

"No book is worth reading at the age of ten which is not equally (and often far more) worth reading at the age of fifty—except, of course, books of information."—C. S. Lewis

"All children's books are on a strict judgment poor books. Books written entirely for children are poor even as children's books."— J. R. R. Tolkien, author of *The Hobbit*

"Unfortunately, some modern re-makes of great old stories ruin the whole lesson of reward and punishment. I'm afraid this is a disservice to children."—Tomie dePaola, author of *The Knight and the Dragon*

"We do not enjoy a story fully at the first reading. Not till the curiosity . . . has been given its sop and laid asleep, are we at leisure to savour the real beauties. . . . The children understand this well when they ask for the same story over and over again, and in the same words. They want to have again the 'surprise' of discovering that what seemed Little-Red-Riding-Hood's grandmother is really a wolf. It is better when you know it is coming."—Charles Williams

"Good books, like good friends, are few and chosen; the more select, the more enjoyable."—Louisa May Alcott, author of *Little Women*

"One gift the fairies gave me: (three
They commonly bestowed of yore)
The love of books, the golden key
That opens the enchanted door."
—Andrew Lang, author of *The Colour Fairy* books

"A good vocabulary is not acquired by reading books written according to some notion of the vocabulary for one's age group. It comes from reading books above one."—J. R. R. Tolkien

Appendix Four

Children's Literature Resources

Following is information—phone numbers, street addresses, and websites if available—on how to contact many of the publishers and organizations that are mentioned in the book. A children's reference librarian or *Children's Writer's and Illustrator's Market* can provide additional resources.

Websites are resources that can lead parents and teachers to further adventures in the world of children's literature. The authors are not recommending any of these websites for children to visit alone. However, with adult supervision several of them may provide enjoyable multimedia experiences. Many publishers' websites offer downloadable study guides for classroom use, interviews with authors, book excerpts, and other goodies.

Book Publishers and Other Book References

Amazon.com (*http://www.amazon.com*) describes itself as the world's largest bookstore, and it is a wonderful way to find books for children. It also features interviews with children's book authors and illustrators, published book reviews, and reader comments. A valuable reference site with some inevitable sales hype.

American Bible Society; 800-32-BIBLE; 1865 Broadway, New York, NY 10023-7505; *http://www.american.bible.org*

The American Library Association (800-545-2433; 50 East Huron Street, Chicago, IL 60611, *http://www.ala.org*) offers pamphlets of Newbery and Caldecott winners, as well as other products promoting children's literature and reading.

Antique Collectors' Club; 800-252-5231; Market Street Industrial Park, Wappingers Falls, NY 12590; *http://www.antiquecc.com*

Bantam Doubleday Dell; 800-323-9872; 1540 Broadway, New York,

NY 10036; *http://www.bdd.com*

Christian Book Distributor (978-977-5000; P.O. Box 7000, Peabody, MA 01961-7000; *http://www.christianbook.com*) will send a free catalog of books, videos, and computer software upon request.

Dover Publications (516-294-7000; 31 E. Second St., Mineola, NY 11501) sells high-quality facsimiles of children's classics and will send a free catalog upon request.

HarperCollins; 212-207-7000; 10 E. 53rd St., New York, NY 10022; *http://www.harperchildrens.com*

Penguin Group; 212-366-2751; 375 Hudson St., New York, NY 10014; *http://www.penguin.com*

Random House Children's Publishing Group; 212-940-7682; 201 E. 50th St., New York, NY 10022; *http://www.randomhouse.com/kids*

Reading Is Fundamental; 202-287-3220; P.O. Box 23444, Washington, DC 20026; *http://www.rif.org*

Simon & Schuster Children's Publishing Division; 212-698-7200; 1230 Ave. of the Americas, New York, NY 10020; *http://www.simonsays.kids.com*

Magazines

American Girl; 608-836-4848; Pleasant Company Publications, P.O. Box 998, Middleton, WI 53562-0998; *http://www.pleasantco.com*

Bayard Presse Canada; 800-551-OWLS; The Owl Group, 179 John Street, Suite 500, Toronto, Ontario M5T 3G5 Canada; for U.S. subscription information write to P.O. Box 11314, Des Moines, IA 50340; *http://www.owl.on.ca*

Carus Publishing Company; 800-BUGPALS; P.O. Box 300, Peru, IL 61354

Children's Better Health Institute; 317-636-8881; P.O. Box 567, Indianapolis, IN 46206; *http://www.satevepost.org/kidsonline*

Cobblestone Publishing; 800-821-0115; 30 Grove Street, Suite C, Peterborough, NH 03458; *http://www.cobblestonepub.com*

Contact Kids; E=MC Square, P.O. Box 51177, Boulder, CO 80321; Subscription Department, P.O. Box 7690, Red Oak, IA 51591

Crayola Kids Magazine; 1912 Grand Avenue, Des Moines, IA 50309; *http://www.bhglive.com/crayolakids/mag*

Disney Adventures; 212-633-4400; Walt Disney Magazine Publishing Group, 114 Fifth Avenue, 16th Floor, New York, NY 10011; *http://www.disney.com/DisneyAdventures*

The Electric Company Magazine; P.O. Box 51277, Boulder, CO 80321

Focus on the Family; 719-531-5181; 8605 Explorer Drive, Colorado

Springs, CO 80920; *http://www.fotf.org*

Guideposts for Kids; 219-929-4429; P.O. Box 638, Chesterton, IN 46304; *http://www.gp4k.org*

Highlights for Children; 803 Church Street, Honesdale, PA 18431; *http://www.teachernet.com/html/Highlights.dna*

Kids Discover; P.O. Box 54205, Boulder, CO 80328

National Geographic Society; 800-NGS-LINE; Attention: [*magazine title*] P.O. Box 63002, Tampa, FL 33663-3002; *http://www.national geographic.com/kids*

National Wildlife Federation; 703-790-4000; 8925 Leesburg Pike, Vienna, VA 22184; *http://www.nwf.org*

Pockets; 615-340-7333; The Upper Room, P.O. Box 189, Nashville, TN 37202; *http://www.upperroom.org/pockets*

The Puffin Club; Penguin Books Ltd., 27 Wright's Lane, London 8 5TZ England

Scholastic; 212-343-6100; 555 Broadway, New York, NY 10012; *http://www.scholastic.com*

School Library Journal (212-463-6759; Cahners Magazines, 245 W. 17th St., New York, NY 10011; *http://www.slj.com*) offers book, audio, and video reviews, recommended reading lists, thematic reading lists, and more.

Sesame Street Magazine; P.O. Box 52000, Boulder, CO 80321

Simon & Schuster; *http://www.simonsays.com/kidzone*

Sports Illustrated for Kids; 800-992-0196; Time & Life Building, New York, NY 10020; *http://www.sikids.com*

Stone Soup; 800-447-4569; P.O. Box 83, Santa Cruz, CA 95063; *http://www.stonesoup.com*

Weekly Reader; Xerox Education Publications, 1250 Fairwood Avenue, Columbus, OH 43216; *http://www.weeklyreader.com*

Zillions; 800-388-5626; P.O. Box 51777, Boulder, CO 80321; *http://www.consumerreports.com/Functions/More/Prodserv/zillions.html*

Zoobooks; 800-992-5034; Wildlife Education, 9820 Willow Creek Road, San Diego, CA 92131; *http://www.zoobooks.com*

Audio Books

Books in Motion; 800-752-3199

Books on Tape; 800-626-3333; *http://www.booksontape.com*

Caedmon Records; 1995 Broadway, New York, NY 10023

Folkways; 632 Broadway, New York, NY 10012

Listening Library; 800-243-4504, *http://www.listeninglib.com*

Recorded Books; 800-638-1304

Spoken Arts; 914-636-5481; 310 North Avenue, New Rochelle, NY

10802,

Film Producers and Distributors
Bridgestone; 800-523-0988
Children's Circle Home Video; 800-543-7843
Children's Video Report (718-935-0600) publishes reviews from child development and media critics.
Coalition for Quality Children's Video (505-989-8076) honors outstanding productions with a *Kids First!* seal. Their video directory can be ordered by calling (505) 989-8076.
Family Home Entertainment; 800-326-1977
Fusion Video; 800-959-0061; *http://fusionvideo.com*
HBO video; 212-512-1000
Movies Unlimited; 800-4-MOVIES
Paramount Home Video; 213-956-5000
Rabbit Ears; 800-800-3277
Random House Home Video; 800-733-3000
Reading Rainbow; 800-228-4630
SONY Wonder; 212-833-8000
Twin Tower; 800-553-3421
The Video Catalog; 800-733-2232
Vision Video; 800-523-0226
Warner Home Video; 818-954-6000
WonderWorks; 800-323-4222

Children's Book Award Addresses
The Children's Book Council (212-966-1990; P.O. Box 706, New York, New York 10276-0706) is an association of children's book publishers. Their annotated bibliographies of children's books include "Outstanding Science Trade Books for Children" and "Notable Children's Trade Books in the Field of Social Studies." (Enclose a 6½" x 9½" self-addressed envelope for each list requested along with first class postage for 3 ounces.)
The Children's Literature Association (616-965-8180; P.O. Box 138, Battle Creek, MI 49016) offers "Touchstones: A List of Distinguished Children's Books" for $1.00.
The International Reading Association (302-731-1600; 800 Barksdale Road, Newark, DE 19714) annually compiles a list of "Children's Choices." (Enclose a 9" x 12" self-addressed, stamped envelope when requesting this publication.) The association also provides a free guide, *You Can Use Television to Stimulate Your Child's Reading Habits.*
Parents' Choice Review (617-965-5913; P.O. Box 185, Newton, MA

02168), a nonprofit foundation, reviews books, audio-visual materials, toys, and computer software in its quarterly publication, and makes its own annual awards.

Children's Book Award Websites

The Caldecott Medal Home Page at *http://www.ala.org/alsc/caldecott.html*

The Carnegie Medal Page at *http://www.la-hq.org.uk/directory/medals.html*

Children's Literature Award Winners at *http://www.eduplace.com/rdg/links/rdg_4.html*

The Evangelical Christian Publishers Association (*http://www.ecpa.org*) lists the current year's nominees for Gold Medallions, as well as past winners.

Kate Greenaway Medal Page at *http://www.la-hq.org.uk/directory/medals.html*

The Newbery Medal Home Page at *http://www.ala.org/alsc/newbery.html*

Author Websites

Louisa May Alcott: *http://www.coppersky.com/louisa*

Ludwig Bemelmans: *http://www.martinburks.com/allison/madeline.html*

Jan Brett: *http://www.janbrett.com*

Eric Carle: *http://www.eric-carle.com*

Learning about the Author and Illustrator Pages (*http://www.scils.rutgers.edu:80/special/kay/council3.html*) provide more than 500 links to author/illustrator sites.

Magic School Bus: *http://www.scholastic.com/MagicSchoolBus*

Katherine Paterson: *http://www.terabithia.com*

Beatrix Potter: *http://www.peterrabbit.co.uk*

Maurice Sendak: *http://www.homearts.com/depts/relat/sendak4.html*

Dr. Seuss: *http://www.afn.org/afn15301/drseuss.html*

Homeschooling Resources

American Homeschool Association; 800-236-3278; P.O. Box 3142, Palmer, AK 99645; *http://www.home-ed-press.com/AHA/aha.html*

Growing Without Schooling Magazine; 617-864-3100; John Holt's Book and Music Store, 2380 Massachusetts Avenue, Cambridge, MA 02140-1226; *http://www.erols.com/holtgws*

Home Education Magazine; 800-236-3278; P.O. Box 1083, Tonasket, WA 98855-1083; *http://www.home-ed-press.com/wlcm_HEM.html*

Jon's Homeschool Resource Page; *http://www.midnightbeach.com/hs/Web_Pages.res.f.html*

National Homeschool Association; 513-772-9580; P.O. Box 290,

Hartland, MI 48353-0290; *http://www.n-h-a.org*
Practical Homeschooling, Mary Pride; 800-346-6322; P.O. Box 1250, Fenton, MO 63026-1850; *http://www.home-school.com*

More Search Engines and Web Guides

American Library Association recommended websites (over 700) at *http://www.ala.org/parentspage/greatsites*

The Children's Literature Web (*http://www.ucalgary.ca/dkbrown/index.html*) is the brain child of David K. Brown of the Doucette Library of Teaching Resources at the University of Calgary, Alberta, Canada. Parents and teachers will be amazed at the resources and links this single website offers.

Internet Public Library at *http://www.ipl.org*

KidsConnect Favorite Web Sites at *http://www.ala.org/ICONN/kcfavorites.html*

Kidsnet at *http://www.familyeducation.com/kidsnet.asp*

Kids on the Web (*http://www.zen.org/brendan/kids.html*) features educational sites, children's books, and information for parents.

Kids Source On-Line at *http://kidsource.com*

Kid Surfer (*http://www.slip.net/scmetro/forabout.htm#homework*) provides links to major libraries and reference materials at

The Ohio Public Library website (*http://www.ohio.lib.in.us*) takes children to Kid World where they can have fun with stories, riddles, and jokes. It also offers links to other enjoyable websites.

Time Warner's website (*http:///pathfinder.com*) features *Sports Illustrated for Kids, Time for Kids,* "Where's Waldo," "Radio Ahs" (a children's radio station network), and provides links to other children's web sites.

Yahooligans! (*http://www.yahooligans.com*) is the children's version of Yahoo!, one of the most powerful search engines available.

Author Index

Author Index

Author Index

Author Index

Author Index

Title Index

Title Index

Title Index

Title Index

Title Index

Title Index

About the Authors

Kathryn Lindskoog is a prolific writer, teacher, and literary critic. She is probably best known for her book *C. S. Lewis: Mere Christian*, an examination of the work of Lewis, who wrote to her, "You know my work better than anyone else I've met: certainly better than I do myself." Among her eighteen other books are *Creative Writing for People Who Can't Not Write* and the three-volume *Dante's Divine Comedy: Journey to Joy*. The mother of two grown children, she lives in California with her husband.

Ranelda Mack Hunsicker, a former elementary and high school teacher, is now a freelance writer of books and articles and a staff writer for Chuck Swindoll's *Insight for Living* ministry. She has written five books, including *In God We Trust: Stories of Faith in American History* (with Tim Crater), *The Hidden Price of Greatness* (with Ray Beeson) and a biography of David Brainerd. She and her husband live in California.